History, Experience and Cultural Studies

Other titles by Michael Pickering

Village Song and Culture

Everyday Culture (co-edited with Tony Green)

Acts of Supremacy: The British Empire and the Stage, 1790–1930
(with J. S. Bratton, Richard Cave, Heidi Holder and Brendon
Gregory)

History, Experience and Cultural Studies

MICHAEL PICKERING

First published 1997 by
MACMILLAN PRESS LTD
Houndmills, Basingstoke, Hampshire RG21 6XS
and London
Companies and representatives
throughout the world

ISBN 0–333–62109–3 hardcover
ISBN 0–333–62110–7 paperback

A catalogue record for this book is available
from the British Library.

This book is printed on paper suitable for recycling and
made from fully managed and sustained forest sources.

10   9   8   7   6   5   4   3   2   1
06 05 04 03 02 01 00 99 98 97

Printed in Hong Kong

Published in the United States of America 1997 by
ST. MARTIN'S PRESS, INC.,
Scholarly and Reference Division
175 Fifth Avenue, New York, N.Y. 10010

ISBN 0–312–17345–8

For Karen, Lucy and Joseph

Contents

Acknowledgements   ix

1 Introduction   1
2 Structures of Feeling and Traces of Time   23
3 The Turn to Ordinariness   54
4 Crossing the Asses' Bridge   91
5 Crossing Horizons   125
6 Relations of Mutual Constitution   161
7 Against the Repudiation of Experience   208

   Bibliography   247
   Name Index   267
   Subject Index   271

Acknowledgements

In writing this book, I have been helped by a number of people in a number of different ways. I would like, first of all, to thank friends and colleagues associated with *Sites*, New Zealand's cultural studies journal, for which I wrote several articles in the early 1990s. The journal's Editorial Board at Massey University provided a hospitable intellectual forum, and in ways which I did not foresee, the production of those articles has subsequently contributed to my thinking for the present book. I am grateful to the journal's current Board for permission to draw on and rework them here. Since then, David Dowling, now at the University of Northern British Columbia, has continued to lend his support and lead by example, while Roy Shuker, during part of his sabbatical leave in Britain, proved a willing and constructive listener when this book was first taking shape in my mind. Another Kiwi friend, Doreen D'Cruz, during her own sabbatical period, planted various seeds of thought which I hope I have nurtured well. Staff at the Pilkington Library have proved very helpful, not only in allowing me an extension on my loan limit while writing the book, but also in assisting me to locate various items of material, and I would like in particular to thank Jenny Chambers, Heather Jennings and Frank Parry. At the point between planning this book and sitting down to write it, Carolyn Steedman was generous with her time and counsel. Her work is for me an inspiration for what can happen when history and cultural studies intersect. Further encouragement and suggestions came from Mike

Gane, David Deacon and, before his tragically early death
in February 1996, Barry Troyna. I continue to feel his absence keenly, and find there are no words, not even the
most simple ones, that adequately configure the loss of such
a close friend. Various friends and colleagues in the East
Midlands read all or part of the manuscript before its submission, and for their helpful and constructive criticism I
would like to thank Alan Bryman, Fred Inglis, Angela
McRobbie, Graham Murdock and Keith Negus. I would also
like to acknowledge the help of Catherine Gray who, as
commissioning editor for the social sciences at Macmillan,
attended meticulously to my initial manuscript, and subjected
the arguments I have developed to careful scrutiny. Any
remaining deficiencies in the book are of course my own
responsibility. My greatest debt is to my immediate family.
A good deal of this book got written in the late hours of
the night, when the house was quiet and I could remain
undisturbed at my keyboard vigils. Yet too often in our shared
daytime I was bothered or preoccupied with the next problem I had to work through in the text. For their indulgence
and support, as well as for their laughter and love, I want
to offer my heartfelt thanks to Karen, Lucy and Joseph. It is
in appreciation of what they bring to my life that the book
is dedicated to them.

                                        MICHAEL PICKERING

Chapter 1

Introduction

History was once life-in-earnest, and all intellectual endeavour, whether worked on human experience or on the oddities of the physical and non-human world, is no more and no less than the effort to wrest what is interesting or useful from the facts of life, and turn it to benign account.

(Fred Inglis)

The Historical Dimension

This book has grown out of a sense of frustration. There has now developed a wide division between history and cultural studies, and my frustration derives from the experience of social historians and practitioners of cultural studies talking past each other, at times in mutually self-righteous terms, and at others in terms of mutual distrust and scepticism. There is now a sort of stand-off between social history and cultural studies, and I view this situation with unease and disquiet. In one way and another, in each of the chapters of this book, I worry over the lost ground between social history and cultural studies, and broach certain ways in which that ground may be reclaimed. It is because I see this lost ground as common territory that I am concerned to reclaim it in the interests of both forms of enquiry. What is at issue is the question of their relationship across this ground, and of how they can fruitfully inform each other. Anthony Giddens has suggested that 'there are no distinctions between the methods of investigation open to historians and sociologists, or the forms of concepts which they can and should employ'

(1987: 224), and this seems to me equally true of history and cultural studies. Yet much cultural studies work today is divorced from the investigations of historians, while historians pay little attention to the disciplinary renegade that is known as cultural studies. This has not always been the case.

When cultural studies was in the process of developing as an area and practice of enquiry, history was widely accepted as a vibrant and critical source of new intellectual work, and the case for developing a historical perspective, in most branches of the social sciences, seemed to gather a real momentum. In Christine Stansell's judgement, the singular achievement of this period when history came to the forefront 'was a tremendous broadening of the field of human experience to scrutiny and questioning' (1987: 24). A diverse range of new areas, new histories, began to be opened up, yet since then, the wind has fallen out of the sails of the case for history in the social sciences, partly because it 'came up against the limits' of uncovering 'this great store of hidden lives', partly because in relation to these limits it failed to theorise its activities adequately enough, and partly because the centre of gravity shifted from interrogation of 'the nature of society to the nature of knowing; experience lost out to epistemology' (ibid: 24–5). History continued to exert an important influence on cultural studies up to the first half of the 1980s, and it did so in various ways. For example, Stuart Hall has noted that for British cultural studies the common meeting-ground between forms of close textual reading and a more social form of analysis first occurred not with mainstream academic sociology – which was generally hostile to cultural studies – but with concrete historical analysis, in the project which saw publication in *Paper Voices* (Smith *et al.*, 1975). In *Resistance through Rituals*, which was published in the same year, it was recognised as 'vital, in any analysis of contemporary phenomena, to think historically; many of the short-comings in the "youth" area are due, in part at least, to an absent or foreshortened historical dimension' (Hall and Jefferson, 1977: 17). This was an important recognition, though the text in question concentrated mainly on the historical specificities of the postwar period when the 'youth question' with which it was concerned bulked large.

What is striking is how little this recognition has been acted on in subsequent cultural studies work. In this respect, there is a stark contrast between earlier texts identified with, or contributing to, cultural studies, and those being produced now, where a 'historical dimension' is usually absent, never mind foreshortened. The development towards this baleful situation was certainly influenced by the Birmingham Centre for Contemporary Cultural Studies in the late 1970s and early 1980s. Although historically informed work was produced there at that time, the interest in history was generally theoretically motivated. The major concerns of both *Working-Class Culture* (Clarke *et al.*, 1979) and *Making Histories* (Johnson *et al.*, 1982) were with social theory and historiography (see also McLennan, 1981). The only significant exception to this – which is where 'people's history' and cultural studies have at times fruitfully converged – is work on popular memory, on the intersections of national constructions of the past and everyday historical consciousness. Patrick White's *On Living in an Old Country* (1985) represents one of the most ambitious and insightful examples of this work, and its focus continues to inform social and cultural criticism. But it is a focus on historical experience in *contemporary* uses, and beyond it, the main lines of the historiographical critique have become commonplace and routinely invoked, so that an interest in the 'historical dimension' in itself appears naive or unnecessary. The result is that the 'historical myopia' castigated in *Resistance through Rituals* has become endemic in forms of cultural studies that have developed in the 1980s and 1990s, particularly as epistemological issues have overridden those concerned with the experience of diverse social groups and different historical periods, with that 'great store of hidden lives'. Cultural studies has ceased to be leavened by a historical sensibility, and it is this deficit which the book seeks to overcome.

The earlier, more convergent interests and concerns of a developing cultural studies and the 'new' social history of the 1960s and 1970s were partly defined by a common relation to Marxism, though increasingly the relation became differentiated by alternative readings of Marx and the Marxist tradition, and by the annexation of that tradition to different

intellectual paradigms and approaches. This is itself a complicated history, and our perspective on it has been profoundly altered by the events of the late 1980s and 1990s in
the former Soviet Union and in the countries of Eastern
Europe. It is as yet unclear how the social sciences may subsequently be realigned with, or positioned against, the different Marxisms of preceding historical periods and formations.
The project of this book is not particularly concerned with
this question, though indirectly its tasks will have some bearing
upon it. The book's primary concern is to foster a more
interactive relationship between history and cultural studies,
and to think through some of the conceptual and theoretical
issues that follow for cultural studies in attempting much
more assiduously to realise Frederic Jameson's injunction
to 'always historicise'. This injunction hardly needed to be
made to those writers retrospectively associated with the
founding of cultural studies, for whom the dialectic of past
and present, the contested terrain of and between different
cultural and political traditions, and the question of historical understanding, were central preoccupations. These preoccupations in the 1970s seemed quite compatible with
cultural studies.

Social history and cultural studies seemed also to work at
that time in a close, if uneasy, alliance because of three
shared concerns: firstly, an effort to take popular culture
seriously; secondly, a rejection of vulgar or mechanically
determinist forms of Marxism, and an attempt to revivify
the Marxist tradition in the face of its Stalinist travesty –
with Gramsci coming to form the major influence on this
attempt; and thirdly, an open acknowledgement of the necessarily political nature of the 'popular', both in itself and in
critical or other commentaries upon it. The cross-fertilisation of social history and cultural studies continued into
the late 1970s/early 1980s. One example is historical work
on popular leisure (see, for example, Bailey, 1978, and
Cunningham, 1980). Stuart Hall's important paper 'Notes
on Deconstructing "the Popular"' (1981) drew upon the
'history from below' movement initiated by people like
Thompson, Hobsbawm and Rudé, and outlined a succinct
neo-Gramscian framework for the study of popular culture.
At the Ruskin History Workshop conference of December

1979, where Hall's paper was first delivered, there were ways in which social history and cultural studies seemed to be marching pretty much in step with each other, an assumption confirmed when the Open University's *Popular Culture* programme (U203) was launched in 1981. But the signs of change, the portents of gulfs opening up, were already there in the late 1970s, and at the self-same conference. Following Richard Johnson's critique of the historical writings of Thompson, came the fierce debate generated by the publication of Thompson's *The Poverty of Theory* (1978), sparks of which flew at the Saturday night plenary, in the chill of an abandoned St Paul's in Oxford. Piece by piece, evidence began to accumulate of a serious gap opening up between history and cultural studies.

It is important not to exaggerate the earlier consonances of social history and cultural studies, for the gap grew on already existing tensions between them, which were especially manifest around questions of theory and method. But it remains the case that a historical outlook and disposition was a vital part of the weft of the cultural studies fabric, and it is one which needs to be woven back in again precisely because it is now largely missing, the major exception to this being the influence of Foucault's iconoclastic historical approach, which is discussed in the final chapter. There are of course real difficulties in attempting this. The historian of popular leisure and culture, Peter Bailey, has spoken of the problem for historians in finding 'a secure footing' in cultural studies, and certainly its tendencies to theoreticism, to an 'often laboured conflation of the abstruse and the banal', to a confusion of textual and historical analysis, and to 'mashing' rather than 'meshing' different 'specialist disciplines or schools', can be obstacles in getting to grips with it (Bailey, 1986: xviii–xix). Bailey has of course attempted to draw on cultural studies in his own work, and it is in part because of this that he has been able to keep in view 'the bigger questions of culture and ideology, agency and structure in a modern capitalist society' (ibid). These 'bigger questions' will crop up in various ways throughout the discussion in this book, and in following up his comment on the difficulties of engagement with cultural studies, I want at this point simply to sketch out

two or three ways in which I find that engagement valuable
for historical practice.

Cultural Studies into History

If, for instance, we take an interest in cultural processes as
a banal connection between social history and cultural studies,
the difficult question which follows is how such processes
may be approached historically. The social relations and
practices in which symbolic expression and exchange have
historically been embedded cannot be known in some prior
sense and then counterposed to the symbolic, for necessarily we are engaged in reconstructing those relations and
practices when we endeavour to explore the contexts of the
senses of historical experience which certain cultural texts
or forms may be said to impart. The past as it is constituted
in historical knowledge is always an organised past, a past
assembled and arranged into sets of evidence and data which
are mediated by the organisation of their presentation as
texts, images or artefacts. The past as told or pictorialised
or physically arranged is always, in its historical condition,
a selective past, which means that what it is composed of
brings various kinds of historical evidence to the forefront
of our attention, there on the page, on the screen, on the
display stands inside the museum. The challenge should always
be to make our attention circumspect when it is focused in
this way. No doubt there are other ways of negotiating this
challenge, but moving between history and cultural studies
is certainly one way of enabling it to be more effectively
met.

What this movement generally serves to remind us is that,
even though the selections are composed of the traces of
what time has left us, in its human organisation, there are
always present-oriented criteria of selection and approach
in play – cultural, ideological and political criteria, or criteria with implications of that kind. History as made is always
history as remade. And it is there that so many of the complexities lie. The choices of what to include and work up in
historical reconstruction need then to be interrogated for
the significance of what is absent as well as present in their
narratives, the evidence and experience that has been

relegated to the shadows and recesses of the smoothly settled foreground of the overall composition. Cultural studies, among other initiatives, is useful in this respect precisely
because it comes poised with a set of pertinent questions to
ask of the unstable relations between symbolic inclusion and
exclusion, of the political implications of evidential selectiv-
ity, of the consequences of acts of historical forgetting as
well as remembering, of the ways in which the organisation
of the telling of tales of the past is oriented to the power
structures of the past or of the relations of these to those
of the historian's present. Historians may turn around and
say that this is all well and good, but they do not need such
counsel, particularly when it is delivered in intellectually
uncompromising terms. And maybe they don't. Yet this will
be an appropriate response only so long as historians themselves ask whose voices and whose views are being privileged
in this or that version of historical telling, and whose voices
and whose views are cast to the margins, rendered insignificant to the story being told. If they do ask such questions,
then it is reasonable to expect that their choices of material and approach should be accompanied by a set of explanations, for without these the charge of mystification is always
likely to stick.

One of the historian's most abiding senses of frustration
in relation to his or her material is its absolute incompleteness, its inevitable existence in the present only as time's
traces. Yet what has at times seemed to me paradoxical, given
this always troubling relation, is that historians often try to
create the illusion of a full canvas of the past as they present
it. As historians, we cannot by definition flood this canvas
with the full colours and textures of the past as it was lived,
variously and contradictorily, yet the problems with having
to piece together the surviving or retrievable odds and ends
of the past, never mind the struggle imaginatively to make
them cohere, rarely surfaces in the texts historians construct.
The fragments that remain have of course been reconstructed
within discourses of their own, produced according to certain modes and conditions, certain principles of organisation, certain frames of inclusion, reference and assimilation,
and part of what is involved in historical analysis is developing an understanding of how their constitutive properties

inform and sustain the material that is studied. But again, this is rarely made explicit – any interrogation of the discourse of the source material too often lies buried beneath the lines of the historian's narrative, or is relegated to asides and notes. At its worst this creates a further illusion of the practice of history writing occurring from some point outside of history and the process of representing it.

The crucial point of bringing cultural studies to bear on historical practice is that it holds up the promise of making history and historiography indissoluble. What this presages is a more developed treatment, alongside the construction of historical narratives and accounts, of the methodological and theoretical issues arising out of their construction. The challenge of historical understanding is to develop an openness to different discourses, different voices, beyond one's own cultural and historical horizon, but this involves problems that stand in need of theoretical elaboration precisely because any form of historical knowledge, apart from the most banal, is necessarily partial, provisional and time-bound. These characteristics of historical knowledge do not spell ultimate damage for what historians do – to the contrary, they indicate precisely the kind of knowledge which historians accomplish through their perilous craft. But it is because of the dangerous illusion of the full canvas, or definitive version of the tale, that historical practice needs to be more reflexive, more openly considerate of its means and conditions of production and the problems these entail. What is needed is, as Carolyn Steedman has put it, 'an abandonment of the *artisanal* tendencies of historians' in favour of a more complex engagement with 'what kind of act the *writing* of history is, what the form they are using permits, what it prevents: what kind of tale they're telling' (1992a: 50). Adequate cultural analysis depends upon a dialectic of conceptual apparatus and object of enquiry, which demands that we think critically about both our methods and our materials. What is advanced as sufficient or appropriate evidence in historical reconstruction, and the constitutive means of such reconstruction, need to be critically set out, and cultural studies provides examples of the ways this can be done.

Yet likewise, a historical framework or perspective of some

kind may help to prevent a critical hermeneutic from becoming locked into a self-fulfilling vindication of its own
conceptual apparatus. History provides a valuable resource
for examining the strengths and limitations of concepts and
theories. In the 1990s, there are signs that cultural studies
is becoming more concerned with forms of empirical enquiry, beyond those involved with media audience studies
and reception analysis, and less centred on modes of textual analysis. In the past, cultural studies has been far more
text-oriented than social history, and while I want to suggest
that the negotiation of time's traces in terms of documentary
evidence, oral testimony and the like may learn much from
such work, cultural studies has at times inclined excessively
towards textualism and theoreticism, and is generally
chronocentric in its preoccupations, which is precisely why
it needs now to be engaged by problems of historical
contextualisation and understanding, and steered towards
imaginative correctives of its recurrent retreat into the present.
Questions relating to text-context relations will be taken up
at various points in the book, but it may perhaps be
worthwhile highlighting one aspect of what they involve as
a way of setting the stage for what follows.

The aspect in question involves the historicality of a cultural text in relation to the historical conditions of its im-
plementation. While one can focus on the particular codes
and conventions which structure a cultural form or narrative, these have always to be understood as historical in at
least two senses. They are historical in the sense that they
can be traced in their development in terms of the ways
they are shaped, are adapted and modified, or become allied with other codes and conventions in a pattern that has
its own story, internal to the form, of use and change. The
problem with this kind of approach is that the treatment of
cultural texts tends, all too often, to operate in a historically disembodied way. This was for instance a tendency in
Williams's *Culture and Society* (1958), but one he eradicated
in *The Country and the City* (1973). The senses in which cultural texts and practices connected with the social forces
and pressures prevalent at particular times, or informed the
cultural dispositions and preoccupations of those who took
them over, in different periods, are too easily lost from view

because of the emphasis on modifications and changes internal to the cultural material or process in focus, though it is in fact questions of process which are what usually go begging. In the face of this generally formalist approach, the alternative approach required for the practice of cultural history insists on the heterosocial dynamics within which particular cultural texts and narratives achieved a certain currency in particular although always loosely bounded sequences of experientially lived time.

In this second sense, cultural forms and narratives are historical in that their uses and changes are always a response of some kind, however complex that may be, to the social and cultural relations in which they operate, and by which they are conditioned. From this perspective, the means by which symbolic expressions are achieved always interact with the historical conditions and structures of social organisation within which those expressions are grounded. This is a crucial, yet exceedingly difficult shift. Cultural analysis which is too exclusively focused on either the means of cultural expression or the conditions of its production and consumption is likely to lead to aesthetic formalism in one direction and sociological reductionism in another. In this light, it can be said that the most decisive impulse of cultural history and sociology arises from the challenge of continually making and remaking the rubric for an intermediate position. It is the relations between cultural practice and historical conditions, in all their unevenness, contradictions and elisions, which the analysis needs to dramatise.

Outline of the Book

The tasks of this book are threefold. Firstly, as already indicated, there is a concern to examine afresh the relations – the common ground – between history and cultural studies, and between history and cultural analysis more broadly. This will involve exploring questions of hermeneutic engagement, as for instance in what is implicated in the interpretation of the relations of past social experience and past cultural forms from a changed historical vantage. At the same time, it is connected with the second task of the book, which is to revisit the earlier formation of cultural studies in the light of the ways in which the field has subsequently developed. Historical questions were integral to this formation, not least because it coincided with the burgeoning of the new, experiential social history of the 1960s and 1970s, which fed directly into it. The tendencies subsequently identified as 'culturalism' spanned both social history and cultural studies. Although I view this term as unhelpful, it has come to be accepted as descriptive of these tendencies. Whether or not they can be taken as paradigmatic is another matter, but their specific characteristics are clear enough, and their involvement with historiographical problems make them obviously germane to the first set of concerns which I have specified.

I do not intend to work through 'culturalist' issues and concerns in a textbook manner or chronological order of appearance. There are other treatments of early cultural studies which move in this direction – see, for instance, Brantlinger (1990), Turner (1990), Milner (1991 and 1993), Inglis (1993) and Johnson (1979a,b) – and there is little point in replicating them here. Instead, I shall take up those issues and concerns as and when they are relevant to the development of my argument. While I regard the opposition of culturalism and structuralism as an intellectual dead-end, it did at the time clarify a set of issues which in my view are still very much with us. If, as Graeme Turner alleges, 'we can consign the culturalism-structuralist split to the past' (1990: 72), we should not view the problems it raised as having been superseded, nor complacently take such consignment to the past as implying a history of progressive improvement. In some recent accounts of the development of cultural studies there are unfortunate evolutionist implications, as if every new step taken moves us onward and upward, and all earlier stages become inevitably inferior by some implicit logic of succession. To the contrary, those tendencies and emphases tidily shovelled together in the heap labelled 'culturalism' continue to exert a diverse influence, to provide a valuable set of map-points and guidelines for cultural and historical analysis, and to show what has been lost from the more fashionable agenda. The story of cultural studies is not one of relentless progression through chapters with fixed beginnings and ends.

It is in the light of this perspective on cultural studies as
an intellectual corpus that I revisit the tendencies identified
with 'culturalism', rather than in some spirit of cleaving
nostalgically to the past, which would be the obvious, yet
facile, charge that could be levelled against this aspect of
the book. I regard many of the the more recent developments in cultural studies – its geographical dispersal and
geo-political discontinuities, for example, or its examination
of questions of cultural identity, diversity and 'difference' –
as welcome not only in enriching what is done in its name,
but also in renegotiating its circulating themes and pluralising
its organising agendas. I also concede that there were various weaknesses and flaws associated with the earlier 'culturalism', and I shall of course be concerned to deal with them,
but I do not accept all that has been said in criticism of the
'culturalist paradigm', and I shall be just as concerned to
tackle the distortions and dilutions of its critical treatment
as to build on its real strengths and values.

In discussing the new social history which emerged from
the mid-1950s, Richard Johnson distinguishes three major
characteristics which, in a rough-and-ready manner, identify some of the major tendencies of 'culturalism' generally.
These were to break with 'cultureless' forms of history and
with elitist conceptions of culture in the interests of writing
'seriously and with sympathy' about the 'ways of life' of ordinary people; to effect a shift from economistic to 'cultural Marxism'; and to give centrality in cultural and historical
studies to the category of experience (1979b: 58–65). This
third tendency could be said to have been a key strategy in
facilitating the realisation of the first and second. Focusing
on the concept of experience is therefore of vital importance in the task of revisiting 'culturalism' in historical, literary
and cultural analysis. It is this which constitutes the third
major task of the book.

The theme of experience is central to the book as a whole,
with much of the discussion turning around it in various
ways. Its centrality is not simply borrowed from 'culturalism'.
It emerged in the process of writing as I found myself continuing to circle back on it as a means with which to bring
together, within one discussion, social history, cultural studies,
historical hermeneutics and feminist history and theory. These

are the major subject-areas which are drawn on in the book, and it is of course no accident that 'experience' has been an important analytical topic or resource in all of them. The need to develop a full-bodied examination of it as a concept has also arisen because of its cursory or hostile treatment in much contemporary work. The term has increasingly come under attack, and is now regarded with drastic suspicion in certain forms of contemporary theory. The critical questioning of the category of experience has pointed both to the methodological inadequacies of the ways in which it has often been employed, and to its general flakiness as a concept. To my knowledge, the attack on it has not yet been substantively addressed. The concept of experience itself has, recently, only been subject to negative appraisal, though its position in cultural anthropology does present something of a significant exception. This book attempts to make good the gap in both respects.

While the concept raises difficult theoretical issues, my underlying concern is to strengthen the case for it as a valuable and, indeed, indispensable category of both historical and cultural analysis. In my view, it should not be hastily dismissed. I shall argue that its analytical use does not necessarily entail a self-validating ground of 'authenticity' and is not necessarily in opposition to the attempt to ground such use in a critical theoretical framework. These are claims often made against it, and I shall be concerned to interrogate them in the course of the book. To some, such is the relentless modishness of cultural studies, this attention to 'experience' will impart to the book a rather old-fashioned ring, but in seeking to go forward I base my defence only partly on earlier cultural studies work. This work seems to me to have been too peremptorily junked, and is not now dealt with satisfactorily in textbook or classroom. Questions of misrepresentation aside, it is more important to take into consideration new areas of work and bring new strands into relation with what are relatively established contributions. If history and cultural studies are to be more closely aligned in the future, this will depend very much on reconceiving the fraught category of experience, particularly in relation to its centrality in previous 'culturalist' history. Such a reconception will be essential in restoring the lost historical

dimension of cultural studies, but that assignment is one I
view from the perspective of cultural studies, and through
undertaking it in this way I hope that it will facilitate alignment from the other side as well.

For this reason, I devote the second chapter to a key concept of early cultural studies which is necessarily bound up
with that of experience. Raymond Williams's concept of structure of feeling is one of the most opaque, yet valuable concepts of early cultural studies, and it is worth examining on
both counts. The intention is to clarify its meaning and
sharpen up its application in cultural and historical analysis. The examination of it also serves as a means of connecting with other concepts and themes in Williams's work.
But the most important reason for putting it under scrutiny
is because it provides a useful key to thinking about the
issues of cultural emergence, discontinuity and innovation.
These issues are the most significant aspect of the second
chapter, for they establish the thread of social and cultural
change that will then get carried forward into the rest of
the book, and around which will turn questions concerning
the relations between experience and social process.

The kind of experience focused on in 'culturalist' work
has characteristically been that of everyday life among particular yet generally subordinated social groups. The third
chapter looks at the turn to ordinariness and to the 'popular' in cultural analysis, and examines the radical implications of these for the subject of 'English' as one of the main
disciplines concentrating on the analysis of cultural texts
and forms. It was against this discipline that the 'culturalist'
moment was defined, and yet subsequently the sociological
aesthetics of experience have not been satisfactorily handled within cultural studies. On the other hand, treatment
of the concept of experience in literary studies remains seriously flawed. The reasons for this are examined through a
reconsideration of the relationship of literary and cultural
studies, which in turn raises questions concerning the
commodification of experience. The chapter concludes by
returning to another lost dimension of cultural studies which
has important historical implications, and not only for literary and cultural studies. This is the dimension of a democratic politics of education. In the past this has involved

the struggle to publicly extend the institutional resources of learning, and to relate the pursuit of knowledge to mundane experience. This dimension is, indeed, another aspect of the turn to ordinariness, but it is one which has become vitiated by the excessive textualism and celebratory cultural populism of recent cultural studies.

The lack of any adequate treatment of the concept of experience in literary and cultural studies has led me to explore the writings of the nineteenth-century philosopher, Wilhelm Dilthey, for whom 'lived experience' was a sort of pivot between our being and consciousness. Dilthey attempted to theorise experience in ways which are not only instructive in themselves, but also sympathetic to its use in the work of 'culturalist' writers like Raymond Williams and Edward Thompson. Their use of the term has been criticised in part because of the failure to subject it to any sustained conceptual formulation, and turning to Dilthey provides a valuable means for doing just this. It is necessary to stress that this cannot be tidily achieved. We cannot stuff everything it involves into a neat little box. The point and purpose of thinking about experience is that there are no obvious models or schemata for dealing with it in its diverse multiplicity. At the same time, this cannot be used as an excuse for not thinking about it systematically. Dilthey simply provides one important means for attempting to do this, and for this reason the fourth chapter is mainly given over to relevant aspects of his work. Devoting such attention to him means that I have not been able, in the present book, to deal with other writers for whom the category of experience has been of signal importance. Dilthey receives the lion's share of attention because he is referred to much less than these other writers, except indirectly, and because his influence has nevertheless been considerable. Although there are problems with his approach, I think it is time for his work to be set once again more squarely on the map of cultural and historical theory.

The term 'culturalism' is generally used to refer to the Anglophone anti-utilitarian body of thought and works traced by Williams in *Culture and Society* (1958), which stretches back to the Romantic period. This use covers both conservative and radical responses to industrialism, capitalism and modernity, in a line of descent from figures like Edmund Burke and William Blake in the late eighteenth century, and has been associated most of all with a literary tradition of comment and ideas concerning the relations between culture and society. It is also used with reference to the work in social history and cultural studies in Britain during the 1960s and 1970s which I shall be concerned to critically review in the light of subsequent developments. As Andrew Milner notes, though, the tradition of cultural criticism surveyed and reworked by Williams has its continental counterparts, most significantly in German literary and intellectual life over the same period: 'In both German and British versions, the concept of culture is understood as incorporating a specifically "literary" sense of culture as "art"'"with an "anthropological" sense of culture as a "way of life"' (1991: 18). Milner, however, concentrates on the theoretical concerns of British rather than German culturalism. One of the purposes of this book is to trace certain affinities and connections between these two culturalist traditions, and not least through the category of experience.

Johnson describes the centrality of 'experience' in earlier cultural studies and social history in terms of its opposition to 'all externalising, mechanical or functionalist accounts of the social world', and its insistence 'on getting inside the minds, perceptions and feelings of the historical agents themselves' (1979b: 64). These features of its use raise important hermeneutical issues, and I extend the discussion of Dilthey's work into their examination in Chapter 5. Part of this involves critically thinking through the notion of empathy – 'getting inside the minds' of historical agents – which is in turn connected with the notion of *Verstehen*, and which provides a link forward to dealing with the project of historical recovery, questions of self-reflexivity, and Gadamer's ideas about cultural and historical horizons of experience and knowledge. The tension between realism and interpretivism runs throughout the book, but it is particularly registered in this chapter. From there, I move in Chapter 6 to a more thorough discussion of the opposition to externalising, mechanical and functionalist accounts of the social world, and I begin this by looking again at the opening of the divide between history and cultural studies in relation to the unfortunate schism between Hall's 'two paradigms' of structuralism and culturalism.

Though I have personally learned a good deal from the structuralisms and their descendants, I have never lost the conviction that these have constituted a series of wrong turns for cultural studies, and now increasingly for those historians who are following them. I do not, however, want simply to call for a return to the 'culturalism' that was excoriated in the late 1970s, early 1980s. The present book is partly a guarded defence of that alternative tradition of work, but my purpose is not one of rearguard revivalism, and consequently this is one reason why the book is not a heated polemic against its adversaries. I am concerned more with thinking through some of the issues and positions which have led to the impasse between history and cultural studies. In doing so, it has seemed to me vital to look at the feminist usage and treatment of 'experience' which was not included in the neo-Althusserian denunciation of the category. Such denunication operated with selective targets, singling out socialist-humanism in cultural studies and the 'new' social history in particular. Feminism has been quite rightly concerned with the category of experience, and the omission of its usage and treatment of the category from any substantial part of the critique was a serious weakness, compounding the neglect and marginalisation with which feminist historians, for instance, have met at various times over the past quarter century.

Realigning Sundered Terrains

While a number of varying intellectual and political currents fed into the earlier feminist history, much of it was driven by the need to open out that 'great store of hidden lives' that had been buried by male-dominated historiographies, and to broaden 'the field of human experience' as it had existed in the past by focusing centrally on the place of women within it. More specifically, it was the distinctiveness as well as the validity of women's changing experience over time which directed this work of recovery and retrieval. Sheila Rowbottom's *Hidden from History* was seminal in this development, while Juliet Mitchell's essay,

'Women: The Longest Revolution', acknowledged the work of Raymond Williams and argued for the advancement of British feminism in an 'engagement of socialist history and cultural studies' (Lovell, 1990: 21; Rowbottom, 1977; Mitchell, 1984). The potential of this was exemplified in the 1970s and early 1980s in the History Workshop movement, which constituted perhaps the most significant parallel strand in historical research and practice to the focus of cultural studies on contemporary cultural processes and change. In the early days of the movement, the challenge to orthodox empiricist historiography joined feminist and radical social history with cultural studies by arguing against 'objective', 'value-free' conceptions of research and analysis, by committing itself to more democratic forms of social knowledge and education, and by urging 'historians to think more critically about the theoretical resources they are drawing on and . . . to engage in theoretical work for themselves' (Alexander and Davin, 1976: 6; Samuel and Stedman Jones, 1976: 8). This kind of attention to theory was certainly germane to the cultural studies project at this time, though even then a note of caution was sounded in describing the dialogue between history, sociology and cultural studies as too often placing the historian in a relation of 'abject dependency, craving recognition and taking theoretical propositions on trust' (Samuel and Stedman Jones, 1976: 7). Again, though more with the benefit of hindsight, we can see an early sign of the unfortunate gap that would soon open up between history and cultural studies.

Feminist history from the start had an obvious yet critical relation to feminist theory as well as feminist practice. In Britain there has been a consistent if fraught dialogue with class politics and theory as well, which is again why the *History Workshop Journal* has been a space for feminist historians both to occupy and contest in developing 'a distinctively socialist feminist approach' (Hall, 1992: 10; see also Taylor; 1983, Steedman, 1986 and 1990; Alexander, 1994; Bland, 1995; and Clark, 1995, for important examples of such an approach). In feminist history, and of course in varying ways, 'experience' – and more specifically in British feminist history, women's experience in particular social classes, with class understood as a gendered position and experience –

raises similar issues of interpretation to those discussed later on in the book. Beyond the vital step of putting women in the frame, there is then the question of what frame (or frames) of interpretation should be developed in dealing with women's experience in past times and past cultures. Linda Gordon, for instance, has spoken of the importance of 'listening' to women's 'voices' in the past, and trying to put herself in their place: 'History needs a subjective, imaginative, emulative process of communication'. This, along with her second recognition of the perils of hindsight, are central to my lines of argument in this book for, as she puts it, you cannot ignore the time that has passed between yourself and your subject, you cannot ignore your own historical place: 'there has got to be a tension between historical empathy and rootedness' in the present, 'a rigorous defence both against presentism and against the illusion that the historian remains outside history' (Gordon, 1983: 75). An attempt to explore what is involved in this tension, and to mount exactly that kind of defence, is one of the key purposes of the book.

If the neo-Althusserian dismissal of the category of experience in early cultural studies and (male) labour history did not take up its importance in women's history, that has subsequently occurred through its poststructuralist repudiation. This has been most directly and comprehensively set out in Joan Scott's deconstruction of the concept, and in the final chapter I deal with this, equally comprehensively, in a critique of her critique. Against her form of linguistic idealism, I continue to argue that the concept should not be regarded as locked hard and fast into an unattested essentialism, but rather taken as a lived register of the contradictions between pressure and practice, limits and freedom. The full story of this lies in the rest of the book, but before this story unfolds it is important to emphasise how certain feminist historians have continued, from the late 1970s to the 1990s, to negotiate a passage for the vessel of historical experience, with its various cargoes, through the war zones of theory. A fine example of this is Leonore Davidoff and Catherine Hall's *Family Fortunes* (1987), a pathbreaking study of the gendered subjectivity and experience of social class in the early nineteenth century. This study marked an

expansion from the earlier preoccupation of feminist history with working-class women to the terrain of the provin-
cial English middle class during the period of their formation,
as well as assimilating the new emphasis of the 1980s on
the articulation of constructions of masculinity and femi-
ninity. As Catherine Hall has more recently put it: 'we drew
on the feminist injunction that you should always start with
yourself and what you know and experience'. Making the
category of 'experience' central to their work in this way,
they 'began to investigate the institution into which we were
born, and which we had in our own turn reproduced, the
middle-class family' (1992: 16). Such work shows that a focus on concrete historical experience neither reifies nor
essentialises perforce the categories of class and gender, since
it conceptualises gender as the social organisation and ongoing construction through time of relations between the
sexes, makes clear the rootedness of historical research in
contemporary concerns while avoiding the pitfalls of
presentism, and provides a valuable counter to the theoretical certainties of poststructuralism.

While acknowledging the important arguments of Riley
(1988) and Scott (1988), Hall questions these certainties,
and asks whether feminist historians need poststructuralism
to develop gender as an analytical category or to realise the
ways in which professional historical writing has often
universalised experience on the basis of masculine conceptions. 'Similarly with ethnocentrism . . . Despite its claims
to de-centre the Western subject, poststructuralism has
given little actual thought to ethnicity beyond the ritual
invocations, as Said's critique of Foucault demonstrated' (Hall,
1991: 209–10). Indeed, the rejection of biologistic or racialistic
explanations of sexual and ethnic inequalities enabled various historians to explore the social construction of those
inequalities, and their reproduction through various social
sites and institutions, before the influences of Foucault or
Derrida began to take hold within gender history or other
areas of historical practice. Moreover, the deconstructionist
take on questions of subjectivity and the subject is representative of its deracinated conventionalist preoccupations,
or what Hall points to as 'a curious loss of feeling' in the
historical writing of Riley and Scott: 'their notion of identity

is without a psychic component'. It is in this context that she refers back to 'the vitriolic exchanges between culturalists and structuralists' in which 'feminists were curiously, or not so curiously, silent ... we certainly wanted to hold on to the possibility of women making their own history, but always, as we knew so well, in determinate conditions. I didn't want to be forced into that choice then, to sign up with the culturalists or the structuralists, and I don't now' (ibid: 210).

In supporting this refusal to dance attendance on either of these or other currently divided camps, I try in the ensuing set of arguments to keep the question of 'feeling' in the sights of historical and cultural analysis, initially through an examination of Williams's concept of structure of feeling, and then through a move from the question of experience itself to questions of identification with the experience of history's others. While recognising that identification with history's others – or by extension, with ethnography's others – is beset with dangers, Hall asks if it is 'really possible to imaginatively evoke difference, the difference of other worlds and times, without those forms of identification?' (ibid). Much of the central part of this book is taken up with an exploration of how we may advance this process, how we may negotiate the problems which Carolyn Steedman, in her fascinating essay 'The Watercress Seller', refers to as the historian's 'massive transferential relationship to the past' (1992b: 201; and see LaCapra, 1985). This involves following through the shift from the crucial yet somewhat naive project of recovery in radical social and early feminist history, to the theoretically difficult ground of identification with and through difference. It is around the engagement with 'otherness' that some of the most vital lessons of historiography for cultural studies may be said to lie. And again, this is where the psychic component of historical experience is a key issue for both historical and cultural studies in their shared concern with the symbolic dimensions of social processes and the subjectivities informing and informed by social relations. What this really involves is a recognition that while, as Cora Kaplan has put it, 'social life is ordered through psychic structures that to some extent organise its meanings, that psychic life in turn is only ever lived through

specific social histories and political and economic possibilities'
(Kaplan, 1986: 4).

It is with this conception of the psychic component in
social life and historical experience that Anne McClintock
operates in her magnificent study *Imperial Leather* (1995).
McClintock examines the ambiguous and contradictory ways
in which ethnicity, class, gender and sexuality have intersected in the imperial relation, and shows how imperialism
and racial ideology have structured white subjectivities and
symbolic exchange in the metropolitan centre as well as in
the colonial peripheries of the British Empire. Her book
should almost be read end-to-end with Davidoff and Hall's
Family Fortunes, not only because it moves forward from that
study historically, but also because analytically it shows how
a feminised domesticity in the nineteenth century worked
in conjunction with the project of imperial mastery. Even
in an apparently simple artefact like a bar of soap, McClintock
reveals how imperialist ideology and evolutionary racism were
brought to the British domestic hearth, contributed to the
disavowal of women's domestic labour under imperial capitalism, and, as an icon of racial hygiene, revealed 'that fetishism, far from being a quintessentially African propensity,
as nineteenth-century anthropology maintained, was central
to industrial modernity, inhabiting and mediating the un-
certain threshold zones between domesticity and industry,
metropolis and empire' (1995: 210). To summarise her analysis in this way does not do justice to its flair and inventive-
ness, which can only be appreciated at first hand, for *Imperial
Leather* abundantly demonstrates the exciting potential of
historical cultural studies. It is to this potential that my own
book is dedicated.

In her book's closing words, McClintock denounces what
she sees as 'the prospect of being becalmed in a historically
empty space in which our sole direction is found by gazing
back spellbound at the epoch behind us, in a perpetual
present marked only as "post"' (Ibid: 396). If history and
cultural studies are to come together again, in a realign-
ment of sundered terrains, then we must strive to fill out
that space and to break out of the beguiling spell of a present-
bound, 'post'-obsessed gaze.

Chapter 2

Structures of Feeling and Traces of Time

> My present position ... is that however dominant a social system may be, the very meaning of its domination involves a limitation or selection of the activities it covers, so that by definition it cannot exhaust all experience, which therefore always potentially contains space for alternative acts and alternative intentions which are not yet articulated as a social institution or even project.
>
> (Raymond Williams)

Connecting with the Past

With these words, Raymond Williams summarised one of the central themes in his work. This theme can be identified as a continual interest in the social and historical genesis of cultural innovation, of changes in cultural forms and practices. He saw these unplanned, yet at the same time willed, new directions and departures as, unless simply modish and hyped-up as alluring novelties, often presenting a challenge to established, accredited ways of providing images and accounts of existing social institutions and relations. While accepting that various critical distinctions have to be made among them, what seemed most to interest Williams were those new directions and departures which are made in the teeth of what serves to legitimate existing social conventions and practices, and of what functions in ways supportive of vested interests, in different areas of social and cultural life. Williams's concern was not only to examine the results of cultural innovation and change, but also to analyse the historically specific processes by which innovation and change come about. Although much of his literary and cultural analysis concentrates on problems of form, Williams's own approach was anti-formalist. His mode of enquiry was always more historical and sociological in orientation, seeking to understand the 'lived' interconnections between cultural texts and practices and structures of social interaction and organisation. It was an approach developed in opposition to attempts to separate and divide social and cultural experience, regardless of the political or educational quarter from which they have come. The emphasis was always on culture *and* society, writing *in* society, individual and social experience as indissoluble. What is keenly arresting about Williams's summary of his position, which retrospectively can be seen as integral to his whole project, is that it was made in relation to the problem which follows from the emphasis given in the general approach. This is the problem of 'explaining in non-metaphysical terms those acts and responses which are not, so to say, prepared by social circumstances as we can ordinarily assess them' (1979: 252). It is this point which I wish to pursue in what follows.

In the work of Raymond Williams, we do not encounter the presentation of evidence and the methodological procedures of a trained historian, yet Williams continuously made reference to the past, in a range of different forms of writing, and his work as a whole can, from one vital perspective, be seen to be preoccupied by the interrelationship of past and present. Williams was a committed interdisciplinarian, impatient with generic boundaries and the institutionalised demarcations of knowledge about human culture, and his work was seminal in the formation of cultural studies, itself identified with the crossing and erosion of disciplinary frontiers. This disrespect for the constraining proprieties of academic method and domain has been salutary in many respects, yet one drawback has been that it has made it easy for more conventional scholars to disregard his work, even to dismiss it as not 'proper' history or sociology. This is unfortunate, not because examples of Williams's writing might be regarded as models of cultural history, which would in any case be unnecessarily prescriptive, but rather because it has mini-mised the beneficial influence and effect Williams's work could have on social and historical enquiry. As Terry Lovell has suggested, his work should now 'flow back to inform the disciplines whose boundaries it rejected' (1989: 139).

The purpose of this chapter is in the first instance to encourage that flow back into the discipline of history, and by extension into the social sciences more generally. There are various ways in which this could be done, although an exhaustive treatment of each would require a book in itself. In the interests of thematic unity, in so far as this can be regarded as a legitimate possibility in these postmodernist times, I intend to concentrate on the problem of develop-ing an analytical understanding of those symbolic acts and responses referred to by Williams which appear not to be 'prepared by social circumstances' and which, by fact of their variation from ordinary patterns and ordinary assessments of those patterns, constitute a moment of cultural disaffec-tion, a movement away from the products and sensibility of any recent and yet relatively settled past. In the hope of adding, to a modest degree, some conceptual fertilisation to what remains a pre-eminently empirical field of enquiry, I take my initial cue from Raphael Samuel's call, following Williams's sadly premature death, for some critical reflec-tion on historical practice, and more specifically for an at-tempt to close some of the distance between Williams's 'version of history' and that of left-wing historians (Samuel, 1989). Samuel has himself sympathetically discussed the ways in which Williams's intellectual identity 'was that of a histo-rian', and it would be useful to begin with a brief outline of these as they are relevant to my purpose.

For Samuel, Williams shared the 'historian's sense of the ambiguities of social change' and was a careful and atten-tive 'eavesdropper on the past'. 'What historians call "em-pathy" – measuring subjects by the accent of their own time – seems to have accorded well with the ecumenical nature of his own sympathies.'[1] In addition, Williams 'could write spellbinding historical narrative when he was moved to it', as he did in his handbook on Cobbett. Yet even in the more usual mode of critical examination against case, one encoun-ters that dense analysis and concern for complexities of detail

and interconnection that is characteristic of historical discourse at its best. This is true not only of studies like Williams's
The Long Revolution (1961) and *The Country and the City* (1973).
Analysis in the light of historical change and continuity is
present in his work on contemporary media, as for instance
in his discussion of television drama or in his positioning
of television watching and the trend towards 'mobile priva-
tisation' in such 'long sequences of development' as 'the
rise of domestic sociability'. There is also in Williams a deep
sense of place and settlement, and a fierce attachment to
local roots, in both the novels and the criticism. This connects with an anti-nostalgic respect for custom and tradition. For example, Williams drew on what he saw as the
strengths of the working-class tradition of mutuality and
cooperation. Although there was something of a tendency
in his writing to generalise and thus essentialise them, Williams
remained keenly aware that these strengths had been developed in the face of the anarchic violence of capitalist business and planning inflicted on the social infrastructure of
communities and lives. Consider, for example, this impas-
sioned paragraph from his final political manifesto, *Towards
2000*, where Williams is talking about the historical record
of capitalist appropriation, dispossession and despoilation:

> What is really astonishing is that it is the inheritors and
> active promoters, the ideologists and agents, of this con-
> tinuing world-wide process who speak to the rest of us, at
> least from one side of their mouths, about the traditional
> values of settlement, community and loyalty. These, the
> great disrupters, not only of other people's settlements
> but of many of those of their own nominal people, have
> annexed and appropriated, often without challenge, many
> of the basic human feelings about a necessary and desir-
> able society. They retain this appropriation even while their
> hands are endlessly busy with old and new schemes in
> which the priorities are wholly different: schemes through
> which actual people and communities are depressed or
> disappear, under the calculations of cost–benefit, profit
> and advantageous production (1983a: 186–7).

It is because of his 'outrage that this has happened and
been allowed to happen' that he was able to write so well,

historically, of someone like William Cobbett: 'a man in whom love of birthplace, love of country, and root-and-branch opposition to the whole social order could be authentically integrated' (1983a: 185; and see also Williams, 1973). What can be taken from Cobbett, despite his harking back to the days of 'good old England', is the fraught, harrowed sense of 'living through a time when an old social order is visibly breaking up', and when the future is 'projected, imagined, exhorted but still quite unknown'. The waves of that future were generated by the forces then coming through, in Cobbett's own time, and it was these which would subsequently 'break on the shore of modernity' and 'run clear to where we now stand' (Williams, 1983b: 58–9).[2] The problems of response to social disruption, to the fragmentation and dispersal of communities occurring by force of external motivations heedless of the social, cultural, psychological and emotional costs involved, and thus of the subsequent deprivations of settled ways of living, were repeatedly returned to in Williams's work. While he felt akin to those who accommodated themselves to an existence of 'exile' or 'outsider' status, the struggle to define and assert viable lines of affiliation, association and community in the interests of a radically open and sustained democracy, was more deeply and insistently felt. There was in Williams a profound sense of the need for human social connections across and through time, for the need, not to be enslaved to imaginary continuities or bewitched by the past's mythic associations, but to be able to draw creatively and reflexively on what past struggles have bequeathed. It is through this sense that he was able to rework 'age-old ideas to meet novel circumstances', and to engage with conservative argument, 'taking on reactionary social thinkers, but turning their perception to radical and democratic ends' (Samuel, 1989: 145).

It is notable that in various aspects of Williams's thinking there are strong yet unenunciated affinities with the political philosophy and cultural ideas of William Morris. Curiously, there is little avowed sympathy for or developed treatment of Morris in Williams's actual writings. It was his friend and colleague Edward Thompson who accomplished, in a long-neglected early book, the task of re-establishing the moral strengths and contesting the falsified accounts in 'the case of Morris' (Thompson 1977a; see also 1976b). Even more curiously, it was this line of critique – uncovering hidden meanings and dispelling subsequent distortions – which Williams undertook in *Culture and Society* for the whole tradition of English cultural criticism. Yet Morris himself was approached with a veiled caution and his contribution to this tradition, as the first significant English Marxist writing within it, was considerably played down (Williams, 1958: 153–61, 165; see also 1979: 128–9). Morris is recognised as a 'pivotal figure' who strived to re-energise the connections between Romantic anti-utilitarianism and working-class politics, yet at the same time he is 'treated out of sequence, as the tail-end of a tradition dominated by Carlyle and Ruskin and left out of the 1880s and 1890s', rather than being seen as 'in historical terms . . . more in touch with the actual and decisive history of the working class than any other writer of the period' (Goode, 1990: 191). His attempt 'to break the general deadlock' is recognised as 'remarkable', but what this gives with one hand is taken away with the other in that the recognition is never properly explored (Williams, 1958: 153). On the other side, in Williams's own work, the significance of contemporary developments was perhaps more sensitively and, where appropriate, more positively understood, as for instance in what he had to say about the potentialities of new communication technologies. The forces and pressures of contemporary social disintegration were also more directly addressed, on their own terms and without, to anything like the same degree, that habitual reliance on the reference backwards, in an optimism more for the past than the present, which at times weakens Morris's work. As Samuel points out, while Williams had no desire for a future that would 'exclude the past', at the same time he 'had a historian's sense of the deceptiveness of tradition' (1989: 146). He had no desire to cling to tradition for its own sake or when its adherences had become, to any significant extent, outmoded.

This leads us back to the rationale for this chapter. Despite the claim that, by any conventional standards, Williams's work does not 'count as history', ignoring as it does the technical procedures and apparatus as well as the systematically developed frameworks and procedures of specifically

historical research, it is high time for a more open dialogue
to be developed between social and cultural history and the
more obviously cultural studies approach which Williams
represented. Dialogue requires, by definition, a two-way flow.
It is with this in mind that we should consider as well the
value for cultural studies of stopping in its current tracks,
turning around from what seem at times to be little other
than intra-referential quarrels – quarrels which begin to sound
more and more like those of an established discipline – and
resuscitating itself at the wellsprings of the historical imagination. The example is there, clearly and abundantly enough,
in the work of its so-called founding fathers – a patriarchal
term if ever there was one – with Williams chief among them.
The historical imagination is nowadays all too often lacking in
media and cultural studies, and for this reason, among others,
Lovell's 'flow back' should not be in one direction only.

While he was deeply intrigued by innovation, emergence
and change, Williams was never simply enthralled by the
new. In his thinking, for instance, about the characteristics
and possibilities of the new media of film and television,
there was never a sense of fixation with the seductive qualities
of contemporary trends, or of being attracted by the temptations of speculating about their consequences purely in
contemporary terms, the terms in theoretical fashion. Through
certain oblique references, through a continual although
varying strategy of connecting from an astute distance, through
a general preference for mature, historically informed consideration rather than intellectually *chic* conjecture, there
was a sceptical unease in his work with the *beau monde* of
cultural theory. Rather, the concern was always to situate
current developments and discontinuities within a broader
historical framework, and most particularly one encompass-
ing the past two centuries or so, for it is within this period
that the key terms of our thinking about culture and society, and past and present, were formed. The effort was always to try 'to combine close attention to the present with
historical awareness' (Tredell, 1990: 61), and so then to
understand not only past and present in their historical
relations, but also the present itself as history.

For example, in considering the relations of the term *culture*
to those of *class, art, industry* and *democracy*, in his early years

as a tutor in adult education, Williams grasped the need to give 'an historical shape' to the connections between their changing senses. Out of this realisation developed the inter-disciplinary project in historical semantics that led to the publication of *Keywords* (1976), a study in the changing meanings and associations of historically significant terms, in their relations of usage and context, in the connections between their past senses and their recent or contemporary variations, and in the ways specialist discourse enters into everyday linguistic practices. The study focuses on the major informing words, often highly charged with ideas and values, in our vocabulary of social change and continuity, and of culture and society. Yet the exercise is not simply philological. In tracing the genealogia of related model concepts and signs, it is concerned with the elements of a lexicon which are integral to particular ways of seeing culture and society, social pattern and process. The key elements of this lexicon demonstrate, in their variable and highly mutable forms, the shifts, interests, struggles and reversals (as, for example, in a word like *individual*) that are part of a broader dynamic of social production and relations: 'what enters into them is the contradictory and conflict-ridden social history of the people who speak the language, including all the variations between signs at any given time' (1979: 176). As Williams put it in his introduction to the book: 'The emphasis on history, as a way of understanding contemporary problems of meaning and structures of meaning, [was] a basic choice' (1976: 20). This touches on the book's political implications, for it is 'not a neutral review' of lexical 'innovation, obsolescence, specialisation, extension, overlap [and] transfer', but rather an exploration of a shifting, highly mutable vocabulary of social and cultural argument: 'a vocabulary to use, to find our own ways in, to change as we find it necessary to change it, as we go on making our own language and history' (ibid: 22).

Although there are numerous passages in Williams's work which attempt to set forth a record of past forms of social organisation and relations through historical narrative, dealing in a treatment of the past on its own ground, so to speak, this approach operates more generally in conjunction with a critically reflexive form of regressive method and a

demystifying purpose – the attempt to get at what he liked
to call 'the real history' behind the various occlusions and
mythical variants of the official record. These principles of
enquiry involved seeking the originations of tangible contemporary forms in the less tangible shadows of the past,
feeling out present issues and problems in terms of their
historical echoes, traces and counterparts, stripping away
reactionary or highly partial associations in order to reas-
sert the historically 'lived' pattern, and to make visible the
hidden strengths of past cultural evidence. Such principles
are far from merely presentist, though they always carry the
danger of presentism; the intent instead is the creation of
dialogue, of movement back and forth, across and through
time, of looking backward in order to look forward, without either perspective monopolising the work of reconstruction and analysis. The questions of how we think with what
we have inherited from past generations and periods, of
how and why we tell our stories of the past, must then be
addressed in any historiographical activity which goes beyond a naive enchantment or a false objectivism of stubborn facts.

Structures of Feeling, Forces of Change

These are difficult questions, and not ones which should be
settled by recourse to easy targets. As a beginning, in an
early discussion of the relationship of past and present cultures, Williams used the instructive analogy of chemical precipitation as a means of distinguishing the changes wrought
by the movement of historical time. In a 'lived' culture of
the present, all the elements of cultural experience exist
'in solution', as inseparable parts of a complex whole, dissolved and suspended in the fluidity of social and cultural
processes in an experience of the present. It is 'only in our
own time and place that we can expect to know, in any
sustained way, the general organisation' (1961: 63). As time
moves on, and places, institutions, cultural practices, language and the symbolic worlds of particular social groups
and strata change, in whatever direction or form, certain
elements are lost, displaced, even become irrecoverable, while
others are 'precipitated' out from that previous lived solution

and become the readily identifiable features of a particular period, generation, institution, project or movement. Our experience of the past is of a range of series of precipitate elements, whereas 'in the living experience of the time every element was in solution, an inescapable part of a complex whole' (ibid: 63). These precipitated elements are not conserved and arranged in some organic way, though; they are subject to both selective organisation and preferred representation as a version and view of the past. The past is therefore always a produced past where certain events and episodes, certain expressions and forms, become fixed and explicit to the exclusion and concealment of others. The task for cultural analysis in this respect is that of trying to get behind such features of time's traces in order to regain a fuller sense, once again, of the felt 'social character' and experiential specificities of past cultures, past 'ways of life'. This is one of the hardest goals we can set ourselves. 'The most difficult thing to get hold of, in studying any past period,' according to Williams, 'is this felt sense of the quality of life at a particular place and time: a sense of the ways in which the particular activities combined into a way of thinking and living' (ibid: 63).

There will always be a gap between 'lived' cultural experience and any attempt, in history, biography, film or novel, to reconstruct intellectually and imaginatively the texture of that experience across time, in a different period, when the very language and technology which we use to communicate our attempt has changed from those used in the former time. Although the attempt is, at almost every step, beset with snares and obstructions, the difficulties that are involved do not mean that the task should not be attempted; indeed, it is those difficulties which partly sustain the task and its fascination in the first place. There is no one best way of trying to close the gap, but for historical cultural analysis, which cannot satisfactorily operate with the illusion of any pristine recovery of the past, or even specific aspects of it, certain conceptual tools are necessary if we are to get an interpretive handle on the relationship between cultural experiences of the past and the attentuated historical forms which constitute our basic working materials. A central term for Williams in this respect was *structure of feeling*. The term is rather loose and inconsistently applied, and yet, contrary to its detractors, I find it conceptually useful in the practice of doing both social history and cultural analysis. It is, firstly, for this reason, and because of the difficulties associated with it, that I intend to concentrate on it. A second reason is its centrality in Williams's approach to writing about history and culture. He made reference to it throughout his work, from *Preface to Film* (Williams and Orrom, 1954) right through to its fullest formulation, in *Marxism and Literature* (Williams, 1977), along with his defence of its usefulness and validity in *Politics and Letters* (1979). Indeed, its continuous presence in his work indicates the artificiality of any sense of a rigid divide between the early and later stages of his intellectual career.[3]

That said, the main purpose of the concept at the outset was in its provision of a unit of analyis which can be utilised in defining and describing that 'sense of the ways in which the particular activities combined into a way of thinking and living' for 'a particular place and time'. Structures of feeling are generated by specific social groups in the course of their experience of and participation in everyday social life, and what follows before too long is that as they arise out of the need to give shape and identity to the localised nature of characteristic social experiences, and to articulate a group's sense of itself in the social world, so they then act back on subsequent experiences by structuring the ways in which such experiences are understood as characteristic and significant. Emerging from the urge to understand what is experientially new and different for a generation or group, and to express a sense of identity which crystallises in differentiation from what has been inherited from the past, structures of feeling come to mediate the group's collective understanding of social experiences and of relations between the social world and a group's place within it. The movement is one of thinking about the process of living to living through the product of that thinking.

This requires an immediate qualification in that what distinguishes a structure of feeling is that it is emergent and provisional, not so much a fully articulated realisation or achievement as one in the creative throes of becoming articulated. Structures of feeling are the external or visible cultural manifestations of an interiorised engagement with the various elements in the general organisation, interiorised not in any imagined private sense but rather as a collective, imaginative response to the relations between what is inherited and what seems contemporary. They involve a general move towards the realisation of a pattern that is not yet a pattern, but which is nonetheless acutely felt in the need to move towards it. In one place, Williams identifies this striving towards identity in terms of certain characteristic 'elements of impulse, restraint and tone' (1977: 132), which can be identified in particular cultural and linguistic forms, and yet in a stronger historical sense these elements relate to a deep and widespread possession within a particular grouping which, in their linking of the personal and social, allow for a very definite form and process of communication among its members. As a collectively realised pattern of response, a structure of feeling is emergent and so only in the stage of becoming anything quite as recognisable and fully defined as a pattern, which is then usually only clearly seen and understood as such with the benefit of hindsight. For this self-same reason a structure of feeling can neither be formally learned nor passed on over time. This in turn means that structures of feeling inevitably change, from period to period, and from generation to generation, so that while continuities are taken up and many aspects of the overall organisation are reproduced, each new generation feels 'its whole life in certain ways differently', and shapes 'its creative response into a new structure of feeling'. (1961: 65)

'Structure of feeling' is an elusive concept because of the inchoate 'moment' of cultural process for which it attempts to provide a general formulation. As a concept, it is difficult to define because, in a sense, it is made up of the formally undefined (Gallagher, 1980: 645).[4] It refers to how social events, encounters and relations in solution, in a 'lived' experience of the present, are met, and how meanings begin to be made of them. It is the still-being-shaped experience of experiences, and conceptually it is directed to the ways in which experiences are culturally experienced and responded to by a particular social or distinctively generational group as it pushes up against the limits and constraints of institutionalised social and cultural forms. A structure of feeling is significantly different from ideology, referring to a different aspect of social consciousness and a different process of holding and shaping experience within consciousness; it is, if you like, 'ideology' before it becomes ideology, and so must always be defined in relation to ideology as a fixed and self-defensive formation, since what it refers to comes either before or after the creation and maintenance of an ideological position in that sense. Structures of feeling can and do become ideological, but at their inception are always distinct from the ideological formations to which they stand in relation. They are generated in the first place through the efforts of a collectivity to make sense, to realise meaning and significance in the form and process of everyday social life. Structures of feeling emerge in the lacunae between widely recognised values and their failed or inconsistent realisation; they develop out of the contradictions between public ideals or standards, and their 'lived' social experience among different social groups and categories.

In certain ways, then, these efforts will draw on and so be accommodated by existing, formed ideologies, but when those existing ways of seeing and thinking fall short of the explanatory mark, when they seem stale or inadequate in relation to the creative thrust of the response to actual experience and the struggle to develop a sustainable identity within changed conditions and circumstances, or when there arises a palpable sense of contradiction and unevenness between ideas, and between ideas and experience as these are actually lived out and responded to in mundane social affairs, then the moment of generation of a new structure of feeling is ripe. At such junctures in the social living of lives, a structure of feeling represents an attempt to reach beyond, to transcend and develop an alternative to established, often socially dominant ways of viewing and accounting for a social order, ways which are always derived from the past, in time's habitual or legitimated traces. When such efforts become collectively emboldened, what is associated with the past may come to appear outmoded, historical in a perjorative sense in relation to the effort to cast new light on a general feeling about the existing order and the place of a certain social category at odds within it. That feeling is then structured according to a particular sense of being placed

in the world, a particular sense of how the social itself is
constituted and inclined to operate, and a particular sense
of what is now socially and culturally possible, of what can
be traced into time future.

Structure of feeling is thus a concept relating to a moment
or stage of social and cultural life existing in necessary tension with cultural processes and forms which are mobilised
in defence of the ideological status quo, which gather their
forces behind the effort to provide warrants for 'the way
things are'. That tension is necessary either because the
generation of a structure of feeling is always in danger of
becoming contained, incorporated or cast to the inconse-
quential margins by existing socio-cultural modes of legitimation, or because the cultural shape and identity given to
experience which goes beyond existing, received ideological positions always poses a danger of transformation or more
limited damage to those positions. The analytical force of
the concept derives from its attempt to provide a descriptive term for cultural practices which are in the process of
active formation as part of an always ongoing social life,
whose forms in modernity are impelled by the dynamic of
continual movement and transition, of creation and destruc-
tion, and what is crucial to it is that these emergent or pre-
emergent practices always in some way pose a challenge to
established conventions or accepted forms, for what they
represent are creative challenges to what has become stable, fixed or outworn. Such challenges take shape in contradistinction to that which no longer provides the means
for articulating the general 'feeling' that is striving to be
realised, to what indeed may appear as so many blockages
and hindrances to the struggle for articulation. The concept
of structure of feeling tries to provide a means for referring
to what happens culturally in moments of disruption or
dislocation, in innovative breaks from what can, with relative ease, be reproduced in terms of the inherited and already
available resources. A structure of feeling becomes manifest
as potentially transgressive or as at least having the potentially equivalent force of the transgressive, so that moments
of pre-emergence of new cultural meanings, practices and
relationships are experientially and symbolically in tension
or conflict with 'official' culture and accredited cultural insti-

tutions, and appear to betoken and register for the first time certain breaks and new directions in general cultural life.

Yet exactly why 'structure' and why 'feeling'? The short answer to this is that the conjunction of the two terms at the centre of Williams's thought is intentionally oxymoronic. A fuller response might run along the following lines. To begin with, Williams's insistence on the dimension of feeling is important because it captures that which is in the process of emergence in a specifically affective mode of social consciousness and relationships: 'not feeling against thought, but thought as felt and feeling as thought', an intimate and at the time not fully tangible combination of 'consciousness, experience and feeling' occurring in an existentially forceful *present* tense (1977: 128 and 132). This is then set against experience in the sense of any ensemble of social relations or practices already formed and established in meaning and valuation, or in other terms against social semantic figures in their precipitated forms, rather than that which is incomplete because in the process of becoming articulated – a tune in the historical air that has yet to be grasped and notated, a shift in the rhythm of social movement that has not yet become firmly attached to socially abstracted and agreed signs or codes. The relevance of feeling is to that which is not yet manifest in any moment of cultural change: 'it is primarily to emergent formations (though often in the form of modification or disturbance in older forms) that the structure of feeling, *as solution*, relates' (ibid: 134). Yet Williams carefully distinguishes 'this specific solution' from 'mere flux', and this is then the importance of 'structure' in what appears initially as its paradoxical coupling with 'feeling': 'It is a structured formation . . . at the very edge of semantic availability' and in that sense is a pre-formation, an affective force struggling to realise a specific cultural and historical structure through its 'particular linkages, particular emphases and suppressions, and in what are often its most recognisable forms, particular deep starting-points and conclusions' (ibid: 134). These qualities can be noticed retrospectively, as precipitates rather than as cultural elements in solution; at the time of their present tense they are more deeply suffused through the whole process of living and are not formally identified, learned and reproduced, though they connect *as structure* in their challenge to what is ordered and settled, and in terms of their own 'specific internal relations, at once interlocking and in tension' (ibid: 132).

A Shifting Signifier of Time's Traces

In speaking earlier against any sharp demarcation between the earlier and later stages of Williams's work, my intention was to emphasise the continuity of his work. This continuity can be traced in his use of certain concepts, but also more broadly in a long-lasting opposition both to idealised conceptions of culture as text, artefact or value, as manifest for example in the critical leanings of Eliot and Leavis, among numerous others, and to reductionist accounts of culture, art or aesthetics, particularly in vulgar or mechanistic forms of Marxism operating with rigidly determinist applications of the base-superstructure metaphor. Yet an insistence on this point should not be made in detriment to any recognition of the development of his work. So, for instance, with the concept of structure of feeling Williams continued to refine and hone its formulation, along with the senses in which it could be applied. The early association simply with the art or literature of a period, and the methodological stress on forms and conventions, expands into an identification of 'a much more general possession' drawn on in the 'interaction between the official consciousness of an epoch – codified in its doctrines and legislation – and the whole process of actually living its consequences' (1968: 9; 1979: 158). It is that process which at certain conjunctures leads to the emergence of potentially disjunctive or counter-hegemonic elements of culture. Further to this, as Williams continued to work on the concept, there developed a keener sense of distinction between emergent elements and those which were simply novel, and hence relatively amenable to assimilation, while the realisation of structures of feeling in both experiential and artistic dimensions of cultural life became more fully emphasised.

The earlier focus on the realisation of the structure of feeling of a historical period in our experience of its artistic works was self-limiting in the sense that it presupposed an almost singular and certainly holistic understanding of the particular 'lived' quality involved, not to mention the possibility of any general agreement as to its veridical representation in such works.[5] As Nicolas Tredell has pointed out, this calls into question who is referred to in talking of 'our' experience, for if different readers or viewers identify different structures of feeling, in the art of a particular period, in what way 'do we judge between them, when the only court of appeal is constituted by witnesses who have already differed in their accounts'. The 'verification' of a structure of feeling in the experience of the work of art as a whole entails a return to the experience of the work which was the means of locating and realising the structure of feeling in the first place. This circularity of argument was a definite weakness in the initial uses to which Williams put the term, precisely because its 'cognitive status' was seen as dependent on the culturally privileged work of art (Tredell, 1990: 13–14). The assumption of this dependence had to be challenged before a more satisfactory account of the relation between a structure of feeling as a collective response and its more specific expressions could be developed. The seed of that challenge was sown in the insistence that artistic works should neither be elevated to an absolute, timeless position of aesthetic pre-eminence, nor separated from the 'ordinary experience' of which they variously partake. It could be argued that the whole point of the term 'structure of feeling' was, from the start, that of attempting to respond conceptually to the pressure of this insistence, despite the hesitancies, inconsistencies and ambiguities attendant on its earlier formulation and application. As such, it implies for Williams the intellectual effort of breaking with the ties of his Leavisite inheritance. What is still left open is the question of acknowledging and working with a sense of the specificities of artistic and cultural forms without abstracting them out of history or material conditions, or, in what is the opposite danger, without dissolving them 'into some indiscriminate general social or cultural practice' (Williams, 1981: 129). In the interests of an emphatically historicising approach, it is perhaps best that the question remains as such, open *because* resistant to any fixed or definitive theoretical closure. In *Marxism and Literature*, Williams defined open questions in exactly these terms. Their characteristic quality is that they entail 'a set of specific historical questions, which will give different kinds of answer in different actual situations' (1977: 197).

What was never satisfactorily resolved, however, was the tension between the stress on the ordinariness of culture and the claim that his methodological hypothesis has a special relevance to the 'high' art and literature of a generationally specific formation. This seems to me true despite, for instance, his close attention to the ways in which the 'popular' has been mediated in modern forms of culture by market-driven criteria, or again, despite his distinction between postmodernism as 'pseudo-radical' and merely novel, and the 'more properly innovatory, pre-emergent "structure of feeling" . . . in the politics of the contemporary new social movements' of peace, ecology and feminism (Milner, 1993: 60; Williams, 1983a: 250). The 'culture is ordinary' formula can be taken as directed against the hierarchisation of culture where any selective 'high art' tradition serves as the aesthetic or intellectual collateral of educational and social privilege. It can also be taken as directed against the associated disembedding of cultural texts and objects from the conditions and currents within which they are socially and historically formed. Yet it has also in practice to be realised in a cultural history and in forms of cultural studies that attempt analytically to treat 'high' and 'low' in their cultural and historical interrelatedness. While it is easy to say it, and to point to movements in other directions, Williams's work in this sense never properly dissociated itself from its early literary-critical preoccupations, with the result that proportionally there is much more detailed attention to 'letters' in his work than to the close reading of popular cultural texts in themselves, or in their relations with canonical forms.

The same point could be made, more forcefully, of other critics, and in Williams's case the shortcoming is more than made up for by his extremely productive thinking around the terms 'culture' and 'popular', from *Culture and Society* and *Keywords* onwards, as well as by his radical commitment to cultural democracy, his influential awareness of the politics of culture, and his heartfelt aversion to the exploitation of culture in the interests of easy money and emotional manipulation. The substantive historical cultural analysis of specifically popular forms has in any case been taken up by others, who in many cases have been influenced by his work, itself diverse and prolific. Yet the problem relates also to the tendency mentioned earlier of referring to structure of feeling in the singular. This is one of the criticisms raised by Williams's interlocutors in *Politics and Letters* (1979), where they point out that any given historical period contains more than one generation, while in capitalist social orders there are clearly differentiated classes, 'not to speak of many intermediate strata with their own sensibility and history and memory' (1977: 157–8, 173). To use the concept in the singular may also imply a lack of conflict within any particular generation (O'Connor, 1989: 84). Applying it in that way may then occlude other significant intra-generational categories, such as those of gender and ethnicity. In *Marxism and Literature*, Williams had written that the 'effective formations of most actual art relate to already manifest social formations', whereas structure of feeling relates conceptually to what is emergent or pre-emergent, '*as solution*' (1977: 134). The generational or class points, as well as those of gender or ethnicity, to be identified in relation to the historical moments of new structures of feeling, are therefore those of significant social cleavage and disruption from which new cultural sensibilities and practices arise. In response, Williams quite rightly concedes the criticism of singularity, although he adds the important rider that the diversity of alternative structures 'is itself historically variable' (1979: 158). Precisely the same could be said of the social category associated with, say, a particular semantic figure which articulates the historical experience that in its precipitate forms becomes recognisable as a particular structure of feeling. However, the problems of defining the boundaries between generations, not to mention periods, and of dealing with alternative or variable manifestations of the phenomenon within the same temporal span, remained unresolved, and in this respect Tredell is justified in describing the term structure of feeling as a shifting signifier (Tredell, 1990: 31; also O'Connor, 1989: 84).

Tredell poses a further question in asking how structures of feeling change, 'and in what sense, when they do change, they remain "structures"' (1990: 31). The answer to this, in abstract terms, should be clear enough from the foregoing, in that such social-semantic figures change because of historical movement, and because of the historically specific and contingent quality of social experience where particular generations or groups struggle to articulate this in cultural and symbolic forms. This is to talk of succession and supersession, but if by 'they' is meant any particular structure of feeling once it has been developed, then, as already acknowledged, it becomes subject to the shaping constraints of its social institutionalisation, and to the pressures to entrench once it becomes widely taken up, in a broad range of media and channels of communication.

Connecting with the Social

Another criticism of the term led Williams to reverse his earlier claim that it is easier to grasp and interpret an emergent structure of feeling in the present in which it is 'lived', rather than in the opposite direction. The tangible and fluid texture of lived experience becomes lost over time, with its immediate historical participants and witnesses relegated to the interminable silence of the grave. Contrariwise, whatever has precipitated out from that experience as a time's traces is for that very reason more easily recognisable as characteristic and central. In the stultifying face of this, it should always be emphasised that the point of such features as variability and fluid boundaries is that, as a key historiographical principle, what is claimed to be characteristic and central for any particular historical formation should always be taken as contestable. The revision which Williams makes is in saying that while 'a structure of feeling always exists in the present tense, so to speak grammatically', it is not 'more recoverable or more accessible in the temporal present than in the past'. 'For the structure is precisely something which can only be grasped as such by going beyond the indiscriminate flux of experiences that are contemporary with one' (1977: 163).

Williams's appeal to 'lived experience' as a source of perception and knowledge, and as a locus of meaning-production in social life, has been criticised as populist, voluntarist and empiricist. The category of experience has in fact been derided as the soft centre of 'culturalism'. I shall deal substantively with this category in subsequent chapters, but at this stage it is important to be clear about two features of the way it has been employed in this particular area of work. Firstly, Williams did not operate with a naive or sentimental view of experience, any more than did Edward Thompson, who has also been attacked for reliance upon the term. Even a cursory acquaintance with their writing, never mind their politics, should establish this. It is therefore quite misleading to claim, as does Fred Inglis, that Williams had 'absolute trust in the truths of his own experience' (1993: 54). It is exactly this sort of 'absolute trust' of which the concept of structure of feeling is suspicious, and it is designed to avoid two consequences of it in particular: on the one hand, the failure to trust other people's experiences, and 'to change in relation to them, [to] refuse an education anew' (Johnson, 1994: 359); and on the other, the kinds of appeal that the term 'experience' itself sometimes appear to entail – 'appeals to a direct unmediated access to something real' being the most easy and dangerous (Middleton, 1989: 52). Secondly, it is important to remember that the reference to experience was directed against various fronts, economism and cultural idealism initially, as mentioned above, but also more latterly, structuralist variants of Marxism and formalist versions of semiotics, both of them anti-historical in theoretical conception and direction. Althusserian structuralism, in particular, considered experience as so thoroughly permeated by ideology that it could be seen as little other than a realm of delusion within which ordinary people were hopelessly trapped. The semiotic distrust of experience is more complicated, and not only because it has greatly enriched the whole field of textual analysis. The point to emphasise here is that Williams approached the basic units of communication – sign, language, speech – not as mechanical structures requiring only a synchronic understanding of their assemblage, but equally as social practices in a historically contingent, changing and continuing process: 'the sign itself' is 'part of a (socially created) physical and material world' (1977: 38).

This is a crucial emphasis, and it is theoretically consistent

with the position identified by Williams as cultural materialism. As a modernist thinker, Williams accepted that social
and historical reality does not come to us unmediated, and
that 'lived experience' does not 'presuppose some pristine
contact between the subject and the reality in which this
subject is immersed'. But he pointed to the danger, in much
linguistic theory, discourse analysis and semiotics, of swing-
ing over to 'the opposite point in which the epistemological wholly absorbs the ontological', so that we must say that
we live only and wholly within signification and discourse,
'that it is only in the ways of knowing that we exist at all'
(1979: 167). The shift is damaging for historical understanding, for if it is the case that 'every signified is also in the
position of a signifier', that is, part of 'a system of floating
signifiers pure and simple, with no determinable relation
to any extra-linguistic referents at all', then history as such
becomes 'randomised' or, as Edward Said put it in describing the structuralist philosophy of history, 'legislated accident' (Anderson, 1983: 46–8; Derrida, 1981: 20; Said, 1985:
311). Williams's whole approach to history and culture was
relational, seeking to move against both the reified document and the textual object isolated from social process. In
a lecture given in Oxford in 1986, he reminded his audience of the irony involved in the derivation of both 'text'
and 'canon' from the same vocabulary:

> A text: an isolated object to be construed and discoursed
> upon: once from pulpits, now from seminar desks. Nor
> could it make any useful difference when this isolated ob-
> ject began to be opened up to its internal uncertainties
> and multiplicities, or to the further stage of its entire and
> helpless openness to any form of interpretation or analy-
> sis whatever: that cutting loose of readers and critics from
> any obligation to social connection or historical fact. For
> what was being excluded, from this work reduced to the
> status of text or of text as critical device, was the socially
> and historically specifiable agency of its making (Williams,
> 1989a: 172).

It is to that agency in its specifiable forms that the concept of structure of feeling is addressed. This may appear
to suggest that there is too much indeterminacy about it

(soft-centres again) when in fact what we are facing is its self-acknowledged limits, its refusal 'to be "proven" in terms of a material model which is somehow anterior in any "settled" sense' (Wallis, 1993: 134). The concept is intended as a device for thinking about the active processes involved in social and cultural change, and for illuminating the 'lived' textures of historical experience in ways which go beyond both formal political histories and formalist approaches to cultural texts or documentation. It is an analytical tool which seeks to connect with a particular dynamic in historical and cultural processes. It does not claim to provide a panoramic view of everyday past social and cultural life, or reveal every aspect of the social structure of different historical formations. Further, Williams conceded that 'there are historical experiences which never do find their semantic figures at all'. As suggested above, it may be that these have in fact existed in specifically popular forms of culture, but the forms themselves have not been recorded or duly attended to. That point aside, Williams was surely right to say that one cannot fill historical silences 'with other people's structures of feeling' (1979: 165). This is important not only for its critical humility, but also for its recognition of the dangers of alien implantation in any act of historical recovery and explanation.

Structures of Feeling, Forces of Power

Alan O'Connor has correctly noted that despite the centrality of 'structure of feeling' to Williams's sociology of culture, attempts to clarify it 'have not been very successful' (1989: 83). In attempting to redress this situation, I have suggested that its real cutting edge lies in its application to liminal forms of experience, as a category of pre-emergence referring to developing forms of change that are not, at the stage which is addressed, realised as characteristic.[6] This sense is obviously blunted by its alternative use in reference to any later settlement into a relatively habitual way of seeing and thinking. This alternative sense of the term is equally, if not more frequently employed, even by those who are credited with Williams for laying the foundation stones of cultural studies. For example, Thompson, in reviewing *The Country and the City*, talked of our being 'trapped within certain

structures of feeling: the prevailing rationalising urban mode
on the one hand, the evasive, retrospective rural mode on
the other. And you can't *argue* people into a new structure
of feeling' (1994: 253). He was right on both counts; it is
the particular application of the term which is unfortunate.
Examples of this application are legion, and many have surely
taken their cue from Williams himself, who wavered between
these two senses of the term, so that at times his writing
tended towards an elision of structure of feeling as pre-
emergent and structure of feeling as an accomplished formation. In some ways this is not surprising, for the two senses
stem from the attempt to grapple with the movement from
cultural elements in solution to those in precipitate forms,
which are then identifiable with hindsight precisely because
their historical interconnectedness has become bedded into
a more or less accepted story or pattern of how a time's
traces signify. But there are certain uses which are incred-
ibly loose. For example, Williams spoke in a mid-1970s arti-
cle on his position in relation to the Marxist tradition, of
having learned from personal experience and observation
of the experience of incorporation, and the reality of hegemony, and then immediately conflated these with 'the
saturating power of the structures of feeling of a given society' (1989a: 75). The effect of this is to drain his own term
of its conceptual force, for as he also said at around the
same period, once the defining characteristics of structures
of feeling have become formalised, classified and institutionalised, then by 'that time the case is different' (1977: 132).
The significance of that difference should not be lost.

Yet Jim McGuigan is surely right to point out that Williams's
use of the concept of structure of feeling in *The Long Revolution* as an analytical tool for unravelling the class-cultural
formations of 1840s Britain can be read as 'a concrete illus-
tration of why Williams later found the concept of hegemony
so useful' (McGuigan, 1993: 168). The connection is a vital
one, firstly because it highlights again the continuities in
Williams's work in its attempt to overcome the presup-
positional categories and reductive tendencies of the base-
superstructure model. In this respect, and despite its
inadequacies, the early formulation of 'structure of feeling'
grappled for an alternative to notions of cultural practice

as reflection, homology or correspondence. But it was only through the engagement with Gramsci that Williams was able to realise the analytical limits of the concept by narrowing it down to address questions concerning challenge, disruption and change, and substituting the earlier formulation with the concept of cultural hegemony. Additionally, Gramsci's concept improved on that earlier formulation because of its constitutive emphasis on forces of power. The appeal of this concept for Williams clearly lay in its compatibility with his emphasis on history as process as well as product, and with his preference for thinking about ideology in terms of how it is 'lived' through cultural practices in their widest sense, ranging from works to lives, not so much as 'false consciousness' or even error and illusion, but rather as the conscious use of 'alien' or contrary elements in the construction of meanings and values.

This use in practical consciousness is integral to hegemonic processes, though it could be argued that hegemony as a concept does not sufficiently acknowledge the active elements of thinking and feeling that are paradoxically wrought up in the reproduction of common sense. The point here is that the disjointed, fragmentary, contradictory and incoherent themes and values of common sense should not be set in complete contradistinction to either 'good sense' or avant-gardist 'solutions', for, as Michael Billig has argued, the 'contrary character' of common sense, the variability of the elements it contains, should not in itself be downgraded, for it is exactly this variability which 'permits the possibility of argumentative critique. The elements of common sense can be used to criticise common sense' (Billig, 1991: 22). If 'culture is ordinary', then we must not lose sight of the 'ideological subject' thinking with, and manoeuvring around, the contrariness of 'ordinary sense' in his or her everyday life. It is in this way that, for Williams, culture is fundamentally connected with the ways in which people make sense and meaning out of their social experience, which they do through the variable cultural forms and practices available to them. This activity in its acutest modes can then lead to challenge and change through the collectively formative processes which are generative of new structures of feeling. Yet the significance of the link to Gramsci is that all the variable ways of making meaning and communicating meaningfully do not occur outside of relations of domination and subordination but within them. The concept of hegemony relates cultural and communicational processes to 'specific distributions of power and influence', to specific inequalities in people's means and capacity to shape and define their lives: 'What is decisive is not only the conscious system of ideas and beliefs, but the whole lived social process as practically organised by specific and dominant meanings and values' (Williams, 1977: 108–9).

In his later work, Williams typologically distinguished between different elements of culture, with the distinction sometimes extending to different cultural formations, as a contribution to further theorising the variability of elements within a 'lived' cultural whole. As we have seen, in any given period, a cultural formation has determinate dominant features by which we identify it; they constitute what are taken to be its centrally defining characteristics. But to speak in this way, particularly when the period in question covers a relatively broad time-span, suggests a comprehensive conformity among these dominant features and a lasting stability to them. Obviously enough, any broad descriptive labels need immediately to be qualified and refined, and what has always to be identified and recovered are the significant variations within them, for that which is dominant has continually to deal with these in order to maintain its hegemonic status and influence. It is when such variations are on the upward curve of their emergence – when they appear as radically new departures and are encountered, particularly in their manifestation as new structures of feeling, as potentially challenging – that a dominant culture is most alert to them. It is usually these which are subject to the most insistent attempts at suppression or incorporation, whereas residual elements are usually taken to be more accommodative. To the extent that this is so, that which is dominant accedes to certain residual forms, ideals or conceptions because it has not found alternatives to them, expressed in its own terms in the present. Residual elements which are simply archaic are generally the most accommodative, but others remain actively residual, and may disturb or at least chafe up against dominant ideas and beliefs, as for instance when religious values are asserted against capitalist 'free market' practices, or at any rate against their excesses when these are seen to damage the social fabric. Another contemporary example is represented by ideas about nature and the human axis within nature as these have fed into the 'greening' of ecology and the active opposition to environmentally destructive government policies and globalised business practices. It is for these reasons that residual elements connect up with the notion of selective tradition, for as Williams put it, it is in 'the incorporation of the actively residual that the work of the selective tradition is especially evident' (1977: 123).

All these variable elements are part of ideology as 'lived thought', and are woven into social experience and practices, and it in this sense that culture is a site of continual negotiation and conflict. It should not of course be conceived as only and always this, but any general approach or definition which does not include this conflictual sense will be deficient and unable to deal adequately with questions of cultural change. Not that these questions are easy. To quote Williams again: 'No analysis is more difficult than that which, faced by new forms, has to try to determine whether these are new forms of the dominant or are genuinely emergent' (1981: 205). It is in the light of this statement that we should understand the definition of popular culture offered by Williams as 'a very complex combination of residual, self-made and externally produced elements, with important internal conflicts between these' (ibid: 228), elements which he suggested need to be characterised by the degree to which they are part of the dominant, are alternative to it and require space within it while being at the same time incorporated by it, are alternative without yet having being incorporated, or are more directly and actively oppositional in the sense that they radically challenge that which the dominant axiomatically represents. This is to put it all too mechanically, and thinking of these elements in terms of their place on a continuum is not much of an improvement, for it is with the complex movements and relations between them, their concrete historical dynamics, that cultural analysis must engage, and engage with historically, for they are themselves variable over time and occur in different traces, patterns and combinations in different historical contexts.

In these ways, then, the distinctions between dominant, residual and emergent categories are closely related to the concept of structure of feeling, with the concept itself defining 'the field of contradiction between a consciously held ideology and emergent experience'. To put it another way, 'the peculiar location of a structure of feeling is the endless comparison that must occur in the process of consciousness between the articulated and the lived' (Williams, 1979: 167–8). A structure of feeling, then, is located in a yet to be defined space between discourse and situated experience; and characteristically, it 'comes through as disturbance, tension, blockage, emotional trouble' (ibid: 168). As a concept, structure of feeling illuminates a particular area of cultural praxis in a way which overcomes the subjectivism sometimes associated with 'experience', but which retrieves the process of agency that operates within active modes of experience where relatively new collective feelings and meanings are emerging, and yet are still in the process of attaining adequate and distinctive expressive forms. In what is the most insightful and succinct treatment of the concept, Peter Middleton describes it as 'a state of unfinished social relations that have not yet found the terms for their reflexive self-comprehension' (1989: 54). As such, it does not relate to experience and understanding as anterior to language, but rather to the struggle to express these in terms that are different from anything already articulated in dominant or residual cultural forms. It is in this sense that it is always potentially involved with cultural and social change.

From a historical perspective, 'structure of feeling' is conceptually useful in thinking about the dynamics of change, not from some Olympian position of detached observation and reflection, but rather from a position sensitive to participant experience, experience which is always realised intertextually and intersubjectively. For cultural analysis, the concept is useful as a methodological principle in that it requires attention to be focused on intersubjectively felt, yet historically structured moments which cannot 'be described in either wholly formal terms or paraphrased as assertions about the world' (ibid: 52). This returns us to the paradoxical coupling of the terms 'structure' and 'feeling'. Middleton rightly identifies the point of using the term 'structure' as a way of indicating that the patterns of feelings involved are socially mediated, while the point of using the term 'feeling' is to indicate the 'unfinished, partially articulated urgency' that is involved is 'the emergence of new forms of life' (ibid: 56). He also astutely connects the use of feeling, and the associated term 'emotion', with the sense in which they were taken by Plato and Aristotle as socially located, and socially learned: 'Far from being the ultimate ground of private authentic subjectivity, emotion was bound up with the social processes of education and rhetoric. Emotion did not really belong to a psychology in the modern sense at all' (ibid: 57). The analytical strength of the concept therefore resides in its attempt to overcome our own dualisms of the 'subject' – emotion and reason, experience and articulation, intuition and abstraction – and dualisms of the 'social' – language and social process, lived and recorded experience, individual and society. It is on the dialectical interactions of these categories that the concept insists. For these reasons, among others, McGuigan's judgement seems entirely appropriate when he writes that Williams's 'research programme cut a path between the twin pitfalls identified by V. N. Volosinov as long ago as the 1920s: "idealistic philosophy of culture and psychologistic cultural studies"' (1993: 174; and see Volosinov, 1986: 11). This judgement in turn relates to the concept of structure of feeling in that its fusion of 'structure' and 'feeling' 'epitomises Williams's approach in all his work – a search for system combined with the desire to acknowledge "the most delicate and least tangible parts of our activity"' (Tredell, 1990: 31; cf. Eldridge and Eldridge, 1994: 112; and Inglis, 1995: 167).

   The task of grappling with the difficulties in this kind of approach should be joined not only for the possible analytical gain which may ensue, but also for directly political reasons. What is at stake is historical consciousness itself. The fewer attempts that are made by those whose 'way of life' is generally subordinated, disrupted by forces outside of their command, or caught in the cross-rip of opposed historical currents, to tell their tale, whether of past or present, and record their experience of the cultural practices through which they have grown, developed and been shaped, then the more assertive, and difficult to deny, will be the accounts of those who, socially, politically and economically, are the most dominant and powerful. To the extent that there is no countervailing tendency to this, then the more likely it will be that hegemonic ways of seeing and thinking are generally reinforced. This connects with Williams's sense of selective traditionalisation whereby the relations of present 'lived', and documented 'period' cultures, are subject to rearrangements which, directly or indirectly, support particular interests and values, and we have then to ask how these in turn relate to more general structures and relations of social power. For that, in the end, remains the most crucial question.

Notes

1 The concept of empathy is usually rather ill-defined, though in its relation to the functions performed by imagination in processes of interpretation, it remains a useful term in the critical vocabulary. I shall critically return to it in later chapters.

2 For a harsher and more peremptory judgement, see Foot, 1980: 40. As I have argued elsewhere (Pickering, 1987), during much of the nineteenth century the past served *inter alia* as a source of aspiration for the rural proletariat. Among the points argued were that, historically, popular tradition cannot be interpreted simply as an unambiguously conservative process of serial repetition, and that there is no straightforward or absolute demarcation between conservative and radical functions in popular culture. Howkins and Dyck (1987) develop a similar approach in another study of the popular song and ballad tradition. Their study is based interpretively around Cobbett's social philosophy, husbandman agrarianism, and the 'cottage charter', and advances a persuasive case for the relativisation of the notion of political action.

3 There is a considerable difference of opinion over questions of development and continuity in Williams's work, sometimes within the same texts. For example, in the critical collection edited by Morgan and Preston, Wallis refers to Williams's earlier 'separate self' whereas in the very next chapter McGuigan talks of Williams's 'self-conscious linking of new work to past work' (see Morgan and Preston, 1993, chapters 7 and 8). The evidence of Williams's work itself clearly supports McGuigan's emphasis.

4 Despite this insight, Gallagher seems to me to misunderstand the purpose and potential of the concept. In saying this, however, I do not mean to suggest that any once-and-for-all, definitive meaning for it is possible.

5 The shifts in Williams's references to the term may be illustrated by contrasting the early formulation that 'it is in art primarily, that the effect of the totality, the dominant structure of feeling, is expressed and embodied' with the later stricture imposed on its use: 'I now feel very strongly the need to define the limits of the term' (Williams and Orrom, 1954: 21; and Williams, 1979: 164).

6 In this sense the concept may be suggestively compared with the term 'figurability', which Fredric Jameson employs in his analysis of the film *Dog Day Afternoon*. This term, like structure of feeling, is a category of emergence, of 'something more basic than abstract knowledge', implying 'a mode of experience that is more visceral and existential than the abstract certainties of economics and Marxian social science'. Jameson refers to the need to 'sense the abstract truth of class through the tangible medium of daily life in vivid and experiential ways' (1985: 719).

Chapter 3

The Turn to Ordinariness

Culture is ordinary: that is the first fact ... The growing society is there, yet it is also made and remade in every individual mind ... We use the word culture in two senses: to mean a whole way of life – the common meanings; to mean the arts and learning – the special processes of discovery and creative effort. Some writers use the word for one or other of these senses; I insist on both, and on the significance of their conjunction. The questions I ask about our culture are questions about our general and common purposes, yet also questions about deep personal meanings. Culture is ordinary, in every society and in every mind.

(Raymond Williams)

Introduction

An obvious step from a discussion of the concept of structure of feeling is to a consideration of the category of experience. Williams continually referred to experience, across the diverse range of his writing, but it was also crucially linked to 'structure of feeling' itself. As we have seen, it is through the attempt to make sense and meaning of social and historical experience, in ways which challenge existing ideological positions and discourses, that structures of feeling are generated. Summarising what has been said somewhat over-schematically, in the movement from the 'lived' experience to the articulation of emergent expressive form, consciousness becomes crystallised in a particular social semantic figure or set of historically defined thematics which then come to stand as a collective response to a collective experience. Experience in its manifold sense is then in this movement a site of emergence, and in this respect it grounds the structured process of crystallisation from 'lived' solution to precipitate forms. We need therefore to go on from what I have described as the 'experience' of experiences to deal with the relatively indeterminate category of experience itself. There is perhaps a somewhat less obvious reason for doing this in immediate connection with Williams's concept, and this is that in thinking about both 'structures of feeling' and 'experience', we cannot have recourse to any easy, off-the-peg forms of explanation. Alfred North Whitehead referred to 'experience' as 'one of the most deceitful' words in philosophy (1928: 19). It is not clear what he meant by 'deceitful'. 'Deceptive' or 'elusive' may be preferable adjectives, for they avoid attributing volitional agency to what is an abstract concept, one which does not have reference to any particular state or process unless it is qualified and made relatively concrete, as, for example, in the experience of love or betrayal. Nevertheless, the general point can be taken, and not only for philosophy. Grappling with the idea of experience is simultaneously fruitful and frustrating, and is so precisely because, in dealing with it, we are 'not at the gates of paradigm-land' (Geertz, 1986: 375). It is in this sense that it presents both a challenge and a risk.[1]

Before dealing substantively with the concept of experience, it seems to me that it would be useful to begin by looking back at certain previously influential ways of handling and utilising it. There are various reasons for doing this. Firstly, it will help in identifying some of the pitfalls and weaknesses in its use; while secondly, it will help in setting out some of its historical and cultural credentials. These credentials were more clearly apparent in early cultural studies than in the ahistorical conception of it in literary aesthetics, and in now attempting to revivify 'experience' as a conceptual unit of analysis, it will be important to draw on the strengths of its earlier use in historical and cultural studies as well as negotiating the problems attendant on that use. Lawrence Grossberg has noted that the now standardised, summary history of cultural studies generally offers a

narrative that is 'too linear and progressivist', ignoring 'the
continuing vitality and influence of earlier moments in the
narrative'. Taking a glance back at these earlier moments
will prove useful in showing that the idea of experience and
ways of conceiving it have been centrally important to cultural studies from the point of its early formation, particularly in its emergence and dissociation from the discipline
fatuously known as 'English'; and that as a key component
of an earlier moment in the narrative, it continues to fill,
however uneasily, what is otherwise a gap in the discourse
of cultural studies. 'The contestation within cultural studies
was not merely around competing theories of the politics
of culture, or the relationship of culture to power, but also
around differing theories of the nature of cultural and historical specificity' (Grossberg, 1993: 23). Experience, I shall
argue, illuminates a particular aspect of cultural and historical specificity. As a concept for handling this specificity,
its days are far from numbered.

Experience as Transcendent

Just as there are various reasons for attending to 'experience' in historical and cultural studies, so there are various
perspectives from which it can be viewed, several of which
have tried to enclose it entirely within their own paradigm-
gates. Exodus from the gilded park-gates of 'English' was a
key defining moment marking the emergence of cultural
studies. It happened initially because of the effort to push
against its limits and limitations as a discipline. Writers such
as Williams and Hoggart appreciated Leavis's emphasis on
'concrete human experience' (Leavis, 1976: 194) as prefer-
ential to a belle-lettrist approach to the study of literature,
but both of them strategically broke with its ahistorical
premises and its elitist claim that the finest human experience of the past was enshrined in the 'selective tradition'
of an aesthetically sublimated art and literature: 'To put
upon literature, or more accurately upon criticism, the responsibility of controlling the quality of the whole range of
personal and social experience, is to expose a vital case to
damaging misunderstanding' (Williams, 1958: 249). It was
Williams who more decidedly worked toward a rejection of

Leavis's nostalgic organicism and cultural pessimism in the face of 'mass society' and its apparent moral and spiritual degeneration. Versions of these attitudes to past and present were retained in Hoggart's *The Uses of Literacy* (1957), where they mar what was nevertheless a richly interpretive 'thick description' of working-class culture and an important attempt to fuse ethnography and cultural criticism. More generally, the contemporaneous emergence of cultural studies and 'history from below' questioned the assumptions as to whose experience was and is significant, and expanded their focus of study to include forms and representations of experience outside of those which were canonically privileged and historically aggrandised.

The humanist emphasis on experience in mid-century criticism was also an approach to study, and there is a link back to feeling in the kind of response encouraged. An emphasis on feeling and emotion was derived from the experiential basis of 'practical criticism' in literary study, where methodologically it was assumed that without prior knowledge of the writer or text, and without the application of other forms of knowledge, the reader of a literary work could directly identify with the experience dealt with – 'the finest human experience of the past', as Leavis put it (1930: 5) – and thus commune with the writer who had distilled its felt essence. Experience here was conceived as aesthetically transcendent, and so not in any way dependent on cultural or historical context. Similarly, the conception of feeling and emotion involved was quite at odds with that outlined towards the end of the previous chapter. In short, the idea of the autonomy of the literary text supported a psychologistic approach to the reading.[2] Terry Eagleton has jocularly compared this procedure with wine-tasting, with the analogy extending to those intensely felt discriminations of quality, character and tone (1983: 43). Of course, the approach went beyond a technique of tasting, or even 'tasteful' reading. In particular, it advanced a highly prescriptive response to the questions of 'how to live' in a secular, technocratic society, and how to engage with questions of moral and cultural values when they are overridden by 'mass' democracy and a rampant commercialism of cultural production and distribution. It is here that the connection of reading with cultural 'taste' becomes apparent. For I. A. Richards, for example, the experience of literature could be 'a training ground for general experience so that we will be more adequately equipped to respond to the changing modern world' (Eldridge and Eldridge, 1994: 58). In the Leavisite emphasis, the idealist value placed upon moral experience was not only linked to pre-lapsarian mythical notions, but was also anti-theoretical and anti-utilitarian in orientation: value lay in the illuminative sense of the life conveyed in literature and artworks conceived in the Arnoldian sense.

Where cultural analysis is concerned with experience, the characteristic emphasis is on its socio-historical singularity, and on the ways in which it is socially learned, shared, transmitted and constructed. Attention is directed towards specific and changing forms of experience, and the specific and changing ways in which such experience has been coded. The focus is on the definite imprint of social and historical conditions, and the transformations in experiential modalities induced by social and historical process. There is also an interest in intellectual border-crossings or making interpretively congruent areas or dimensions of experience which are otherwise studied in defensively insular disciplinary patches, with their tendential pull towards the fragmentation of human knowledge. This is obviously opposed to assertions of the primacy of any one particular mode of study, as in Leavis's 'Queen of the Humanities' ideal of literary criticism. What also follows from this is a refusal of the conception of experience as something static, absolute and unassimilable to other discourses. Experience is understood not only as historically relative and culturally variable, but also, in what is for various reasons a hazardous switch of emphasis, as only made available in the contextually determinate language and discourse in which it is articulated, received, and in both moments made possible. I shall turn to the difficulties later, for the initial point that needs to be underlined is that whenever experience is posited as transhistorical, in the sense of the immanent transmission across time of putative human universals, the theoretical problematic of 'difference' – which raises questions of cultural heterogeneity and historicity, and of intercultural communication and understanding – is occluded. Experience is naturalised, and such naturalism conceals the cultural and historical implications of the uses to which the term is put. Even if we agree with Edward Said that 'there is an irreducible subjective core to human experience', those involved in cultural and historical analysis would obviously want to go on to argue, with him, that what is most significant in this experience lies in its worldly affiliations in history and in culture (1983: 4; 1994: 35).

Worldly Affiliations

From its early days, cultural studies has rejected any exclusivity of focus on what have been aesthetically elevated, hierarchically scaled at the apex of cultural expression and experience, and thus of any claim which holds up certain fields of cultural production over others as the most significant access we have to 'human experience', a formulation which is itself contested as essentialist and ahistorical. Though an inventory of its objects of study would show that cultural studies has developed its own forms of exclusivity, neglecting various cultural practices and institutions which have not figured on the fashionable agenda, the turn to ordinariness has in general terms been beneficial. A complementary shift was to move beyond the restriction of attention to formal textual features. Again, there have been definite tendencies to text-centredness, but at its most promising cultural studies has been concerned more broadly with the interactive dynamics of cultural forms and social formations, with the intersections of social structures, situated and mediated experience, and social subjectivities and relations. Instead of the idealised aesthetic qualities of experience deriving from the study of the isolated literary text, the objects of inquiry are a range of heterogeneous cultural texts, practices and experiences, with an emphasis on the generation of meanings and values as an active social process occurring in particular forms of life in definite historical contexts. Now of course not all literary criticism has been concerned with an empiricist focus on the text 'as it is'. Marxist literary criticism, for example, constitutes a varied body of work opposed to those 'technocratic' modes of criticism exemplified by American New Criticism, just as feminist criticism works paradigmatically in opposition to literary history. Such alternative forms of criticism challenge the kind of scholarship which is ostensibly distanced from the structures of power it actually sustains, even if only in the very silence it maintains about them. It is for this reason that the most valuable work in literary studies has been simultaneously some form of social and cultural criticism, a fine example being Williams's *The Country and the City* (1973), which dramatises the tensions between the social relations of capitalism and literary figurations manifesting those opposed meanings, values and sensibilities associated with the shifting categories of city and country. The force of the book derives from its engaged analysis and its attempt to relocate literary texts within the historical processes and experiences from which they emanated but from which, all too often subsequently, they have been abstracted.

The abstraction of such texts from the social and historical contexts of their production is not only a question of methodology, but also of the ideological division between people's everyday experience and art and literature as formally conceived. This relates to the problem of the alienation of art from labour and technology, a problem that has produced a dualistic tendency in left and left-liberal studies of art and culture. In literary studies, for example, there has developed on the one hand work with a focus on literature's vindication of human creative impulses and possibilities in the face of a capitalist social order which either regards them in a utilitarian or philistine manner or threatens to commodify them. On the other hand, criticism strives to expose the ideological values of particular writers, works or genres, to show the way they have obscured people's actual experiences, sustained hierarchical conceptions of gender, 'race' and nationality, promoted misrecognitions of social inequalities and injustices, or mystified the real contradictions out of which history itself has been spun. In very general terms, the shift in approach can be characterised as moving from learning to love the mystery of the Word to learning to unravel its beguiling sophistries. It hardly needs emphasising that the utopian-humanist position of under-politicised aesthetic enchantment and the demystificatory position of over-politicised disenchantment are somewhat at odds. More importantly, as Eagleton has observed, neither 'criticism as utopian project' nor 'criticism as negative hermeneutic' provide a sound basis for an academic discipline. Added to this, both that form of writing designated as 'literature', and appreciation of its aesthetic features, are of considerably less significance to most people's everyday experience than other symbolic forms, while 'literature' itself, as a category, is of an inherently unstable nature (Eagleton, 1982: 48–9).

The assignment of value to art in articulating and contributing to the quality of social experience, or its variably attributed lack, is always relative, contingent and mutable. A socially and historically rooted cultural analysis not only refigures what is studied as 'culture', but also has to negotiate the problems of a politicised relativisation of what is of value in cultural texts, practices and experiences, rather than swim with the tide of a catch-all pluralism. Recognition of this does not entail the devaluation of literature and the fine arts, but it does mean that extra-aesthetic arguments have always to be made about quality itself, which cannot therefore be taken as absolute or objectively given in the Leavisite sense of 'this is so, isn't it ?' Nor does it mean that the value of writing is exclusive to each specific text. What is at issue is making visible the point and purpose of an evaluative position, working critically with a sense of its social and historical nature, and being receptive to considerations of the political implications of its assumptions, expectations and priorities, to the ways in which value itself is a categorial site of conflict. Frederic Jameson is only restating an explicit recognition in Marxist cultural theory when he says that 'the political interpretation of literary texts [is] not ... some supplementary method' which can be drawn on to add flavour to other critical approaches, but rather 'the absolute horizon of all reading and all interpretation' (1981: 17). Nevertheless, he is surely right to claim that the recognition is more than methodological. Among other things, this means deconstructing any hierarchical ranking of aesthetic tastes in terms of how they endorse as well as embody positions of social privilege and structures of social disadvantage; bringing 'lived' social experience clearly into the ambit of critical concern; avoiding a fetishism of attention to 'texts' by integrating textual 'readings' into contextually oriented forms of analysis; and engaging with the real diversity of cultural experience across and within time and space. There is nothing particularly new about these emphases of approach. For example, William Morris dedicated much of his life to denunciating, and attempting to repair the damage caused by, the gulf between the 'greater' and 'lesser' arts (see, for example 1979: 31–56); indeed, dedication to breaking down the distinction between the fine and applied arts became a general avant-garde preoccupation during the second half of the nineteenth century (Mackenzie, 1995: 106). Other examples could be cited to illustrate the points I have made, yet what should be emphasised is that everyday social experience remains interwoven with all sorts of institutionally unaccredited forms of cultural material and practice, and even though selectively they may now figure as reasonably commonplace inclusions in television documentaries or newspaper supplements, the complex ways in which they contribute to the varied textures and conditionalities of social experience continue by contrast to go under-examined.

The use of experience as a key reference point in early cultural studies was directed against two fronts in particular – aesthetic idealism and cultural elitism on the one hand, and economistic Marxism with its rigid application of the base-superstructure formula on the other. The point of its use was integral to the turn to ordinariness in emphasising that culture is rooted in mundane experience; that it cannot be uprooted from such experience without losing in vitality, reference and connectedness; that culture has a determining power in itself, and is not simply the reflection of certain social forces or conditions; and that the study of history or art and culture which erases the everyday experiences and symbolic practices of 'ordinary' people is not only substantively incomplete, but also ideologically supportive of an unequal social and political order in its historical distortions and incompleteness. Now if the Althusserian challenge to the socialist humanism of early cultural studies had a point it was, as Grossberg has noted, in criticising the 'assumption of a series of necessary correspondences between cultural forms, experience and class position' (1993: 28).

But in then asserting the relative autonomy and specificity of the cultural, structuralist Marxism had no actual ground in everyday life on which to locate it since it had already dismissed the socially and historically located subject, and his or her own experience, out of court, and was not able to recognise that although the correspondences are not necessary or by preordination homologically aligned, connections between experience and elements of culture are nevertheless made, intersubjectively, by people with diverse cultural affiliations and identities, in every walk of life. Where social class is involved the process is not a politely made match of elements with structural position, but an unevenly balanced struggle to articulate various elements in combination in such a way as to realise or contest particular class identities and interests. If experience was sometimes construed as an essentialist category in early cultural studies, paradoxically it inhibited the intellectual elitism implied by reducing subjectivity to ideological or discursive 'effects', though at the same time so-called culturalism was thereby weakened by the lack of any satisfactory theoretical engagement with ideology until it was assimilated in its Gramscian formulation as hegemony.

The actual moves were of course complex and uneasy, and were not conducted by a straightforward passage into or out of any firmly fixed paradigm-gates, which in themselves contributed to the difficulty of the moves. For Williams, Hall and many others the process of development involved attempts to build a more sociological framework for cultural analysis and a more theoretical approach to the leading questions of cultural studies, as well as the take-up of new models of textual analysis, especially that of semiotics. The different assessments of the methodological and theoretical significance of semiotics, however, particularly in its alignment with structuralism, marked the initial point of new divergences. These will be addressed more fully later on. What I want to connect back to here is the emphasis on intersubjectively generated and reproduced meanings and values. Although it has undergone numerous articulations and transmutations, this emphasis has remained a leading one in cultural studies. A concern with the dynamics of the relations between determinate structures and the mutabilities

of meaning-production, in what is always a politically implicated field of social possibility and restriction, has become
a defining feature of cultural studies. This should be related to the dual focus of cultural studies, which addresses
the intersubjective areas and relations between public representations, including those of the communications media,
and the 'lived' consciousness of individual subjects. It is in
these areas and relations that experience is sited, and it
has, accordingly, both situated and mediated dimensions,
neither of them clear-cut or phenomenologically distinct,
but nevertheless sufficiently different, in some ways tangen-
tially so, to warrant the definition of the dual focus.

It may be worth spelling out a little more closely what
this can involve. Given the salience of contemporary media,
it may seem at times that their general cultural reach in
(post)modern societies is such that Baudrillard's simulational
model of social reality becomes entirely persuasive: 'TV is
the world', and TV's world of hyperreality dissolves the social, renders it an illusion – semblance is all, and reality
flickers. Yet for most people there remains a crucial distinction between media representation and social experience.
Much of the ideological critique of media studies, of feminist interventions or Marxist analysis has operated with this
distinction, making the claims of misrepresentation or mystification of real antagonisms and differences of identity or
experience a characteristic aspect of the examination. How
we think about and understand the social world is of course
influenced more than ever before by media forms of narrative and representation, but the crunch always comes when,
in terms of particular identities and memberships which are
not simply those of media consumers, we feel that publicly
mediated representations do not accurately or faithfully
portray, or comprehensively typify us, in our situated forms
of social life and sense of cultural belonging or dislocation.
Critically as well we may extend these feelings to representations of other groups or collectivities, so that, where possible, we dissociate the processes of 'speaking as' and 'speaking
on behalf of' a social group or category as a way of ap-
proaching the problems of over-representation (stereotyping),
under-representation (marginalisation), and misrepresentation (caricature, distortion, lies). We then soon arrive at

the point where we say that media or other cultural representations do not make sense in the way we make sense. We say that they do not match our own experience, in the social situations we know, or do not tally with what we understand of other people's experience and with what characterises them sociologically or culturally. If we then go on to attempt to realise the political and ideological implications of this, we are beginning to do cultural studies, whether we do it at a university, in extra-mural classes or in a corner of a local pub.

The distinction involved here can be extended to that between media culture and everyday situated cultural forms and practices which arise out of ongoing, localised social interactions, in situations of co-presence. These cover a considerable range, from the stories we continually tell each other of mundane events and encounters, to rites of passage and rituals of inclusion and exclusion, the vocabularies of subcultural identity and style, forms of social remembrance and remembering, and so on. These items of cultural bricolage are interwoven into individual life-experience and biographical episodes, and continue to mark the symbolic connectedness of groups and communities as they draw on their diverse and ever-changing funds of cultural resources, regardless of any practical dependencies on a far wider system of national and international organisation. As repertoires of distinct or partially distinct collectivities they contribute to the interpretive frameworks through which individualities are mediated. The interest of cultural analysis with individual subjectivity does not then operate with the individual conceived as a monadic entity, but rather in terms of her or his place and participation, as well as formation, within various cultural groupings: it is such groupings and the symbolic constellations in which they orbit that constitute the focus of enquiry. The life-course, grounded cultural manoeuvres and quality of life involved for particular people are then studied in relation to the social categories which are bound up with and experientially inflect specific conceptions of identity and subjectivity, rather than in relation to any described qualities of subjectively known or assumed uniqueness.

There is much more that could be said about the

distinctions between situated and mediated forms of culture, but just as we should be sceptical of apocalyptic exaggerations of the pervasive influence of the latter, so we should be careful of temptations to idealise the former, either in contemporary social life or in retrospect. The massive cultural transformations and extensions to communication ensuing from the development of the modern media render any sharp division between them increasingly artifical, if not ideological in itself. It is because they are to a great extent imbricated within each other that they can be grouped together under the general category of popular culture, although as soon as that is done the immediate caveats have to be made about attending to the multiple and pluralised nature of the term, and about steering clear of easy assumptions of any neat functional 'fit' between mediated and situated cultures. Indeed, one of the hallmark achievements of cultural studies has been its critical challenge to such assumptions, and this is again to emphasise the importance of the dual focus. This challenge has arisen, at least in part, through its insistence that both situated and mediated cultures as well as their interrelations are structured by asymmetrical relations of power, conflicting forces and interests, unequally competing forms of explanation and evaluation, unequal access to resources and to means of communication, and differentially validated competences of use and application. As Gramsci noted, such phenomena exist in a state of 'unstable equilibria' (1978: 182), and this requires continual work in sustaining the legitimacy and authority of a society's directive values at all levels of social activity and consciousness. It is then the active winning of consent to the existing social order, to existing relations of power and subordination, which is the central structuring force in the field of culture, and not only in class terms but also in terms of other forms of domination as they are delineated by categories of gender, age, ethnicity, sexual disposition, and so on. Everyday symbolic acts and the social identities and relationships to which they give shape and form are deeply permeated by hegemonic processes which are continually 'renewed, recreated, defended, and modified' in response to the ways in which they may be 'resisted, limited, altered, [or] challenged by pressures not at all [their] own'. This then leads to what Raymond Williams called the 'most interesting and difficult part of any cultural analysis in complex societies' – 'that which seeks to grasp the hegemonic in its active and formative but also its transformational processes' (1977: 112–13). It is when it attempts to control or incorporate alternative and oppositional elements that a cultural hegemony is at its most active and most exposed, outside of the 'crisis of authority' which a resort to coercion indicates. Cultural studies is then itself an active intervention within the whole social process which constitutes its field of enquiry.

It is because of this kind of concern with the relations between culture and power that cultural studies has operated through a continuing and diverse engagement with the Marxist tradition, which has considerably added to its critical edge. When it then became engaged with a developing feminist criticism, the mix made for a more complex and sophisticated perspective on the earlier humanism while retaining, in its more productive forms, an emphasis on creative agency and cultural struggle. Following this, and refining its dual focus, the 'specificity of cultural studies was located in the realm of intersubjective meaning which mediated between culture and society' (Grossberg, 1993: 41). The reformulation of culture as a process of meaning-production occurring through determinate structures of social communication then took for granted a rejection of an Arnoldian conception of culture and of experience as transcendent. The alternative sociological and ethnographic conception meant focusing on mundane experience and intersubjective meanings, but increasingly this focus was directed through the lens of ideological critique, particularly where such experience and meanings were being taken up and re-presented by the communications media.

> The field of contemporary cultural studies opens up the interplay between everyday life and cultural articulation. Every determination of this interplay is itself a political intervention in the cultural field tied at once to denunciation and the precarious vision of something better (Angus, 1994: 85).

What were not resolved in this critical focus were the disparities between intersubjectivity and cultural difference, and

one aspect of this irresolution was an increasing unravelling of the semiotic/structuralist, and then psychoanalytic
strands of cultural studies, away from its sociological and
social-communicational strands. In the process cultural studies
became, especially through some of its most influential variants, more and more dehistoricised.

It is easy to see why literary studies aligned itself much
more closely with the formal approaches of structuralist semiotics and Lacanian psychoanalysis as ways of enriching textual readings, and then aligned itself with these influences
in the re-theorisation of literary studies in the late 1970s
and 1980s. The result was not only a relative loss of the
historical, but also in many ways a dissolution of the turn
to ordinariness, the turn built on the conception of culture
as ordinary 'in every society and in every mind' (Williams,
1989a: 4). The issues involved in this for cultural studies
will be taken up later, for what has first to be reviewed is
the failure of 'English' to be transformed by cultural studies. The turn to ordinariness involves examining the construction and consequences of a broad variety of forms of
cultural production, rather than focusing only on the historically determinate category of 'literature', and understanding these as inseparable from the social relations and
arrangements in which they are embedded. In other words,
all aesthetic and cultural experience is seen as social, as
integrally folded into forms of sociality and necessarily bound
up with different interests and identities which are historically conditioned, and historically in struggle. If, then, we
see the quotidian and vernacular as legitimate objects of
study pursued in this way, where does this leave the peculiar object of 'English'?

Broken English

Currently, 'English' is in a state of disarray, and now finds
not only that its empiricist epistemology has been seriously
undermined, but also that the identity of its traditional object
of study, the 'literary' text, has begun to blur and dissolve.
There are of course vociferous defenders of conventional
literary studies, who fight a rearguard action for anti-demo-
cratic educational reform on the basis of a return to its major

paradigmatic features (see, for example, Bloom, 1987; Hirsch, 1987; Kernan, 1990). But what is more widely recognised is precisely a paradigm crisis in 'English'. This has occurred as a result of an inability to sustain any longer its privileging of this essentialised kind of text, and of the collapse of basic assumptions underpinning its traditional practices of aesthetic discrimination and evaluation, technical dissection and ostensibly disengaged moralism, all of them ahistorical in orientation. The received corpus of canonical texts, each with their assumed unity, the static periodisation which has often accompanied their study, and their false discrimination from popular culture, have all been seriously questioned, particularly by feminists, minority intellectuals and those interested in contemporary writing and the popular media. There is now a greater recognition than twenty years or so ago of the need to engage critically with a broader range of writings and with processes of signification and communication more generally. Yet this is a rather frantic response to the crisis. It is as if taking on more cargo would help resolve the problem of where the good ship, the Pride of the Humanities, is headed. A character in David Lodge's *Nice Work* observes that 'English' has today come to accommodate a host of diverse pursuits and fields of study. 'Now we have linguistics, media studies, American Literature, Commonwealth literature, literary theory, women's studies, not to mention about a hundred new British writers worth taking seriously.' As his Dean goes on to comment, English has become, since the 1960s and 1970s, 'like a three-masted ship with too many sails aloft and a diminishing crew. We're exhausting ourselves scrambling up and down the rigging, just trying to keep the damn thing from capsizing, never mind getting anywhere, or enjoying the voyage.' But he then concludes: 'With respect, Bob, I don't think your committee has addressed itself to the fundamental problem' (1989: 351–2). Unsurprisingly, this consummate example of donnish evasion and gracious buck-passing leaves the 'fundamental problem' undefined, since it is not in the end that of the incompatibility of humane letters and the discourses and practices of capitalist business, which is the novel's central theme. The 'fundamental problem' is that of 'English' itself.

Reloading the ship with different, and additional cargo,

without changing direction and seeking out alternative destinations, is a sign of desperation which should be clearly distinguished from a commitment to interdisciplinarity. There is also a sense in which this desperation is diagnostically signified by the turn to theory in literary studies. While this turn has been a fruitful one in a number of ways, it is not unconnected to a realisation of the impending bankruptcy of the traditional appeals, denials and procedures of literary criticism, and of the danger of 'English' becoming little more than a form of institutionalised cultural nostalgia. It could be argued that, unlike linguistics or sociology, 'English' has never had a theoretical core of any significance, and its institutional history would appear to bear this out, yet it has nevertheless been built around certain implicit theoretical assumptions and values, which would include its alleged humanising functions, its curator role of preserving morally edifying and spiritually uplifting 'great works', its trust in the virtue of intuitive insight in lieu of a rigorous conceptualisation of object and procedure, or its self-serving resistance of 'junk' culture. These largely celebratory appeals, amounting to what Greenblatt aptly describes as 'a kind of secular theodicy', now carry little cogency (1990: 78). Indeed, one could could go so far as to say that it is because 'English' has become academically outdated, and either philosophically or politically has failed to provide any durable basis or justification for its founding credentials of transcendent value and individual self-improvement, that it is now fractured and in crisis as a discipline. 'English' is broken, as MacCabe has had it (1988: 12), and it now faces the task of reconstituting itself in the light of this condition.

It is a moot point whether this can be achieved without it becoming radically different, where frantic repair would lead to complete overhaul and thus to some quite different kind of vessel for sailing after knowledge. Many critical responses to its broken condition actually involve abandoning the model of its conventional architecture. Some of the most arresting examples of recent cultural studies have actually come out of the discipline of 'English', though characteristically they are works of divergence. Stallybrass and White's *The Politics and Poetics of Transgression* (1986), or Moretti's *Signs Taken for Wonders* (1983), are just two cases in point. Yet the moves away are becoming steadily broader. In general terms, this is manifest in attempts to articulate the interest in how the meanings of symbolic communications are constituted by language and other semiotic forms, to an interest in how they operate subjectively within the social formations in which they are realised and apprehended. Where there is a shift away from purely textualist concerns and from decontextualised considerations of sensibility and moral attitude towards an engagement with how symbolic forms operate in their social and historical fields, and with how these fields exhibit a complex dynamic within which symbolic forms acquire resonance and significance, and are ideologically endorsed or contested, then literary analysis moves closer to cultural studies. In this respect, feminist criticism, Marxist approaches to literary analysis, cultural materialism in its literary analytical variant, and New Historicism, provide examples of the degree of convergence which has already occurred.

Yet these developments and potentialities still exist to a great degree at the margins, and have not radically transformed the moribund disciplinary centre. Moreover, their challenge, while worthwhile, is limited too often to new methodologies of studying literary, rather than other cultural forms and genres, as for instance in the cultural materialism approach to Shakespeare ('the imperial hero of culture', in Malcolm Evans's description). In addition, it is not just a question of making more democratic the critical examination of things human in the humanities, but also of attending to the neglect of cues offered by other fields of study. An example here is anthropology, which in the work of scholars like Geertz, Turner, Douglas and Sahlins has increasingly drawn on methods of literary critical analysis, and which sits happily enough with cultural studies as I understand it. The failure to provide any sound theoretical self-justification, and to take up these cognate developments, is all the more distressing in the light of Richard Johnson's suggestion that the humanities, 'which are pre-eminently concerned with identifying the subjective forms of life, are already cultural studies in embryo!' He goes on to note that 'forms, regularities and conventions first identified in literature (or certain kinds of music or visual arts) often turn out to have a much wider social currency', and gives as an example the way in which feminists working on romance 'have traced the correspondences between the narrative forms of popular romantic fiction, the public rituals of marriage (e.g. the Royal Wedding) and, if only through their own experience, the subjective tug of the symbolic resolutions of romantic love' (1986/7: 59). The move this suggests is between public storytelling, social institutions, experience and subjectivities and then back again, in a cultural/ideological circuit through which real lives are lived, and actual destinies are shaped.

From Literary to Cultural Studies

The distress is occasioned by the potential that is abundantly there, albeit embryonically, and in the light of this I want now to take up a particular attempt to move the kind of studies Johnson refers to beyond their reluctant gestation into a different kind of project. In the early 1990s, Anthony Easthope argued for the transformation of literary into cultural studies on the democratic principle of studying 'every form of signifying practice' and 'the discourses of all members of a society' (1991: 6–7). This relates to what Johnson encourages as the most significant future application for the techniques of formal analysis developed in literary studies. Easthope certainly pursues his case well so far as 'English' itself is concerned, but the kind of cultural studies he advocates is excessively centred on textual analysis or analyses based on the textual analogue. Before dealing with this revamped formalism, it should be acknowledged that he does not dissolve texts (whether literary or otherwise) into the variable interpretations made of them, as certain deconstructionists have done. Certainly, the meanings of cultural texts need to be considered as an active and unstable field, though one arising out of the interaction between the formal characteristics of such texts and the situations and circumstances in which they are produced and consumed. Yet as a result of operating with a sense of the dialectical interaction between text and reader, Easthope rightly insists that the text has a relatively fixed identity. Conceiving of the idea of unity as not so much intrinsic to the text but rather as an effect

produced through its relation to who interprets it does not
mean that the text is solely constructed by the interpretation. If we deny the text any identity, we remain locked in
a binary logic because our denial requires a mirror image
of the text 'in itself'. This makes for a proper rebuttal of
the position claimed, most notably, by Stanley Fish. Easthope
shows that he has a sharp nose for the flaws of either/or
modes of thinking, and he takes various literature-as-con-
struction theorists to task for reproducing the metaphysical
concepts of the 'literary' against which they are opposed
(the influence of Rorty is noticeable here). This is important in that, across time, texts are obviously a key medium
of time's traces, but this leads to the first problem with
Easthope's approach in that, despite his stance on the limits of polysemy, he underplays the constructedness which
occurs relationally in the reinterpretations made across time
of those traces. He writes that 'good texts are not always
the same but always significantly different' without immediately specifying what he has in mind in using the enormously
problematical epithet 'good'. It would seem that what he
has in mind is the capacity of a cultural text to exceed the
historical conditions of its production (or in Easthope's words
its 'original context'). This is a troubling issue.

Easthope argues formally against essentialist notions of
the 'literary text' and takes an anti-foundational approach
to literary studies, but there lingers in his writing the idea
of an autonomous quality in certain (literary) texts which
enables them to ride through the waves of historical change
when others sink beneath them. In view of this, it would
seem necessary to underline yet again the truism that the
ascription of quality to certain texts is not made in an ideological vacuum, for when Easthope writes that 'a text of literary value can be distinguished from one with merely historical
interest by the degree to which its signifiers have actively
engaged with new contexts' (1991: 58), it could be assumed
that the progress of these enterprising signifiers is generated solely by some protean source of energy in their textual combination. Again, he writes of certain texts functioning
intertextually 'to give a plurality of different readings
transhistorically' (ibid: 59), and the sense is repeated of some
metaphysical filtering mechanism – the thinly coded texts

slipping away into the dust of oblivion while the gold nuggets of 'great texts' remain shining forever across the wastelands of memory and time.[3] It is surprising to find someone alert to, among other historical determinations, patriarchal values and pressures on a selecting and selective tradition, and the consequent need for gendered readings in textual study, wanting to preserve the conception of literary value in this way. It not only impoverishes Easthope's central argument, but also displays an impoverished sense of the historical. Whether and how a text exhibits value by continuing 'to function in a contemporary reading' (ibid: 60) are not questions innocent of broader social and ideological values. Easthope knows this well enough, but at times by-passes its difficult implications by coming at 'culture' more from the perspective of 'literature' than from that of the 'popular' (literature's 'other'), from literary rather than cultural studies.

Easthope takes his general cue from the various theoretical interventions which have undermined the defining assumptions of literary study and authorialism, and draws out six conceptual categories – institution, sign system, ideology, gender, identification and subject position – as the necessary terms for the analysis of texts and textuality. Significantly, he has greatest trouble with institutional analysis. He treats what it involves either highhandedly ('it cannot really distinguish between one text and another' (ibid: 28)), or with an excessive caution of the pitfall of sociological reductionism ('the two analyses of texts [and] institutions cannot be brought together in theoretical coherence' (ibid: 135)), and this despite the cogent and sobering institutional analysis of academic literary studies by Richard Ohmann (1976). The problems of text–context relations are certainly a veritable briar patch, for sociology and cultural history as well as English studies. But if what Easthope alleges is true, we are seriously in trouble. In response to the difficulties, and fearful of the reductive or functionalist ways in which the relations can be handled, Easthope clings to an analytic privileging of the features distinguishing signifying practices over other practices, rather than trying to work towards a more valid conceptualisation of the 'social' as the field in which cultural texts are disseminated, and signification is embedded and made intersubjectively possible. The consequence of this is threefold. Easthope offers only a limited conception of the social formation, claims that 'texts cannot be adequately analysed in relation to . . . social and historical context' (1991: 113), and allows the idea of semiotic multiplicity to shield the lack of attention paid to social dynamics. Without an adequate approach to questions of institutional analysis, treatment of Easthope's other conceptual categories will inevitably remain stunted.

In face of the certainty that 'literary study as presently conceived won't last much longer' (ibid: 179), Easthope seeks to transform 'English' into cultural studies always from the starting point of that which he seeks to transform. This gives his book a particular perspective and edge, but this perspective is both provisional and limited. It is provisional in the sense that, although he argues against encouraging in students a position of assumed intellectual unity and mastery, and is otherwise wary of the possible authoritarianism of authoritative readings, he doesn't seek to offset these dangers in relation to his own argument. Work of the syncretising kind which Easthope is offering tends to build up a sense of its universal validity. Easthope's proposals represent but one version of cultural studies, with its central progressive call being for a comprehensive opening up of the cultural texts to be studied. One of the central lines of my own argument, however, is directed against this version of cultural studies, which I find flawed in its sociological and historiographical attentuations. In the light of what has been said of literary studies, there is a tremendous irony here. Over the last twenty years or so, too much cultural studies work has become excessively text-focused as it has built on and elaborated the semiotic model, thus seeing social phenomena predominantly through a synchronic-textualist optic. A present-centred preoccupation with the textuality of the social, and with the social as a text, has among other things contributed to a retreat from any sense of a developed historical aspect to its project. This is what Williams referred to as an 'awful loop in time' leading to a recrudescence of formalism, and to its accommodations in 'a self-consciously modernist Marxism' (1989: 170). The irony is that if we strip away the poststructuralist and postmodernist refinements, then Easthope's position is not that far away from Hoggart's in the applications of forms of textual analysis to social and historical phenomena.

In view of this and Johnson's earlier point, it is instructive to review why it was that literary criticism proved inadequate in realising Hoggart's aspiration (as expressed in his inaugural lecture 'Schools of English and Contemporary Society', which launched the Birmingham Centre for Contemporary Cultural Studies) that it should constitute the preferred mode of analysis for dealing with the key issues of the culture–society relation (1973, vol. 2). This may be explained partly by the subsequent reaction to Leavisite 'culture and environment' analysis, to which Hoggart was deeply indebted, and partly by the shifting of a concern with literature to the margins of CCCS work. Cultural studies in the 1960s and 1970s defined itself against much humanities scholarship through a critical engagement with the 'unstated presuppositions' and claims to 'disinterested knowledge' of such scholarship – a demystification of 'the regulative nature and role the humanities were playing in relation to . . . national culture' (Hall, 1990: 15). In addition, the open hostility and miserly attitude of 'English' to the work of Hoggart on the relations between working-class and 'mass' culture can hardly be said to have provided a conducive ground upon which to establish the field of study Hoggart had in mind.

Equal in importance, though, was the incapacity of an aesthetically oriented perspective for dealing with the relationship between culture and society, or between ideologies and institutional structures of power. Yet Hoggart was much more sensitive to the need for treating popular culture in its own right, and the innovatory nature of this recognition within 'English' has now perhaps to be emphasised. Furthermore, I don't think he was wrong in the way he expressed his own stake in the discipline, which he said was 'to do with language exploring human experience, in all its flux and complexity. It is therefore always in active relation with its age; and some students of literature . . . ought to try to understand these relationships better' (1973, vol. 2: 243). We may want to extend what is meant by 'language', and we may want to stress more the historical constituents of experience to which he pointed, but the point seems to

me basically sound, and task enough for any field of intellectual inquiry. Hoggart also called for 'better links with
sociologists', and while his sense of what intrepretive sociology can achieve was rather limited, such links have proved
immensely significant for cultural studies. These acknowledgements and qualifications are important, but they do not
detract from the point that beneath the surface of Hoggart's
lecture lay inappropriate assumptions about the 'popular'
which at that time had not been sufficiently thought through,
and critically rejected or modified. Reference to 'unpromising
material' is just one example among others that have been
more commonly identified, and extensively raked over.

Straw Targets

This criticism of Hoggart should not be exaggerated. There
has been a definite tendency to do this, for in methodologically arrogating to itself more than it could analytically
deliver, literary critical method *vis-à-vis* Hoggart's blueprint
for cultural studies has to some extent been dealt with more
harshly than approaches from other disciplines which include the category of culture among their areas of concern.
On a personal note, it took me some while as a doctoral
student to wake up to the ways in which the sociological
tradition has such extensive scope for the analysis of culture, since my first sociological encounters as an undergraduate in the late 1960s/early 1970s were largely with its positivist
and functionalist branches. Their application to the
conceptualisation and study of culture seemed to me then
to be grossly inadequate. I should add that my own ways of
thinking about culture, as an undergraduate at that time,
were also grossly inadequate, and yet subsequently it struck
me as odd that cultural studies did not define itself as much
against these particular sociological approaches as it did
against 'liberal-humanism', in what was in any case often a
rather straw-target version of that tradition of scholarly thought
and approach. The pathway of many people from literary
to cultural studies, and an embarrassed need to cover their
tracks, is only part of the explanation for this. Other reasons may well lie in the somewhat destructive frustration
deriving from the failure of cultural studies' various attempts

at theorisation of the culture–society relation to move 'much beyond what Williams, Hoggart, and Thompson originally offered' (Brantlinger, 1990: 63). This is for me a radical re-evaluation, and it is central to my own argument in this book.

There has, then, been a tendency to scapegoat the moral limits and political naivities of liberal-humanism in literary studies. As David Buckingham has put it in relation to media studies: 'It is as if media studies needs to construct an enemy, in the rather vague shape of "liberal-humanism", against which it can define itself' – and he cites Masterman's work as exemplifying this kind of rhetorical strategy (1990: 8; and see Masterman, 1980 and 1986). It is ironic to note that among the advances of the recent concerted return to theory in 'English' has been the detailed exposure of exactly those humanist inadequacies and malconceptions which it is accused from outside the discipline of continuing to perpetrate. For Buckingham, the key differences between literary and media/cultural studies are defined in terms of concepts and practices, with the latter being 'predominantly concerned with conceptual learning', the critical application of concepts to cultural texts, and the former concentrating more on the affirmative practices of reading, writing, speaking and listening, and, in the same spirit, on 'the expression of feeling or the articulation of experience' (1990: 10). Here, of course, experience is often taken as self-evidently authoritative, as some vague yet potent source of appeal outside of questions of method and critique, and yet there is a curious parallel in the alternative pedagogical authority of theory. Both can be either tyrannically or complacently wielded.

Since we are talking of straw targets, this is often what 'high' or 'bourgeois' art has often become in latter-day cultural studies, and it is 'too easy a target . . . for a new generation of intellectual populists to attack' (McGuigan, 1992: 75). For example, think only of the respect which Marx had for such canonical English figures as Shakespeare or Shelley (Prawer, 1978; also Foot, 1980: 227–8). The same easy-target syndrome is true of the claim that the implicit adoption in literary studies of 'an idealised, asocial view' of cultural production and consumption, in their historic modern transformations, serves as an automatic result to perpetuate the idealist conception of the culture/commerce opposition (Buckingham, 1990: 10). This may or may not be the result; there is nothing automatic about it. Various branches of literary studies, far from simply celebrating the alleged creative freedom of the writer, have stressed the circumscription of that freedom in capitalist as well as communist societies, and have examined through the medium of literary works the opposition of moral ideas about beauty, and of the ethical postulates of being good to each other or arriving at some conception of a collective good, to the economic imperatives of capital accumulation and the practices of 'good business'. This is not, of course, to say that forward-thinking moral ideas, or a critical or utopian dimension, are necessarily absent from popular forms. As Ros Coward has suggested, in looking forward to 'a wider, more self-conscious and critical notion of value', any 'preconceptions about the superiority of one genre over another, or the superiority of one medium over another', must be abandoned, and in its place must be substituted an interest in 'how certain texts criticise our everyday perceptions and make us see our surroundings and our emotions in new and critical ways' (1990: 91). The interest is in their potential for questioning and expanding experience, for generating an 'experience' of experience, and for making what is experientially ordinary extraordinary rather than the other way round.

Commerce and Cultural Experience

Earlier in this chapter, I spoke of cultural studies defining itself in opposition to reductive forms of economism that relegated culture to an always determined superstructure. In a paper published in the late 1980s, Graham Murdock has returned to his claim of the late 1970s that one of the abiding problems of cultural studies is 'its continuing refusal to incorporate a critical political economy of culture' (1989: 45). In his view, recent writings on postmodernism only exacerbate this condition, and he points to the lack of any theoretical linkages between work on postmodernist forms of representation and aesthetics, and commentary on new, so-called post-Fordist economic regimes organised around flexible accumulation and an increasing commodification of information and communication. Yet the lack of theoretical integration is not wholly one-sided, for the political economy perspective has not yet completely unhitched itself from the problems of economism, has not overcome the problems involved in its tendency to assign greater weight to economic and production issues than to the politics of cultural representation and consumption, has not engaged adequately with such concepts as experience, intersubjectivity and practice, and has tended to remain rather thin in the 'thick description' characteristic of cultural analysis. Because of this, although he is right, McGuigan can do little other than gesture affirmatively at the need to integrate cultural studies and a critical political economy of culture.

An additional problem is that both cultural studies and the political economy of culture continue to remain stuck over the problem of determination, moving uneasily between the mechanistic rigidities of the base-superstructure model and its opposite pole where everything seems overdetermined by everything else. Williams's formulation of determination as the setting of limits and the exertion of pressures is still something of a holding operation, as Stuart Hall first pointed out (Williams, 1977: 83–9; Hall, 1980b: 104). More importantly, it suffers from a overly negative view of structure, failing to acknowledge the constitutive role of structures in grounding and enabling social activity. Conceptually Marx's own less dichotomous metaphor in the *Grundrisse* of 'a general illumination in which all other colours are plunged and which modifies their specific tonalities' still seems preferable (Marx, 1977: 107). Yet in any less general formulation, the term begs a number of explanatory questions, such as whether economic organisation is determining in the last or the first instance (Hall, 1980b: 84). Further, it does not help us move beyond the dualistic impasse between commerce and culture, creativity and economic control, business and pleasure, commodity production and popular authenticity. The problem remains that of striving to avoid both reducing questions of cultural politics to the power of economic forces, and abstracting cultural politics from the complex play of those forces in their local, national and international manifestations. Yet we still founder on the question of how 'relative' is 'relative autonomy'. How 'overdetermined' can

symbolic forms be before they become socially indeterminate? The problem is that attempts to avoid determinist forms
of thinking tend to develop concepts which are by contrast
too capacious. How far, then, do you go before you reach
the 'ultimate' in 'ultimate determination'?

Cultural critique has long moved awkwardly between positions which place relatively greater stress on the power of
capital and the market in determining popular cultural forms,
and those which tend to emphasise more the creative possibilities either of resistance to these forms or their adaptive
reworkings in a patchwork synthesis that functionally suits
the identities of particular groups and allows the development
of distinct symbolic cultural worlds. Since the work done in
the 1970s on the analysis of youth subcultures, and since
the advent of the ethnographically oriented media audience
studies in the 1980s, it is the latter position which now holds
sway. While there are tremendous strengths in such work,
at their weakest they display a tendency to re-invent an authenticity of the 'popular'. There have been various manifestations of this in the postwar period, examples being the
essentialist 'folk' culture paradigm, labourist notions of some
genuine working-class voice beyond the reach of 'bourgeois'
aesthetics or commercialist hype, the romanticisation of 'subversive' appropriations of what Paul Willis once called 'the
shit of capitalist production', and the kind of celebratory
populism elaborated by John Fiske (see, for example, Fiske,
1989a and b). The identified tendencies may be there, in
some form or other, but in either descriptive or analytical
terms they are hyperbolically rendered. It is as if the credentials of radical cultural critique require the invocation
or construction of an inverse image of the object of critique
in idealised forms. In particular, Fiske's benign faith in the
open possibilities of subversively resignifying the products
of the culture and leisure industries serves, in the end, only
to polarise the cultural pessimism which entails an *a priori*
rejection of commercial popular culture and an assumption
of the complete ideological effectivity of its products. Likewise, Connell's championing of what he sees as the revital-
ising forces and socially accountable features of commercial
television – as opposed to the elitist paternalism and sub-
servience to the State of public service broadcasting –

engenders the same end-result (Connell, 1978, 1983; Connell and Curti, 1986; see also Garnham, 1983, and Robins and Webster, 1987). Mica Nava advances a more tentative approach when she points to the need to understand consumerist culture as 'variably (sometimes simultaneously) both a form of subjection and a form of resistance' rather than 'inherently one thing or the other, since, if consuming objects and images is potentially subversive, this potential is countered always by its potential reappropriation and transformation into yet another mode of regulation' (1987: 207).

There is, then, a problem of critical oscillation between Adornian melancholia and breezy Fiskean populism, between productionist determinism and what is tantamount to an endorsement of the thesis of consumer sovereignty (Pickering, 1990: 45–6). In postmodernist theory these polarised approaches are collapsed into each other in the name of stylistic eclecticism, irony, and pastiche, a self-conscious delight in mass-produced art, kitsch and the play of surfaces, and anti-realism and anti-historicism. This collapse is no solution to the problems they pose but rather an abnegation of the responsibility to deal with them. There would, however, be little point in denying that postmodernism has made important contributions to cultural critique in late capitalist societies. If these two evaluations appear contradictory it is because postmodernism itself is contradictory or 'definitionally incoherent' (Simons and Billig, 1994: 5). From one point of view, it might seem that within postmodernist discourse any concern with authenticity, however problematically conceived, is redundant: everything is now interfusion; unities, centres and certainties are fragmented, disjointed; images float free of contexts; individuality is self-parody; and the idea of honesty in self-expression is replaced by the self-bemused pose. All is assimilable in the whirlpool of commercialism. All that's left us is some 'playful' shopping, some semio-consumerist dalliance, in the malls beneath the edifice of Cynicism, Inc. (Gitlin, 1989: 354).

Yet in its relentless exposure of forms of essentialism, in its insistence on difference and diversity, postmodernism blends in politically with anti-racism and struggles against oppressively normal forms of (hetero)sexuality. Its radical critique of the great meta-narratives of modernity, its attention to universalising market 'logics', its debunking of the radical pretensions and values of High Modernism, and its de-centring of the 'sovereign subject', have been useful and provocative. However, all the various conceptions of posteriority 'have no intrinsic political belonging in themselves', and in its more apocalytic versions, postmodernism threatens to destabilise the grounds of political action by seeing everything as *imaged*, a mirage world of 'banal seduction' and 'mindless fascination' 'where any kind of judgement – not just artistic but moral and political – becomes impossible' (Hebdige, 1989: 51). As Simons and Billig have put it, 'the flight from foundationalism, and the suspicion against claims of truth, is at the same time a flight from politics . . . The problem is not that the postmodernist spirit lacks a critical impulse, but that critique is running rampant without political direction' (1994: 5–6).

What has also to be said is that the claim that either modernity or modernism has been surpassed is a historically foreshortened view; to echo Mao Tsetung, 'it's too early to tell'. Postmodernism is yet another case of theory running away into the present. It is dazzled by recent changes because it has an inadequate grasp of these as accelerations of longer-term transformations (see Murdock, 1993, for a useful presentation of this case). It may be that postmodernist theory would not have spawned such a proliferation of deracinated writing, which is at once speculative and assertive, if a historically grounded way of thinking had been more prevalent in cultural analysis. One aspect of this, which I now want to pursue, concerns the resolutely modern question of the idea of culture in its relation to the pursuit of democratic forms of education.

The Third Revolution

A democratising pedagogic impulse was central to the emergence of cultural studies, and crucially it became manifest in extensions to the ways in which culture itself is conceptualised. These extensions are now well known and widely accepted, but the insistence on the ordinariness of culture, and the rejection of positions built around the idea of a necessary opposition between 'mass' culture and the Leavisite

notion of a minority culture, were at the time very significant developments. In combination with the application of
an anthropological conception of culture to the societies of
modernity, and recognition of the important historical accomplishments of working-class culture, the sense of a new
scope and vision for cultural analysis seemed intellectually
liberating. This sense appeared to provide fresh justification and ground for the study of popular culture and the
history of majority populations. But it did so as well through
its political grasp – its concrete extrapolations of Marx's final
thesis on Feuerbach – as well as through its analysis of cultural texts and institutions. There was in this a refusal of
the idea of disinterested knowledge, and a recognition of the
need to attend to culture as a multifarious field in which
unequally resourced ways of seeing and speaking about the
social world contend with each other for space and attention. Cultural studies has at best given centrality to a general theoretical perspective on culture as consisting of the
symbolic sites of social power, the diversely patterned but
also inequitably structured terrain upon which the struggle
for and against particular conceptions of how society operates and is constituted is actually played out, in terms of
competing visions and discourses. That, precisely, is the focused achievement of such significant works as *Policing the
Crisis* (Hall *et al.* 1978), or *Women Take Issue* (Women's Study
Group, 1978), which in their relation to particular issues
are political interventions just as much as they are examples
of cultural critique. For cultural studies, cultural processes
are continually intersected by antagonisms of interests and
conflicts of divergent ideological forces.

Yet what has been diminished in various ways in the swing
to a celebratory populism, and rendered critically impossible in anti-foundational variants of postmodernism, is a
popular-democratic politics of education.[4] For Williams, the
project of cultural studies was founded, in part, on such
politics, the politics which he referred to as the 'third revolution', alongside scientific/industrial development and the
struggle for democracy: 'the aspiration to extend the active
process of learning . . . to all people rather than to limited
groups' (1961: 11). This in turn was intimately connected
to the critique of contempory media and the urge to en-

courage and facilitate more democratic channels and forms
of cultural representation. Although hermeneutical questions
are vitally important for cultural studies (and I shall elaborate on them later in the book), cultural analysis itself becomes etiolated when centred almost exclusively around the
interpretive excavation of texts – regardless of how these
proliferate through the attention paid to neglected areas of
experience – and around interpretive questions *per se*. It is
with reference to such tendencies that Williams made the
point that 'there remains the problem of forgetting the real
project' of cultural studies (1989b: 158). The same point
applies to the way in which the fractious skirmishes and
confrontations between different theoretical battalions have,
since the 1970s, obscured in battle-smoke this intended basic
purpose of fostering the democratisation of education and
culture, of educating for citizenship and of developing a
representative public culture. The result is a 'specialised
academicism and loss of historical imagination' (McGuigan,
1992: 27).

For early cultural studies, the emphasis on the cultural
distinctiveness of the northern English working class, among
other regional variants, and on the collectivist cultural achievements of organised labour, was joined to 'the attention given
to the inflections of class and culture inside education'
(Green, 1982: 79), an attention handsomely represented at
the time in the now neglected work of Brian Jackson (1968;
and Jackson and Marsden, 1962). The questions surround-
ing this kind of attention are often underplayed in recent
accounts of what crystallised into the intellectual 'set' of
early cultural studies. Against the text-centred tracing of the
historical beginnings of cultural studies in three or four
founding books by Williams, Hoggart and Thompson, it is
for this reason important to remember that as texts they
grew out of the experience of participation in adult education, extramural extension classes and the like, where socially underprivileged people – particularly women and
individuals from working-class backgrounds – strived to relate fictional representations and intellectual knowledge to
their own situation and experience. Historically, 'English'
itself, in part, had its origins in such pressures from 'below'
during the late nineteenth century and early twentieth century

period, and yet from the outset literary study was deliberately employed in adult education as a means of diminishing class conflict and social discontent among the 'lower orders' (Baldick, 1983: 63–7; see also Eagleton, 1983: 17–53).

'English' was not alone in establishment attempts to bring the classes together and to promote mutual sympathies: these aims had also been fundamental to Christian Socialism, which had developed as an alternative to Chartism, while an ideology of class conciliation was assiduously encouraged in the general areas of sport and leisure (Cunningham, 1980: 110–39). The success of these efforts was never as great as their advocates claimed, and there is evidence that while the middle classes conceived of working-class education in terms of moral elevation and social policing, for many working-class leaders education 'appeared as a useful instrument in the struggle for social and political emancipation' (Harrison, 1963: 4–5; Rée, 1984: 8–9). Nevertheless, education for the people was intended first and foremost as a means of 'shaping society according to dominant middle-class views': 'It was an education designed primarily to strengthen the social fabric, rather than provide cultural or emotional enrichment for the individual; and it was conceived of almost exclusively in literary terms' (Harrison, 1963: 40). The close relation between the rise of English studies and the 'failure of religion' in the late nineteenth century is now widely acknowledged. By the time of the Newbolt Report, 'English' had become so much the new source of sacramental influence that it could be proposed as the keystone in rebuilding the entire arch of national education in Britain and the colonies. As George Gordon, an early-twentieth-century professor of English literature at Oxford, put it in his inaugural lecture, the function of English literature was not only 'to delight and instruct us, but also, and above all, to save our souls and heal the State' (Baldick, 1983: 94, 105).

Having assimilated 'the poor man's classics', the universities converted English studies 'into a fairly normal academic course, marginalising those members of itself who were sustaining the original project' (Williams, 1989b: 153). By the 1920s, the discipline of English had become introverted, professionalised, and promoted as a fundamental means of harnessing those forces generated by the gradual secularisation of attitude and belief, and the drive towards 'mass democracy' and 'mass education', all of which were seen from 'above' as potential threats to the social order. 'English' also became the bastion against which the polluted tides of 'mass' culture could be resisted. As Gerald Graff has acknowledged, academic literary studies operated as 'a means of reinstating cultural uniformity and thus controlling those unruly democratic elements that were entering higher education for the first time' (1987: 12). The spirit of 'the original project', as far as many working-class readers had been concerned, was thus greatly diminished. The only major alternative to it was the Leavisite position, and while this form of cultural criticism was an important precursor of cultural studies – the other, more significant, one being Mass Observation – the new work in what became the new field was an attempt to refashion 'a cultural politics whose lines of development, after the war, became badly blocked' (Green, 1982: 78).[5] While the broader context of this was the New Left response to the 'Butskellite' convergence, the more immediate problem for an emergent cultural studies was that of seeking out new directions beyond the Leavisite blockages :

> And so all the people who first read what you could now fairly call 'Cultural Studies' from that tendency – from Richards, from Leavis, from *Scrutiny* – who were studying popular culture, popular fiction, advertising, newspapers, and making fruitful analyses of it, found in time that the affiliation of this study to the reproduction of a specific minority within deliberately minority institutions created a problem of belief for them, and also a problem for defining what the project was (Williams, 1989: 153–4).

Retrospectively, it seems fitting that, in breaking with 'English' and Leavisite social criticism, cultural studies took up 'a renewal of that attempt at a majority democratic education' in which both the established discipline and Leavisism had failed, but the point of rehearsing these parallel lines of development is also to de-centre the 'founding texts' approach to the emergence of cultural studies, and to underline the significance of the historical context of the New Left and initiatives in adult education (for the most recent

accounts of the New Left, see Chun, 1994, and Kenny, 1995).[6]
While tracing the formation of cultural studies in certain
ideas and accomplishments as encapsulated in founding
texts is of course important, the educational practice and
political context which was crucial to the formation of
those texts in themselves should not be forgotten. The
basic terrain of cultural studies was thus staked out during
the late 1940s and early 1950s by 'many people who were
active in that field at that time who didn't publish, but who
did as much as any . . . to establish this work' (Williams, 1979:
154).[7] It is always the field marshals and generals, rather
than the foot-soldiers, who receive the credit for successful
campaigns.

   Cultural studies has continually grown by displaying an
open-ended, adaptive flexibility. Its vitality depends on its
being responsive to different cultural currents, and new ways
of theorising that which it studies, in the interests of a defining focus on struggles over meaning, experience and values
in their determinate social conditions. This applies also to
disaffiliations from established disciplines and dissatisfaction
with their separation from each other. Cultural studies must
always be turning around to ask questions about how things
intellectual are done and with what end in view, precisely
because institutionalised knowledge is established on the basis
of regulative patterns of designation, obligatory orders of
saying and seeing, and systematised legitimations of statements and accounts whose authoritativeness depends upon
unquestioned and delimited criteria. This raises a perenni-
ally difficult problem, for while the drive towards conceptual rigour and theoretical critique is important, it is not a
sufficient end in itself, and the effect of the theoreticism of
much 1970s and 1980s cultural studies work has been to
deflect the force of the educationally democratic intention
which underpinned the early formation of cultural studies
as a project. If cultural studies research and pedagogy has
any purpose, then it must be connected to the pressing issues of empowerment and emancipation, beyond their often ritualistic intonation, for otherwise the charge of
academicism is always going to stick. As Eileen Janes Yeo
has recently put it:

We must always try to keep analytic space open for people who are 'being studied' to appear as active agents (even if not the most powerful forces) in social life. In contemporary history, a more daunting challenge invites us to develop practices of social study which allow room for people to speak for themselves and thus to represent themselves (1996: 307).[8]

Too much media and cultural theory has operated at a lofty, mandarin height whose elevation above the practical consciousness of those who wish to gain a more critical purchase on culture-and-society issues can prove intimidating, and may undermine rather than help to build up their own insights and self-confidence in relating work within the field to their own situation and experience. Cultural studies needs to regain the impulse to facilitate 'that crucial process of interchange and encounter between the people offering the intellectual disciplines and those using them', and to respect 'the more basic right to define the questions' regardless of disciplinary boundaries (Williams, 1989: 157).[9] In pointing to this further aspect of the turn to ordinariness, I am not at all arguing for a fixed, definitive identity or adherence to some received orthodoxy, but rather, emphasising the need to regain that sense of democratic direction which was lost in the theoretical turn to the new structuralisms and formalisms that has made cultural studies a specialist enterprise where privilege is allowed in again by the back-door, now wearing the cloak of philosophical eminence rather than the crown of artistic excellence.

Notes

1 It may be that is more applicable to history than to other disciplines – Michael Stanford for instance has noted that 'experience' is one of the key concepts of history precisely because 'it contains a good deal of "the contingent and the unforeseen"' (1994: 10) – but for me at least it remains true also of its place within cultural studies, not to mention other subject-areas in the human sciences.

2 This, and the aesthetic elevation of such texts, relate back to the twin pitfalls of cultural analysis identified by Volosinov in the 1920s: see Chapter 2, p. 51.

3 The term 'metaphysical' is used here in the sense of what is

taken essentially as 'transcendence from the temporal toward the atemporal' and which is thus based in 'a refusal, if not a repression of the temporal, and thus of finitude' (Grondin, 1990: 47).

4 Two major exceptions to this limited concern with education are the Education Group's (1981) *Unpopular Education*, which examined the politics of education in postwar Britain, and their follow-up study of Thatcherism's impact on public education, *Education Ltd* (1990).

5 For critical work on Mass Observation, see Jeffrey, 1978; Pickering and Chaney, 1986; and Chaney and Pickering, 1986. See also the useful anthology of MO writings edited by Calder and Sheridan, 1984.

6 In his review of Chun and Kenny, Inglis offers the following capsule account: 'The huge project of the British New Left was to effect the cultural turn, remoralise Marxism by bending power back towards value, and to fashion a cultural and historical theory capable of connecting local backwardness to international possibility, and of tracing the circuits which ran from ordinary creativity to transformative action' (1996: 90). This is of course a summary, but a grand one at that.

7 See also Inglis, 1995, chapter 6; Harrison, 1961; Harrison, 1995, chapter 10; Thompson, 1968a; Hoggart, 1973: 205–30; and McIlroy and Westwood, 1993: 260 on Tony McLean as an example of the many people referred to by Williams.

8 In the light of this statement, it is worth noting the development by feminists of methods in sociology which attempt to place the subjects of study more actively within the research process. See Roberts, 1992, and Maynard, 1994.

9 The work of Henry A. Giroux in the United States is helpful here. See in particular Aronowitz and Giroux, 1991; Giroux, 1992; and Giroux and McLaren, 1994.

Chapter 4

Crossing the Asses' Bridge

The basis of our consciousness of self is the abiding fact that without a world we would not have such a consciousness, and without this consciousness no world would exist for us. What occurs in this contact is life, not a theoretical process; it is what we call an experience, that is, pressure and counter-pressure, expanding towards things which in turn respond, a vital power within and around us which is experienced in pleasure and pain, in fear and hope, in grief over burdens which cannot be shifted, in delight over what we receive as gifts from outside. So the I is not a spectator who sits in front of the world's stage, but is involved in actions and counteractions in which the same actualities are overwhelmingly experienced whether kings figure in them or fools and clowns. This is why no philosopher could ever persuade those involved that everything was appearance or show and not reality.

(Wilhelm Dilthey)

Tracing the Lexical Threads

So far I have been preparing the ground for a broader consideration of the category of experience in historical and cultural analysis. This will involve thinking around some of the problems which are raised by the ways in which the meanings made of any object of study are influenced and coloured by our social and historical experience. But the first question that needs to be addressed is how experience itself may be conceptualised and understood as a constituent in the production of cultural and historical meanings.

Experience as an analytical category in cultural studies and social history remains slippery and elusive. It seems to defy any attempt to use it with precision, and always to become stubbornly tangled in wider senses and associations. It is because of this that it generates both fascination and frustration. This chapter will therefore explore the term conceptually in an attempt to clarify and sharpen up its various references and meanings. I shall begin by tracing certain aspects of its historical usages and development.

All words have a history and so in themselves provide us with threads back along the indistinct, overgrown pathways of their past meanings and applications. Etymologically, the term *experience* derives via Middle English and Old French from the Latin *experientia*, which was itself related to *experior*, trying or proving, from the root *peri*, 'try', hence the connection to *peritus*, experienced, practised, skilled, that is having learned by trying or trying out. The historical connection with the word *experiment*, in the sense of putting to the test, is thus clear, but while *experiment* became more directly just the test itself, *experience* came to refer also to a consciousness of the results of such a practical test, and by extension to a consciousness of an effect or state. The threads variously converge, intertwine and diverge, both within and across languages. Needham, for example, notes that these two senses remain compounded in the French *expérience*, a word that has thus become a '*faux ami* to neophyte translators into English' (Needham, 1972: 172). From the sixteenth century, the association of the term with the past became more prominent, as in 'the tried and tested', and the word was increasingly used to denote knowledge based upon historical events or particular observation. The link with *experiment* has been retained, however, in a further association with *empirical*, as in 'testing by empirical means', that is attaining proof by direct observation or replicable demonstration. These lexical traces persist, but the more usual senses of the term refer both to the assimilation of experience on the basis of what is observed, encountered or felt, as in 'experience shows', or 'it is a question of experience', and to the resultant knowledge which is derived from living socially through events or from the shared perception of things happening, as in 'common experience'. The first sense here is of experience as *process*, and it is this process from which experiential knowledge emanates; in the second, it is of experience as *object*, the cumulative body of knowledge associated with it. In this second, more general sense, the term can then be personified, as in Disraeli's description of experience as 'the child of Thought' (1926: 177) or generalised, as in Mills' reference to 'the results of Indian experience' (1910: 426). In the second sense, experience refers to 'lived' experience of the past not so much in itself, but rather in terms of the congealed knowledge that is derived from it, both individually and collectively. It consists as well, though always contentiously, in the 'lessons of the past'.

Conceptually, experience can therefore point in at least two directions. The first refers us to a subjective involvement in a particular range of activities, which is to see it as a participation in a sequenced phasing of events and actions, and this can be linked to the 'lived' moments of experience. Experiences in this sense are of course rarely met in the 'lived' encounter in any raw, unmediated form in that they are, biographically and collectively, cumulative and recursive; they are assimilated in aggregated, synthesised forms and patterns that subsequently act back on the processual dimension of experience. There are a myriad of ways in which psychologically and culturally such mediation may operate and become manifest, but what is implicated here in general terms are context-specific questions of appropriate conduct and demeanour, relevant modes of feeling and response, and so on. It is when we take the other direction that questions of change become relevant, for assimilated experience does not necessarily entail inert reproduction. The reference is then – or at least when it is actively and positively accented – to what is learnt from experience, intentionally taken from it, consciously used and reflected on, and perhaps subsequently adapted in future participation and action. Needless to say, these different conceptions are not mutually exclusive, and there is nothing inevitable about the avoidance of negative experience. We may even want to say that more generally experience is no teacher at all, that its lessons for the future are often ignored or inadequately assimilated. History contains no shortage of examples, and contrapuntally they raise the difficult issue of the grounds

on which valid or useful experience can be defined and
evaluated.

Williams notes a particular historical development of the
processual sense of the term, associated with the present,
referring to 'a particular kind of consciousness', full, open
and active, including feeling as well as thought, and thus
distinct from reason and empirical procedure (Williams, 1987:
126–9). There is a strong appeal here to wholeness, to forms
of thought which are not exclusive or specialised in mode,
abstract or aridly rationalistic in character. Despite its first
generative association with Romanticism, it would be too
easy to lock it solely into the (albeit fraught) historical terms
of that association. It has in fact a much wider application,
and what it evokes is often culturally, aesthetically or reli-
giously revered as a significant creative attainment or in-
tense form of engagement involving what John Dewey referred
to as 'those moments of fulfilment [which] punctuate experience' (cited McDermott, 1981: 537). These moments may
not have any long-term transformative consequence, and may
not entail what is subsequently viewed, in a different period,
as valid or extendable experience. Nonetheless, in the associations with feeling and the active engagement with concrete occurrences and symbolic exchange, there would appear
in some ways to be an obvious connection with the generation of a structure of feeling, in the sense of its urgency of
creative effort towards articulation in a 'lived' present, as
opposed to what has become a relatively settled and readily
identifiable thematic ensemble. The experientially holistic
nature of this particular inflection of the term is also akin
to the appeal in early Williams to grasp analytically that felt
wholeness which characterised for him the immersion within
a 'lived' present. On the other hand, the connection should
not be pushed too far, for there are various differences, which
would include the sense that what is culturally and historically emergent precludes neither the faculty of reasoning
nor an empirical grounding of the resultant expressive form.

Dilthey and the Development of Hermeneutics

It is instructive to compare these semantic developments in
English with similar developments in the German language,

not only because they mutually illuminate each other but
also because it is important to take up and discuss the influential formulation by Wilhelm Dilthey (1833–1911) of the
term *Erlebnis* – that which is 'lived through' – in his philosophical writings. In this new linguistic and conceptual term
of the late nineteenth century, the sense of experience as
direct, actual and immediate comes together with the sense
of what this yields, the more durable residue that acquires
resonance, weight and significance over and above the relatively transient, and soon-to-be-forgotten elements of day-
to-day experience in the perpetual flow of events. Victor
Turner suggestively notes that Dilthey's emphasis on living
through connects with the syllabic component *per* in 'experience' in that *per* threads hypothetically way back to an Indo-
European root 'whose central concept is perhaps the base
of prepositions and preverbs with the core meaning of "forward" or "through"'. It could of course be said that this
tentative connection begs questions about the temporal,
realised meanings and usages of categories, yet even at a
strictly philological level the connection is fruitful in keeping up in the air the active aspect of the term. This particular root sense of traversal can then be traced in the related
Erfahrung, but what is important in Dilthey's description of
Erleben is that the 'living through' a sequence of events is
incomplete until one of its 'moments' attains the status of
'performance', 'an act of creative retrospection in which
"meaning" is ascribed to the events and parts of experience'
(Turner, 1982: 18).

In this double sense, we are presented again with both
process and product as interdependent. The process renders
up the fluid material for interpretation which is then given
the emphasis of what lasts, in its precipitate forms of time's
traces, but this also in various ways mediates experience as
ongoing process in what Dilthey describes as 'a translating
back of the objectifications of life into the spiritual livingness
from which they emerged' (Gadamer, 1975: 59). As Turner
puts it, experience is then 'both "living through" and "thinking
back". It is also "willing or wishing forward", i.e., establishing goals and models for future experience in which, hope-
fully, the errors and perils of past experience will be avoided
or eliminated' (1982:18). The connection with Dewey's

'moments of fulfilment', in the most general sense of that accomplishment, is clear enough. So also is the sense of process where these moments become formative in the on-going interpretive engagement with what happens in the course of our lives, and in our participatory experience of historical processes which involve, in Dilthey's conception, always a dual movement of retrospection and prospection, action and counteraction, pressure and counter-pressure. It is important here to sound again a note of caution, though in a rather different sense, against an over-aestheticised emphasis on experiential attainment. It is important because many 'moments' in individual and collective lives prospectively exhibit a negative vitality, or become retrospectively a corrosive force. The recognition of this is clear enough in Dilthey's thought, as the epigraph at the head of this chapter demonstrates. The assimilation of such 'moments' may entail a sinking under rather than a rising above the crushing weight of unwanted or unwilled experience, of change, disruption or pressure which people are unable to come to terms with because of the definite, unadaptable positions their individuality has become identified with. Arriving at such passes, their own *habitus* permits only a negative, sometimes hostile self-defensive response, though in other cases an individual may struggle, perhaps unsuccessfully, against these internalised limitations. This is what Dilthey referred to as the 'tragedy of finitude' (Hodges, 1952: 280).[1] Less dramatically, the assimilation of pain, suffering, failure or excessive burdens on one's time, energies or patience may be only retaliatory or compensatory, rather than, as with moments of fulfilment, carrying a sure sense of movement forward in growth, learning or the satisfying accomplishment of specific purposes in individual life and collective projects.

In German as well, however, the positive connections with Romanticism are important. It is not merely coincidental that Dilthey's earlier thought on the concept arose in the context of a discussion of Goethe and Rousseau. Throughout the nineteenth century, as in England, experience as 'lived' and felt carried associations of opposition both to an excessive rationalism and to trends towards the mechanisation of social life and labour. While this has at times been a valuable counterweight, it has also at others veered off into mystical vapourings and pantheistic credos. These tendencies are, for example, apparent in the English literary tradition in the work of rural writers like Richard Jefferies (see, for example, 1983). Dilthey, by contrast, attempted in his approach to 'experience' to bring together opposed currents of thought relevant to it. Throughout his life, he drew centrally on the two traditions of Romanticism and Empiricism. His project can be described as an attempt to reconcile these traditions, and in doing so he gave to hermeneutics its most significant expression in nineteenth-century thought. Hermeneutics first developed as a historiographical method in the sixteenth century, when it was applied to the exegesis of theological texts, but towards the end of the eighteenth century it moved 'beyond the mere critique of texts and began to ask difficult questions about the nature and the objectives of historical knowledge as such; indeed, of social knowledge in general' (Bauman, 1978: 8). Romanticism was important here in locating the meaning of the work of art in the artist's life-experience; the challenge of understanding a work of art was felt to require an imaginative re-engagement with the depths of that experience. In taking up this task, and applying it to the study of social texts, hermeneutics could only employ philological critique as a starting-point; the interpretation of meaning entailed a grappling with difficulties for which such critique was methodologically inadequate. The influence of Romanticism on a developing hermeneutics was then an important factor in the hermeneutic challenge to conceptions of social science as based on the model of natural science. Positivist approaches could at best 'explain' social phenomena; they could not properly 'understand' them, in the romantic depth-sense of the term. As with a work of art, so with social action: 'Both cases required above all the forging of affinity into shared experience, a sort of sympathetic self-identification with another human being'. Understanding 'could not be reduced to a set of rules which eliminated the role played by subjective purpose and purpose-subordinated decisions. Thus understanding was an art, not a science' (ibid: 12), and as such was always incomplete, always in production, arriving at no final truth and reaching no absolute value.

One form of response to this was to deny 'subjective meanings' and subjective forms of experience any place in sociological research, since they are simply not relevant (Horkheimer, 1939: 434–5). This response is not possible for the kinds of historical and cultural analysis with which I am concerned, for as we shall see, experience, subjectivity, identity and their specificities are central to them. Dilthey is interesting precisely because he is an unacknowledged forbear of such forms of enquiry. His significance for them is in the way he tries to bring together the opposed currents of rational criticism and emotional involvement. The Culture-and-Society tradition remapped by Williams, and its extensions in the 'radical earnestness' of English social thought from William Morris and T. H. Green to postwar socialists like E. P. Thompson and John Berger, have been concerned, among other things, with 'rewriting the deep contradictions of Romantic feeling and Enlightenment rationalism' (Inglis, 1982: 23). Cultural studies is an inheritor of these attempts to challenge the damaging rift between methodical reason and imaginative engagement, and in this Dilthey's thinking remains instructive. The influence of Romanticism in his thinking is manifest in his denial that social and historical analysis can be confined to the rigorous application of empirical method, and that reason can be elevated to a position above and impervious to the social and cultural phenomena which are studied. Dilthey's epistemology is grounded in experience, and experience cannot be studied solely by 'objective' techniques or understood only in terms of abstract rationality or formal theory. Yet at the same time, Dilthey followed empirical procedure to the extent of canvassing a comparative anthropological approach to culture as ways of living and thinking, and rejecting all forms of apriorism.[2] He took up a critical position with respect to both sides of his cultural inheritance, viewing the Romantic tradition as insufficiently social in conception, and limited in its contribution to social improvement; and viewing empiricism as inadequate in understanding the dynamics of the historical process and the social and psychological complexities of experience. Hodges aptly sums up this dual approach in describing Dilthey as 'a positivist trying to do justice to a poet's vision' and 'a romantic trying to analyse himself in positivist terms' (1952: 2). This is the measure of Dilthey's intellectual ambition. It is his struggle to work towards a synthesis of these cross-cutting tendencies that makes him such a fascinating figure.

The basis for a historical form of hermeneutics was laid by Friedrich Schleiermacher (1768–1834), whom Dilthey called the 'Kant of theology'. Schleiermacher's enquiries led him to raise wide-ranging questions about how meanings are generated from texts and how an objective knowledge of them may be possible. Dilthey then broadened these questions out to deal with symbolic structures in general. This extension of Schleiermacher 'brought the problem of understanding and interpretation' into relation with 'the practice of living, in daily life, in lived experience' (Bauman, 1978: 29). Hermeneutics was thus reconceived around the tasks of understanding the 'quotidianity' of experience in cultures or historical periods other than our own. As Zygmunt Bauman comments: 'One can easily see the Romantic origin of this remarkable shift of attention. Romanticism's paramount legacy – the elusive, polysemic notions of *Leben* and *Erlebnis* – have from then haunted forever the self-reflection of the humanities.' In replacing *Geist*, the term *Leben* became 'both the central ontological concept and the leading methodological principle' (ibid: 29–30). This was crucial to Dilthey's extension of Schleiermacher's hermeneutics. Schleiermacher's approach was twofold, involving firstly a comparative method which interprets texts in terms of characteristic linguistic, stylistic, syntactical and discursive features; and secondly, a 'divinatory' aptitude, which is akin to intuition or imaginative insight in literary criticism, and is directed to the 'inner' conception and germinal source of the text. While in some ways this second approach to understanding recognises that we need to be receptive to the strangeness or stark difference of experiences encountered in the texts and practices of past times, it nevertheless remains an earlier instance of understanding experience as transcendent, primarily because it conceived of understanding itself as an atemporal psychological process. Dilthey rejected this second aspect of Schleiermacher's approach, firstly because his 'concept of understanding has nothing whatsoever to do with intuition' (Rickman, 1960: 309); and secondly, because it ignored the social and historical contexts of experience in favour of absolute conceptions, values and principles. A cultural text bears time's traces, not some timeless essence. For Dilthey, Schleiermacher's 'divinatory' method could deal only with formal change in the object of study in time and over time, and was thus historically impoverished. There is nothing anterior to historically lived lives apart from the history of which they are a part. Whether we are thinking historically of a particular individual, a particular social institution or a body of cultural texts, 'lines of influence from the past meet... intersect, and are directed afresh into the future' (Hodges, 1952: 14). The ground of this action is experience, through which, for Dilthey, all historical knowledge is mediated.[3]

Das Erlebnis

A central Kantian distinction in Dilthey's concept of *Erlebnis* is that between 'mere' experience, which is characteristically transient and caught up in an ever-moving, indistinguishable flux, and *an* experience within which, or in relation to which, significant meanings and values are condensed, and given a forward-carrying coherence and intensity. This distinction of Dilthey's connects with that of Williams's between 'mere flux' and a structure of feeling as a pre-formation whose emergence is structured by the effort, as a prospective force, to characterise itself against what is settled and fixed in place within an existing social order. These distinctions are significantly different from Whitehead's contrast between 'the world as disclosed in immediate presentation, gay with a thousand tints, passing, and intrinsically meaningless', and 'the world disclosed in its causal efficacy, where each event infects the ages to come, for good or evil, with its own individuality'. Whitehead gives as an example of this contrast the inscription on old sundials, *pereunt et imputantur* – the hours perish and are laid to account – where the immediate, fleeting world of time present is caught in *pereunt*, while the influence of the past in the formation of the present is condensed in *imputantur* (1928: 55–6, 69; and see Smith, 1885: 372) Apart from other points of variance one could note, the distinction here is different in that for Whitehead the emphasis given to the contrast between time passing and time's traces is that which underlies the senses of pathos and nostalgia, whereas the stress in Williams's distinction is on moments of emergence which underlie the forces of aspiration and hope.

It is then, significantly, experience conceived as *an* experience, helping to coalesce meaning and significance retrospectively and prospectively, which has been seminal in the development of autobiography as a distinct form of writing, and the development of an increasingly reflexive historical consciousness, both of which are characteristically modern in their questioning of and willingness to remake what is empirically given or transmitted in tradition. In autobiography, this willingness cannot become wilful without the particular form of narrative employed being lost or transformed into some other kind of storytelling. Autobiography achieves the form in which it is apprehended through a present view of life, which acts upon the process of looking back and reshapes what is yielded by this process in the light of the understanding which it confers. The biographical importance of *Erlebnisse* is that they constitute the key points in which thematic meanings and concerns are anchored, and from which identity and the life-process are most intensely illuminated, backwards and forwards: 'past and future are related to experience in a series that forms itself into a whole through such relations' (Warnke, 1987: 29). So what is also generically distinctive about the autobiograpical form is that its activity of reconceiving what is significant in a specific past is itself 'determined by the same past experiences whose significance it reveals'; it is, as Dilthey puts it, these dialectical relations of meaning which 'constitute the present experience and pervade it'. To adopt Hodge's gloss: 'the object to be apprehended enters into and determines the apprehending subject' (1952: 274). By means of this to-and-fro movement past and present mutually frame and reframe each other. So with history, which initially at least we approach in the same spirit of inquiry and interrogation as we do our own experienced movement through time: 'The power and breadth of our own lives, and the energy with which we reflect on them, are the ground of historical vision. It is they which enable us to give a second life to the bloodless

shades of the past' (Makkreel, 1975: 379–80). This is in some
ways exaggerated, and in itself is a recipe for chronocentric
reckonings of past forms of life, but at the same time it
provides a valuable counter to empiricist notions of a past
speaking strictly for itself. As with autobiography, our own
positions as interlocutors of the past render these notions
impossible. What constitutes *an* experience, and what is
considered significant historical experience, are interpretively
mobile. For this reason, *an* experience may exceed any significance which is retrospectively invested in it; its realised
significance is in the way it lasts and is never finished with,
even after long assimilation. 'Because it is itself within the
whole of life, in it too the whole of life is present' (Gadamer,
1975: 62).

Yet the distinction between *an* experience and those which
are merely mundane should not be conceived as dichotomous, for it is the tension between different forms of experience which is always significant. When we extract any
particular experience from the habitual flux, when we single
it out and express its significance in story, song, chronicle
or account, there is a danger of isolating it from the living
stream in which it first emerged. As Abrahams suggests, by
'elevating our actions to stories and even more dramatic
replayings, we lose some of the spirit that resides in actions
simply because they are humdrum' (Abrahams, 1986: 48).
In focusing on the unusual, the atypical or overtypical, we
need to avoid reproducing certain polarised valuations which
may be associated with their distinction and the contrarieties which often underpin them. Particularly relevant here
is the symbolic economy of experience in our culture which
greatly inflates the currency of *an* experience as opposed to
the small coin of the quotidian. The opportunist version of
this is what I call experiential sentimentalism, where those
intangible elements of community or things-in-common in
everyday life are emotionally bathed in a soft moral light,
and often idealised in reference backwards. Experience in
this sense is benignly rendered as an unquestioned positive
value, and it can be used ideologically to validate certain
propositions or policies.

To give an example of this, there is today an irritating
form of public address which invites audiences to 'share'

certain experiences with the speaker. For me, a recent encounter with this form of address occurred at a small lunch-
time gathering on a university campus. The speaker invited
his audience to share his experiences of what he called key
moments in the history of postwar popular music. What ir-
ritated was the unspoken presumption that his audience could
and would 'share his experiences', and that those experiences transparently defined the 'moments' that went undefined. This kind of public address seems to assume not only
that communication as sharing is unproblematic, but also
that it offers such participation as a guarantee of truth-tell-
ing in human interaction. The guarantee is unsound not
because experience is inherently individualistic, but because
it assumes that 'sharing' experiences provides a communicational warrant for the speaker's honesty in the telling
of it. The assumption of experience 'being shared' establishes
an entitlement to speak in public, and invests the communication with the authority of a truth to historical experience that is implicitly claimed as being held in common.

In experiential sentimentalism, then, the words 'experience' and 'communication' are deployed as complacent ali-
bis of each other's authenticity of sense and reference. The
task for analysis is then to cut through their lines of mutual
connection, to make problematic the ease with which they
support each other in the claim to being true to common
experience. It is a mistake to assume that communication is
about telling the truth. There are of course statements which
are incontrovertibly true, just as there are those which are
a pack of lies straight down to their middle, but there is
also a lot of haziness between truth and lies, in everyday
social intercourse just as much as in public forms of communication, and there is no absolute gauge that we can apply
to see which is which (see, for example, Barnes, 1994; cf.
Eco, 1976: 7, 58–9). We do not normally equate the communication of anyone's personal experiences with lying, yet
there is no general reason why we should not. I shall want
to qualify this later on, but the point to drive home here is
that we should stop thinking of 'communication' as auto-
matically a positive term, which is for instance what we do
when we emphasise its value in creating a sense of social
bonding. Telling is only potentially to share, which means

that we should ask how such sharing is itself possible, and on whose terms, in whose interests, from what perspective, and for what duration. Asking such questions may help limit the incidence of experiential sentimentalism in everyday discourse, though the questions themselves carry no guarantee of that. In Geertz's terse observation, 'the announcement of some Smiling Jack that he is about to share an experience with you is enough to make you reach for your wallet'. Such fatuous uses of the term, however, do not mean that there is a cast-iron case for dismissing it, even though in such instances there is. What they do mean is that a more thorough conceptual understanding of it is imperative. As Geertz goes on to say, 'it is equally true that without it, or something like it, cultural analyses seem to float several feet above their human ground . . . Perpetual signification machines can do no more than perpetual motion ones; occurrence must break in somewhere.' Cultural analysis 'must engage some sort of felt life, which might as well be called experience'. For this reason, at least, 'experience' is 'the asses' bridge all must cross' (1986: 374).

The complex ways in which the routinised ongoing movement of everyday life interacts with those moments of experience which stand out in their felt intensity, symbolic framing, stylised performance or ritualised drama are what cultural analysis grapples with. This interaction is there in the very term 'experience', in its multi-valencies and tensions of sense, in its reference to radically contrastive modes of being and becoming. For Dilthey, experience is most significantly represented in the expressive forms which constitute what is historically and culturally 'lived through'. These expressive forms encapsulate 'structures of experience' which emerge out of, but are clearly differentiated from routine, habitual experience in the regular flow of everyday life. Experiences of this kind are far more diverse than any distinction between flux and form can capture, but it is in their most vital and scintillant sense that they connect with structure of feeling as emergent. In this sense they are held, as it were, on the cusp of cultural meaning where past forms of linguistic utterance and cultural practice are brought together, and yet moved beyond in a new articulation which embodies a felt sense of the forces and conditions that have coalesced around a particular moment of being in the social and historical process, a sense crystallised out of the formative experience of what has been 'lived through'. This conception of experience is a vibrant prefiguring, an electric connection forward, to Williams's concept of structure of feeling. Significantly, though, for *Elebnis* the same tension obtains between its immediate, emergent sense and its sense as 'discovered yield' and 'lasting residue' (Gadamer, 1975: 55–6). Expressive meanings in this latter sense are what is *pressed* or squeezed out of experience, or as Victor Turner has put it, turning the process around to its more active 'moment' : 'An experience is itself a process which "presses out" to an "expression" which completes it' (1982: 13). As such, and because of this creative process, expressive forms are more than simply evidential driftwood left at the historical shoreline of human lives. They are, to quote Turner again, 'the crystallised secretions of once living human experience, individual and collective' (ibid: 17).[4]

We need here to clarify more precisely what Dilthey meant by this particular quality of the 'lived' in social experience. For him, we are not conscious in *Erlebnis* of experience *as* experience; we 'live through' it in the sense that its constituent parts exist in solution; these are subsequently and selectively apprehended through introspection or recollection, though these processes can also involve a 'living through' when there is no awareness of them as such. 'In a word, *das Erleben* is the mode in which we experience our own states or psychical acts in the actual having of them, and it differs from all other modes in which we can be conscious of ourselves in that it is an *immediate* experience' (Hodges, 1952: 38). In *Erlebnis*, distinctions between observer and observed, apprehension and what is apprehended, are during the experience dissolved, or as Dilthey puts it, the *Erlebnis* 'does not stand as an object over against the observer, its existence for me is not distinguished from that *which* in it exists for me' (ibid: 39). 'Lived experience' is thus described as 'immediate knowing', that is, knowing before it is objectified, knowing as pre-emergent. When we think of what is happening to us we become conscious of it as an experience, we identify it as such in thought, in utterance, and where we can in relation to some expressive cultural form or practice which often acts as a way of mediating the sense and meanings we give to the experience thus identified. When we think back and rework time's traces, we order our lives by distinguishing between such experiences, but again, because of this process, these are different from their immediate 'living through' in that their content has become objectified and given expressive form.

It is obvious that 'lived' experience and 'immediate knowing' are dependent on pastness, memory and self-reflection over time, but the point of *Erlebnis* is that it also denotes the structural and thematic coherence (such as it is, in anyone's actual biography) made out of the life-process where vibrant elements of experience 'dovetail' through memory and recollection into the present as a 'dynamic unity', and thus 'are experienced as a determining force' (Hodges, 1952: 47). 'Immediate knowing' thus involves an intensity of experiential presentness, but precludes for its specific temporal span awareness of its broader connections with social institutions and historical currents even though it is intimately wrought up in them. It is because *an* experience tends to generate a self-reflexive process that the structural relations within it are brought to light. For Dilthey, then, 'lived' experience is 'the basis on which imagination, memory, and thought arise', and which work 'to clarify and amplify what is ours' in such experience over time (ibid: 50–1; Makkreel, 1975: 386–9). As Georgia Warnke has put it: 'In Dilthey's conception understanding and experience spiral around each other: new experiences revise the way in which the past is understood and the future anticipated; at the same time, those experiences are interpreted in the context of an understanding of past and future' (1987: 29).

In *The Stone Diaries*, Carol Shields notes that at 'the edge of every experience is the refracted light of recollection, snagged there like an image in a bevelled mirror' (1994: 175). What is crystallised in an expressive cultural form is always what is remembered and what is constructed out of that remembrance, in a continuous sequence of temporal succession. Remembering involves recognition, in both senses of the term, and this means that 'everything past is a reproduction, structurally related to a former experience' (Dilthey, 1976: 185). As we have seen for those past-creating forms

of autobiography and historical narrative, that it is a re-pro-
duction is undeniable, for what is past can only be expressed,
pressed out and given form, in a newly contingent present.
Representing a past experience means re-fracting it in that
present, creating an image in a bevelled mirror. Yet, at the
same time, the present reproduction of what is past only
attains meaning in its structural relation to former experience, to experience in its cumulative form. For Dilthey, time's
traces are not only continually retraced, but are also integrally bound up in experience within a present, which is to
say in one sense that there never *is* a present: 'what we
experience as present always contains memory of what has
just been present', and so 'every observed moment of life is
a remembered moment and not a flow; *it is fixed by attention
which arrests what is essentially flow*' (ibid: 210, emphasis in
original; cf. William James: see McDermott, 1967: 213). If
we say that the interaction between experience and expression
is dialectical in the sense of a reciprocally structuring and
transforming relation, the restless flow of time 'cannot be
experienced as such because the very observation of time
fixes our attention and interrupts the flow of experience,
leading to periods of reflexivity when the mind becomes
"conscious of itself"' (Bruner, 1986: 8). On the other hand,
such becoming 'conscious of itself' is dependent on the sense
of a present as what was 'lived through', where 'a moment
of time' was filled with 'experience' even though 'that which
constitutes the content of living experience perpetually alters'. The present in this sense is therefore where our little
skiffs of individual life are afloat on the stream of its cease-
less advance, and the most significant moments in this ever-
ongoing flow are 'where we live in the fullness of our reality'
(Hodges, 1952: 44–5). We can bring the two aspects together
by saying that while the present cannot be experienced
because experience is successive, it is only in the present
that past and future can be conceived and given form. This
is the temporal dynamic. Dilthey expresses it thus: 'The
present . . . is a lapse of time whose extension we grasp together as a unit. We grasp together, with the character of
the present, that which, by reason of its continuity, is for us
not separable' (ibid: 46).

Hermeneutic Understanding and History

Thinking of experience in terms of this dynamic inevitably rubs up against the theoretical limitations of structuralism, for in giving analytical priority to the transformational 'deep structures' of culture, structuralism negated experience as a mere surface phenomenon. The volatile relationship between experience and its symbolic expressions was significant only for indicating what lay beneath it, making experience constantly 'spoken for' by its hidden determinants. Poststructuralism avoids the idea of meaning as resting upon stable underlying structures, such as those of clear-cut binary oppositions, but instead delivers only the sense of meaning continuously deferred in endless chains of endlessly sliding signifiers. Far from rehabilitating the historical subject in his or her participatory involvement in the generation or regeneration of expressive forms, postmodernism disperses that involvement to the eventual point of its disappearance: the decentred subject finds its identity only amid fragments of language or discourse (Giddens, 1991: 170). The structuralist and poststructuralist charge that an epistemological focus on 'experience' is empiricist is obviously valid in certain specific cases, and is obviously valid when the evidence of experience is accepted without such acceptance being tempered by any consideration of its external determinants or its internal dynamics. Yet the charge is often indiscriminative.

Dilthey's empiricism, for instance, was distinctive in its rejection not only of speculative knowledge but also of British forms of empiricism, as in Hume or Mill, and in this he can be seen retrospectively as moving closer to forms of interpretive sociology and, not altogether fancifully, to aspects of cultural studies as well. Dilthey particularly rejected those narrow forms of empiricism which define experience strictly in relation to sense-data – Nietzsche's 'dogma of immaculate perception'. In the scale of empirical knowledge, this dogmatic empiricism severely relegates the significance of emotions, memory, presuppositions, value-systems and so on, which for Dilthey were just as much constitutive components of human experience as what the senses admit. This is of course not to say that Dilthey did not value empirical enquiry; the attention to concrete detail and discrimination among factual data was what he admired in historians like Ranke. What Dilthey found wanting among historians of his time was any attempt to follow through the theoretical implications of their work or to develop a theoretical basis for historical studies. In his own theoretical approach to historical knowledge, he attempted always to relate the experience of a particular period and place to the social and cultural processes which grounded its lived and learned possibilities: 'Our observations of life around us are obviously enriched by social and cultural knowledge; this, surely, is what we call experience if we are not influenced by speculative philosophic assumptions' (Rickman, 1979: 54). His reference to Comte's 'crass, naturalistic metaphysics' should then be understood in relation to this way of thinking of the rules and resources generatively drawn on in everyday social interaction (Truzzi, 1974: 8).

Dilthey acknowledged that experience as a source of knowledge derives partly from introspection (though this can degenerate into self-absorbed brooding) and partly from the enabling and restricting contacts of everyday life, but he viewed these as insufficient in themselves for an understanding of our own social and historical experience.[5] This, if we are to begin to realise it, needs to operate within broader parameters of comparison and contrast with places, times and cultures other than our own. The examination of other 'epochs and cultures tends to illuminate certain structures and tendencies within ourselves which we should not have been aware of otherwise' (Horkheimer, 1939: 434). Even in the case of our own culture, though, this is never 'given' to us as individuals but rather, as Edward Sapir insisted, 'gropingly discovered'. 'We never cease to learn our *own* culture, which is always changing, let alone other cultures' (Turner, 1982: 64). If we take this as a palpable aspect of our own ongoing experience in the present, then we are obviously engaged even more gropingly with the problem of what gets lost in the precipitation of time's traces from the manifold elements experienced in a particular time's 'lived' solution. It is never possible to regain for a past period those innumerable taken-for-granted elements which Garfinkel noted as being invisibly present in even the simplest act of talking, and which are integral to the very tissue of living at that time (Bauman, 1978: 31). On the other hand, we may know more historically of the broader contexts and processes in which lived experiences of a past period were aswim. This is the brunt of Schleiermacher's bold assertion that we may know the authors of particular texts better than they knew themselves. Through this more extensive understanding, however, we may lose sight of the 'inside' experience in its intricate and manifold qualities. Interpretively, there are dangers both ways.

In whatever way our interpretation is mobilised, we should at the very least always start by trying to develop a sympathetic understanding of others' experience, even though the telling of it, in whatever form it takes, may be suspect, may be unwittingly skewed, or laden with social myths. This is to talk of the need for balancing intellectual humility with sceptical identification. It is to talk of a willingness to attend to the other side of where we ourselves stand without romanticising what we find there. For Dilthey, the lack of this open-minded attentiveness makes the possibility of gaining some sense of others' experience forever elusive. Edward Thompson's 'always listening' approach to historical practice is an instance of this (Thompson, 1976a: 15), and such 'listening' must be acute in imaginative feeling as well as in reasoned doubting. The importance of *Erlebnisse* is that they offer felt immediacy, concrete action and response to action, and not some abstract formulation or scientific principle. In this sense their analytical value runs counter to the 'cold rationalism of the Enlightenment' (Gadamer, 1975: 57). Dilthey took the view that the concepts and categories we use to organise experience do not exhaust its significance, and because of this our attention and response to data should not be sustained solely by 'the diluted juice of reason'. 'Thought clarifies and generalises lived experience, but experience is charged with emotion and volition, sources respectively of value-judgements and precepts' : structures of experience 'are not the bloodless "cognitive structures", static and "synchronic", so beloved of structuralism' (Turner, 1982: 13).

Dilthey was opposed to any mechanistic form of explanation which reduced the complexity of human experience to external, causal processes, thus analytically eschewing or diminishing the significance of the subjective dimension of social life. The historical school of late-nineteenth-century Germany, of which Dilthey was the *fons et origo*, rejected the scientific paradigm as a basis for the conduct of historical and cultural studies. For this reason, although his attitude to it was often ambivalent, there was a definite suspicion of positivist methodology in his general approach. Among other things, positivism holds that 'since experience is the sole source of knowledge, the methods of empirical science are the only means by which the world can be understood' (Stent, 1975: 1052). In this sense positivist methodology seemed to Dilthey 'to mutilate historical reality in order to adapt it to the ideas of the natural sciences' (Holborn, 1950: 98), and in doing so it effectively left the questions of symbolic meaning and value, and the interpretive processes of cultural participation, clear out of its framework. Positivism distorts knowledge in discounting reflexive life-experience and the intersubjective mediation of this experience. Now we can of course say that Dilthey's approach was empiricist in the sense that he rejected any form of metaphysical construction, and refused attempts to force empirical inquiry into the strait-jacket of any rigid rationalistic, theological or moral assumptions. But if by empiricist we are referring to the tendency 'to believe that the world "out there" is isomorphic in every respect with the image the detached observer will form of it' (Nash and Wintrob, 1972: 529), then Dilthey hardly fits the bill. Indeed, he condemned empiricism in this sense as no less abstract than philosophical speculation: 'It bases itself on mutilated experience, distorted from the outset by an atomistic theoretical view of mental life' (Rickman, 1979: 54). Dilthey was a methodological anti-naturalist. He was concerned with a human world 'which he saw suffused throughout with meaning arising from the consciousness, feeling, purposes and valuations of human beings' with particular social and historical identities (Rickman, 1961: 61). Hermeneutic understanding for him meant 're-translating' the 'objectifications of life' (in historical documents, cultural texts, social institutions and so on) back into the life-relationships in which they have, or once had, existence. He was interested in developing an analytical approach which

works out from particular cultural forms – and the understandings of experience which these in some sense embody
– to the broader cultural formation which in part sustains
them. He conceived this as an approach which would integrate pragmatic, subjective understandings, experiences and
interactions within the cultural and historical complex of
which they were constituent parts. This holistic methodology parallels the insistent emphasis in Williams's work on
seeing cultural elements in relation to a whole social process, and is similarly historical in conception:

> Dilthey opposed the reduction of understanding to psychological
> categories and the reliving of the experience of others.
> Hermeneutic understanding seeks to produce *historical knowl-
> edge* – not psychological knowledge – of the part to the whole.
> Understanding is, therefore, not a form of empathic penetra-
> tion and reconstruction of individual action and consciousness,
> but an interpretation of cultural forms that have been created
> and experienced by individuals (Swingewood, 1984: 132).

The cultural sciences, which in English means cultural
studies, included for Dilthey the humanities and the social
sciences, with history as their go-between. These were clearly
different from the natural sciences in their concern with
meaningful social conduct and the experiential meanings
'expressed' in cultural forms, and it was because of this,
most of all, that he regarded the natural sciences as an inappropriate model for cultural and historical enquiry. Similarly, he considered that the romantic hope of grasping the
hidden meaning of nature, in the same way as we may come
to understand the concrete meanings of social experience
and cultural texts, was misconceived. Nature cannot be understood in this way; it is not open to understanding in the
same way as a cultural expression or act of linguistic communication. It is only social practices which 'may be said to
be comparable to historical documents or poetic expressions
and analysed for their significance' (Makkreel, 1975: 248).
This significance is distinguished by the fact of their historicity, just as our understanding of it is historically conditioned and perspectival, and the folly of both humanistic
rationalism and romantic intuitionism is to believe otherwise. In methodologically dissociating the natural and cul-

tural sciences, Dilthey stressed that while the 'quest of the
unconditioned, and the belief that it can be found by reason, is inveterate in human thinking . . . it is an inveterate
illusion' (Hodges, 1952: 81).

The point of this was 'to preserve the cultural sciences
from dogmatism', to guard them against any tendency to
think that experience can be transcended (Horkheimer, 1939:
430–1). For Dilthey, there are no absolute values, no universal 'laws' and no final outcome: 'there is no such last
simple word of history, uttering its true sense, any more
than there is such a thing to be abstracted from nature'
(Masur, 1963: 165). It was in this sense that he criticised
Comte's sociology, as well as for its vague analogies and lofty
generalisations across different historical periods (ibid: 431–
2). In history there are no purposes but 'human purposes,
the purposes of actual historical agents'. Hand in hand with
this was a conception of historical process itself as teleology
without a *telos*. 'An individual life may have an assignable
meaning, eg in devotion to a cause, and so may a group, or
a movement, or an aspect of social activity, but not history
as a whole' (Hodges, 1969: 54). In this sense, Dilthey turned
against St Simon, Hegel and Marx, but not against Simmel
(Horkheimer, 1939: 432; Hodges, 1952: 189–90). This of
course poses the problem of historical relativism. Dilthey
was firmly committed to the position that 'every world-view
is historically determined and, therefore, limited and relative', and yet aware that this raises general problems about
the possibility of reliable knowledge. If everything historical
is relative, what we assemble as historians may seem to slide
inexorably towards an inescapable subjectivism, and on the
basis of a relativising impulse we may appear to be 'condemned into sceptical inactivity, or, worse still . . . tempted
into a type of higher opportunism, into bowing down before the forces which seem to be carried vigorously by the
tendencies of history' (Rickman, 1961: 57).

Dilthey tackled this problem in roughly the following way.
For him, values are units of consensus enabling groups to
act in concord, or to some common purpose; they help to
construct and maintain a sense of community, or to justify
a desired or achieved result. All human agents give value to
experience, and respect for this evaluation – regardless of

how we may morally or politically judge it – is vital for historical enquiry if it is to achieve more than the confirma-
tion of its working assumptions or pre-existent positions. This
approach was characteristic of Dilthey the man, of his toler-
ance and open-mindedness; he belonged, as Gerhard Masur
put it, to that invisible community 'who have left sectarian
loyalties behind' (1963: 171). For Dilthey, texts or text-ana-
logues such as moral and cultural values have to be understood in their own terms just as much as in ours: interpretation
is not the handservant of doctrine. In his view, since the
times which historians attempt to retrace have already been
experienced as meaningful by those who lived through them,
a historical period is always in a sense centred upon itself
and is not just a preliminary stage to our own time (the
error of evolutionism and Whiggery). 'We cannot properly
understand a past age by applying to it our own notions of
politics or government, our own ideas and valuations. We
can only understand it in terms of the institutions then
prevalent, the ideas which animated the people in it and
the purposes which were then pursued' (Rickman, 1961: 47).
Respect for the meanings and values of people of the past
and the experiences they signal as starting points for historical enquiry implies a necessary recognition of human
agency, in that women and men are always to some extent
free to respond in some way or other to the conditions of
their unfreedom, and to that extent, individually or collectively, able to 'make their own history', however high the
cards are stacked against their effective realisation of this
ability.

The creative response this involves occurs in varying circumstances and is concretely conditioned by them. For this
reason Dilthey opposed any belief 'in timelessly fixed moral
codes and static eternal values'. It is because people respond
to their own time and place that they are able to take new
directions, set themselves new purposes, and appreciate new
values. As Rickman summarises it: 'the relativity of values is
only the reverse of the coin of man's creative freedom', and
for this reason 'history is not the orchestration of an eter-
nally fixed theme' but a remarkably diverse array of stories
of the creative struggle of men and women to come to terms
with, or challenge, the conditions of their existence and

the values and shibboleths of their cultural inheritance (Rickman, 1961: 59). We cannot predict anything other than the obvious on the basis of this position, but in considering past struggles, in this sense, we can at least guard ourselves against dogmatic narrowness, widen our vision, and perhaps fertilise our own creative struggles, in the quite altered circumstances and conditions of our own immured times. To quote Dilthey :

> The historical consciousness of the finitude of every historical phenomenon, every human or social state, of the relativity of every sort of belief, is the last step towards the liberation of man. With it, man attains the sovereign power to wring from every experience its content, to surrender wholly to it, without prepossession . . . Every beauty, every sanctity, every sacrifice, re-lived and expanded, opens up perspectives which disclose a reality . . . And, in contrast with the relativity, the continuity of the creative force makes itself felt as the central historical fact (Hodges, 1969: 33–4).

Against the enormous influence in his own time of evolutionist ideas, with their biological metaphors and analogies, Dilthey aimed to avoid any specious conflation of the world of nature and what is specific to the human world of social action and cultural practice. On these grounds, he distinguished the cultural sciences from the natural sciences 'on the threefold planes of difference in fields of research, in forms of experience, and in attitudes on the part of the investigator' (Rossi cited in Hughes, 1967: 195). He further distinguished three classes of statements made in the fields of cultural study: those relating to concrete detail – the field of history; those consisting of abstractions made on the basis of this detail – the contribution of the social sciences; and those which express value judgements and practical rules – the entry points back into a historically contingent everyday life. Dilthey's conception of the *Geisteswissenschaften* was as a counter-tradition to that linking Comte, J. S. Mill, Durkheim and modern functionalism, and in the main because the concern of the former with the 'inner' understanding of 'meaningful conduct' has no parallel in the natural sciences. For this reason the identity of the social or cultural sciences depends not on their continuity with the natural or physical sciences, which was the view of Comte and Mill, as well as historians like Buckle, but on their dislocation from them (for Buckle, see 1904 and St. Aubyn, 1958). Yet as we have already seen, Dilthey was not content with any straightforward 'two cultures' way of conceiving of this distinction; for him it meant also thinking towards a 'scientific' validity for what cannot be scientifically studied. Giddens has approached this intellectual puzzlement in Dilthey's work by suggesting that its central strain stems from the attempt to combine elements of positivist philosophy with the neo-idealist tradition of *Geisteswissenschaften*, particularly in respect of the concept of *Erlebnis*. For the early Dilthey, understanding human action and cultural products involved a 're-experiencing' or 're-living', not in the sense of the direct intuitive identification postulated in 'practical criticism' and Leavisite approaches to literary study, but rather in one which attempted to be far more conceptually and empirically rigorous. The problem of *Verstehen* then lay in placing too much stress on 'immediate lived experience' as a constituent of consciousness, in what was an obviously empiricist conception, at the same time as combining this with an interpretive approach which emphasised the 'inner experience' of consciousness, the significance of subjective understanding.[6] In later life, though, Dilthey came to realise that an analytic emphasis on the need for an imaginative grasp of historical and social experience could not be reconciled with the demand that the study of human conduct should match up to the 'objective' standards of assessment of the natural sciences (Giddens, 1977a: 12–13, 80–1, 135–6).

Yet the tension between descriptive accounts and interpretive meaning continues to have a direct bearing on historical practice, as for instance is borne out in Hajo Holborn's observation that the key problems of historical knowledge 'hinge upon the fact that an objective knowledge of the past can only be achieved through the subjective experience of the scholar' (Holborn, 1972: 79). History is an empirical discipline, but it is also an interpretive one. Historians deal both with the unique or singular qualities of the experience of events, situations and processes, and with the similarities and dissimilarities, continuities and disruptions, between them. This means that they deal in concrete details, and at the same time utilise concepts. Abstract statements provide historical study with the analytical tools it requires, and prevent history from becoming a heaping up of disjointed and meaningless facts, as in pedantry and antiquarianism. And yet, as Hodges put it, 'whatever Dilthey might say about the more methodical side of historical research and the logical scaffolding which underpins it, he always added that it is the imaginative process of understanding which gives life and meaning to the rest' (Hodges, 1969: 19). It is a truism that the historical imagination is disciplined by the contextual evidence on which it operates. What is historically interpreted must be grounded in this evidence, and the validity of the historical work is then assessed in terms of this relation. This is quite different from a Rankean enumeration of facts as the sole source or method for showing 'what actually happened'. Rather, historical imagination helps us to decide what materials are relevant to our inquiry, and our imaginative reconstruction is then, in its turn, based on these chosen materials (Rickman, 1961: 46–8). In all these various respects, historical practice is unlike the experimental sciences in that the spectrum of experiences in daily life and as accumulated over time remain firmly in play, and that history becomes desiccated without an attempt to develop an imaginative grasp of these experiences, their intersubjective meanings and values to participants, whereby 'reality seems to open itself up to experience from within' (Habermas, 1972: 143).

For Dilthey, the temporal structure of experience consists in a dynamic movement from perception through the evocation of past experiences and the revival of feelings bound up with past experiences to the bringing into relation of past and present in felt thought, and thought feeling, a movement which has then to be completed, within particular contextual frames, by the generation of expressive cultural forms, linguistic or otherwise, and the communication of meanings through these forms. For Victor Turner, culture itself 'is the ensemble of such expressions – the experience of individuals made available to society and accessible to the sympathetic penetration of other "minds"' (Turner, 1982: 14). In support of this formulation, he draws directly on Dilthey : 'our knowledge of what is given in experience is extended through the interpretation of the objectification of life and this interpretation, in turn, is only made possible by plumbing the depths of subjective experience' (Dilthey, 1976: 195–6). This could perhaps be said to prefigure Sartre's conception of praxis: moving from objectification through internalisation to objectification (Sartre, 1963: 97). What this processual, yet always conditioned sense of cultural experience entails is that experience of the social world occurs in relation to particular determinants of that world – 'a world which exists independently of individual will although it is only experienced in personal terms' – and becomes 'complete' in the accomplishment of cultural forms which are both individual and collective (Chaney and Pickering, 1986: 37). While accepting the expanded understanding of time and space which language makes possible, cultural forms can be said to articulate meanings in more than a strictly linguistic sense in that they embody, or point in the direction of moral, social and political ideas and institutions. These embodiments can then be 'read' for the ways in which they signal a standing out of certain experiences from the impersonal flow of events which in their expression have become structured units of meaning. 'Only when we stop looking at the extended finger and follow the direction in which it points can we understand that we are confronted by an expression; then we can begin to understand its meaning.' These units of meaning – representations, texts, discourses, performances and what not – therefore arise from people's involvement in the world and 'stand in larger contexts which contribute to their meaning and are modified by them' (Rickman, 1979: 89 and 114, and see 88–108 for Dilthey on the subject of expressions). Experiences in this sense constitute the felt actualities of living at the cross-over points of different and at times contradictory structures.

There are of course different ways in which experience is organised, and experienced as meaningful, and Dilthey distinguished between structural relations between mental acts ('thoughts, for instance, arouse feelings and feelings prompt resolutions'), dynamic interactions with the natural and social environment, and perceptions of significant relationships within our temporal experience of life. Representations of experience can be extended outwards to communities and social institutions, common ways of interacting in social

groups, collective forms of remembering and public conceptions of collective purposes, though as we have seen, any
question of shared experience is inherently problematic.
Although certain historical, social and cultural forces and
relations may impinge similarly on particular social groups
or classes, how these are experienced and what they are
taken to mean, at the time or in the past, varies in relation
to the position and perspectives of actors and interpreters.
This is equally true when 'experiences' and 'expressions'
are studied academically. For example, Dilthey considered
that even what may be said of the same expression varies
between different academic disciplines, and he noted that
social and cultural history would tend to be focused more
on conventional and relatively durable forms of expression,
while psychology would concentrate more on the significances
of 'natural and fleeting expressions' (Rickman, 1979: 102).

   The interest of Dilthey's work thus lies not only in the
emphasis he placed on experience as made meaningful by
historically located agents, but also in the ways he tried to
classify and conceptualise it within the interdisciplinary matrix
of the cultural sciences of his time. Yet Dilthey did not consider that attempting to reconstitute the meanings which
people in the past have given to their experience was the
be-all and end-all of historical inquiry. It was, for him, a
crucial starting point, but he recognised that experience can
be misinterpreted or only partially understood, and that the
experiencing agent in particular events or situations cannot
know all the consequences which his or her actions may
have.

> To the assassin at Sarajevo his act was one of patriotic defi-
> ance. To those who organised his activity it was a move in a
> political game. To us the meaning of the action lies in its hav-
> ing started the chain reaction which led to the First World
> War (Rickman, 1961: 48).

This is so in that historically we now understand the consequences of the murder of Archduke Ferdinand on 28 June
1914 as including not only the evaporation of the optimism
of the *belle époque*, but also the disintegration, following the
deaths of so many millions, of all that was represented by
the old European order. Historical enquiry is therefore

transformed by the ways in which time's traces are historically experienced and understood, though this does not
necessarily fill in all the missing pieces in the puzzle of the
past. As Michael Stanford has noted, we do not know exactly why the consequences of the Archduke's assassination
were entailed in that specific event: ' it is by no means exactly clear why this one incident should have led to four
years of appalling and uncivilised carnage' (1994: 34). All
that can be said, perhaps, is that 'history teaches no simple
lessons . . . [and] never happens as the actors plan or expect.
It is the record of unintended consequences' (Thompson,
1982: 10). Clearly, certain actions and plans are intended,
and certain social events and changes can be explained in
relation to them. This much is obvious. It is 'less obvious
and more difficult to grasp that the intentional sequences
of events planned and intended separately by many interdependent people interweave with each other to produce
structured, directional processes of change which no one has
planned' (Mennell, 1992: 182). What is equally difficult to grasp
is why 'unintended consequences of action may reproduce
the familiar at the same time as they may bring about the
unfamiliar or the unexpected' (Giddens, 1987: 223).

It is for these reasons, among others, that history has always to be revisioned and rewritten. While we are not able
to apprehend the felt qualities of past life in exactly the
ways experienced by those for whom it was a lived present,
we can see that past life, with all its acts, events, episodes
and conflicts, all its dreams, desires and dilemmas, in ways
not available to those who lived through them. In this sense,
though perhaps only in this, we may see them more fully.
Yet this is always a relative amplitude, and in some ways it is
better to see this difference simply as difference. Successive
generations bring changed experiences, alternative points
of view and revised ways of thinking to bear on their interpretations of the past, and so for this reason find different
historical experiences and different aspects of social institutions in the past worthy of or relevant to historical study in
their own time. 'How people view and articulate their experience is a product both of their own place in history and
that of their successive interpreters' (Lowenthal, 1976: 291–
2). According to Dilthey, extrapolating on the meanings of

past events, actions, institutions and practices depends on a threefold process: firstly, on developing an understanding of the points of view of those involved; secondly, on developing an understanding of the meanings that events, actions, institutions and practices had for those who experienced them and who were affected by them; and thirdly, on developing an assessment of these meanings in the light of the historian's own period, as she or he looks back with a hindsight that may prove to be either beacon or burden. This third process is not simply to be tacked on when the other work has been done, for as Dilthey put it, echoing Vico, the first condition for the possibility of historical knowledge 'lies in the fact that I am myself a historical being, that the historical researcher also makes history' (Outhwaite, 1975: 25). We have of course always to remember that, even as we attempt to triangulate between these three approaches to historical practice, only one thing is certain. This is that historical understanding can only ever be partial and provisional; it is never complete and it is always fluid. There is no finality in historical understanding because there is no finality in history itself. The one fixed principle in historiography is that the meanings made of the past are contestable.

Notes

1 *Habitus* is a term taken from the work of the French sociologist, Pierre Bourdieu, and provides a way of explaining the continuities and regularities which are empirically observable in the social world. The enduring practices to which they refer are related to structures of social differentiation and stratification, in Bourdieu's view particularly those of social class, and they operate through those cultural dispositions and competencies which mediate objective structures, on the one hand, and group histories and individual biographies on the other. Social life cannot be disaggregated to what individuals do, since it is *sui generis*, but nor can it be explained simply as determined by overarching structures, since social individuals and groups contribute to it and not simply in a reflex adaptive manner. *Habitus* is a useful conceptual tool for overcoming the subjectivist/objectivist dichotomy because it refers to that which is intermediary between the individual and society, and to what

is regularly transmitted and occasionally modified by experience: it is thus 'the site of the internalisation of reality and the externalisation of internality' (Bourdieu and Passeron, 1977: 205). In Bourdieu's conception, *habitus* is 'the durably installed generative principle of regulated improvisations' (Bourdieu, 1977: 78). It is a *modus operandi* which is initially acquired through processes of socialisation in the family and school, and which becomes a generalised framework for action, perception and understanding that, although accented on the perpetuation of cognitive and motivating schemes, cultural values and standards etc., can nevertheless at times be flexibly applied in making sense of experiences of social contradiction and change, or can at least allow improvisation, adjustment and correction: thus, it operates 'as a system of lasting, transposable dispositions which, integrating past experiences, functions at every moment as a matrix of perceptions and actions and makes possible the achievement of infinitely diversified tasks' (1977: 82–3). In other words, it is not necessarily associated with the 'tragedy of finitude'. A *habitus* is, then, always a practical consequence of given structural conditions and circumstances, but in ways which vary within social groups and categories, as is the case with, say, aesthetic criteria and lifestyle choices. In this way it is handy as, for instance, 'a way of thinking about the development of gentrified inner-city areas which are shunned by those who prefer orderly suburbs', or about 'the phenomenon of post-tourism, which is not understood by those who seek holidays that are "home plus"' and in which 'the desire for experience becomes greater than that for mere enjoyment' (Shurmer-Smith and Hannam, 1994: 25–6, 194; and see Urry, 1990). For the concept of *habitus* in Bourdieu's work, see particularly *Outline of a Theory of Practice* (1977) and *Distinction* (1986); and for a couple of critical treatments of it, see Jenkins (1992) and Honneth (1986).

2 For Dilthey, apriorism in historical interpretation – exploring and examining time's traces from a set of abstract notions or fixed assumptions – was to walk blindfold into the past. Such an approach was for him an impediment to interpretation because of its disregard for experience in its historical and cultural specificities. In his view, apriorism usually operates with the sense of timeless rational principles, and of truths and essences somehow innate in the mind, absolute and therefore always antecedent to experience. It was in this way, perhaps most of all, that Dilthey dissociated himself from the neo-Kantianism of his time.

3 This, in turn, informs his criticism of experimental psychology

as confined to the formal study of behavioural and cognitive processes, and as socially decontextualised in approach. For Dilthey, psychology should study the individual as a social product. What he was after was a social psychology *avant la lettre*.

4 'Expression' can carry the unacknowledged *portée* of an essentialised identity or category, such as masculinism or racial supremacism, and for this reason the currently more fashionable term 'construction' is preferred. But the term 'expression' does not necessarily carry such ideas or lead to such implications. It is not an ideological category *per se*. (For a useful summary of Dilthey's classification of expressions, see Rickman, 1960: 312–14.) There is also the sense in which the term 'expression' carries associations of a spontaneous overflowing of some 'inner' feeling, state of being or response to situations in life, as for instance in Wordsworth's conception of poetic expression. Against this, 'construction' or 'production' are presented as alternative terms because they imply that experience is only possible because of the medium, which is usually language, in which it is given form. I do not use 'expression' in the radical constructivist sense, but rather as a term for signifying representation in words, images or sounds, for designating the discursive and stylistic means of representation, and for loosely covering the symbolic forms associated with these means which register impulses of thinking, feeling and/or willing. Expressions are not necessarily intentional, and ambiguity stems from the difficulties of knowing this (as e.g. with Ryle's twitch or wink), but more usually they retain a sense of the effort to find the appropriate words, contest other representations, or arrive at new ways of giving form to experience. This important sense apart, my use of the term is in many ways compatible with the term 'construction'. 'Expression' is never the 'raw' or direct articulation of experience since it is only made possible by that which mediates it, and which thereby transforms it. The term 'expression' retains the distinction of creative effort, of cultural praxis, but perhaps needs to be fully reconciled with the 'historicist' stress on the inevitability of reinterpretation. In this sense, 'crossing horizons' is an act of cultural or historical translation rather than transposition. As Alisdair MacIntyre (1976) has it, we 'inhabit an interpreted world in which reinterpretation is the most fundamental form of change'. (See Chapter 5 on this.)

5 In this respect, as in others, Ludwig Stein (1924) provides a misleading guide to Dilthey's theory and method. For a more accurate early summary, see Tapper (1925).

6 Though the problems associated with it are considerable, *Verstehen* is an important tool of interpretive sociology, where it is generally taken to refer to an imaginative-sympathetic mode of understanding which tries to grasp the meaning or meaning-complex attributed by participants to their social experience or action. It is a form of qualitative understanding that attempts to engage with the meaningful nature of experience for and in terms of the participants involved, and as such it is differentiated from the explanatory potential of the natural sciences. To put it in a nutshell: experience cannot be understood through experiments. For Dilthey, the human sciences are concerned with the contingent, mutable forms and processes of experience which need, at least in part, to be understood through those meanings which participants strive to realise. How this is analytically possible, and how it is connected with a social analysis of the causes and consequences of experience and action, is where so many of the problems begin. The term *Verstehen* nevertheless provides a vital conceptual resource for considering the process of interpretive dialogue occurring between and across different cultural frames and different historical contexts.

Chapter 5

Crossing Horizons

And just as there are no simple dynastic answers, there are no simple discrete historical formations or social processes. A hetereogeneity of human involvement is therefore equivalent to a heterogeneity of results, as well as of interpretive skills and techniques. There is no centre, no inertly given and accepted authority, no fixed barriers ordering human history, even though authority, order, and distinction exist. The secular intellectual works to show the absence of divine originality and, on the other side, the complex presence of historical actuality. The conversion of the absence of religion into the presence of actuality is secular interpretation.

(Edward Said)

Life and Life Only

My purpose in rehearsing and adapting some of Dilthey's major ideas has been to trace certain tentative lines forwards to a firmer conceptual base for the use of the category of experience in historical and cultural analysis. It seems to me that it is worthwhile going back to Dilthey precisely because of his attempt to ground such analysis in forms of experience by insisting, among other things, that the analysis itself is always part of human life-activity. Dilthey is important because of the centrality of the category of experience in his work, because of his attempt to render its analytical sense more fertile, and because he held that any guarantee of an absolute point of vantage outside of history, society, culture and the intersubjective forms we live

125

by is an illusion, even though in his own work he did not fully reconcile his own position to this realisation. For him, historical experiences were 'nodal points of meaning' and to be respected by the historian for the vitality that clusters around them, so that even before they are fully understood and analysed, 'they colour the life of a community' : 'Experiences, though conditioned by social changes and scientific development, emancipate themselves for a time from the chains of conceptual thought and so affect people's minds' (Rickman, 1979: 118). For this reason, experiences can, on occasion, disturb us out of our set precepts and predispositions, upset our routinised social conduct, jolt us into glimpses of alternative directions into the unpredestined future. There is no guarantee in the generality of experience that these potentialities will become realised in particular forms, yet that is precisely the point of interest. If these moments are carried forward they may lead 'to that openness to experience that is set free by experience itself' (Gadamer, 1975: 320). Such openness, the kind of freedom from dogma which Dilthey cherished, grows out of awareness of fallibility and limits, and creates a capacity for learning, expansion of view and what Charles Madge once referred to as the suspension of intolerance (Harrisson, 1961: 279). This is to come again, from a different angle, at the betwixt-and-between relation of formation and pre-formation, or what Sartre called 'going beyond a situation' to what people succeed in making of what they have been made: 'The most rudimentary behaviour must be determined both in relation to the real and present factors which condition it and in relation to a certain object, still to come, which it is trying to bring into being' (Sartre, 1963: 91).[1] It is in this sense that we reconnect with the concept of structure of feeling. I want now to deal more critically with what Dilthey brings to this reconnection.

First, though, it is important to make the point that Dilthey's achievements still stand in need of being acknowledged in their own right, and fully carried forward into our own period. Too often he has suffered the fate of a relegation to footnotes, to a sentence here or a paragraph there, or else has been used as a foil for other people's arguments. Despite the validity of much of what they say, Gadamer, Habermas and Bauman, among others, have been guilty of using him in that way. No doubt the guilt is mine as well, for I have made very selective use of him, concentrating mainly on his conception of experience, and that in the available English translations. Yet what has also to be said is that the very nature of his work, as he left it at his death, lends itself to this kind of treatment. Dilthey's project was bold, ambitious and expansive, so much so that he was never able to bring together all the elements of his monumental 'critique of historical reason', which survives him in the form of extensive drafts and fragments. This is in one sense a problem in that the critique was never systematised; he was often prey to the allure and excitement of new ideas. Yet his creative instability has something quite admirable about it. Dilthey was a secularised intellectual who refused to pretend to completion in his treatment of difficult issues, but instead returned again and again to the attempt to see them afresh, to see them from a different angle and throw light on some hitherto unrealised aspect of his understanding of them. Apart from its monumental incompleteness, there are, however, other and more definite problems with Dilthey's work.

He struggled valiantly, but in the end unsuccessfully, with the problem of historical relativism, and most seriously undermined himself in this by assuming, at his weakest, the possibility of 'a virtual simultaneity' of historical understanding and past experience, which, as a methodological assumption, 'has so little evidence that it requires a philosophy of vitalism' (Habermas, 1972: 183). Hence at times the rather vague and unconvincing appeals to 'life' : 'Life is like a melody in which it is not sounds that appear as the expression of the realities residing in life. The melody lies in life itself.' Or again: 'Life and the experience of life are the continually fresh-flowing sources of the understanding of the social-historical world.' Here, once more, the influence of Romanticism is persistent, for such appeals can be traced back to Goethe's proposition that 'only life teaches everyone what they are', which is so generally applicable that it is historically and sociologically vapid. But at the same time the emphasis in Dilthey is just as often on the historical, and in this sense the conception is quite different from Bergson's *élan vital* flowing through all things, and 'revealed in all its fullness at any moment by the act of metaphysical intuition', nor was it comparable to Pareto's psychological foundation for his theory of history and society (Holborn, 1950: 103; Horkheimer, 1939: 435, 440).[2] This is an important qualification, though at the same time 'life and the experience of life' are usually rendered far too benignly. There is insufficient recognition of lives running experientially in conflict with each other, of discord between experiences, and of the struggle to assert and place the meanings of certain experiences over those of others, which are then marginalised or made insignificant. Experience cannot be divorced from the clashes of interests, structural denials of opportunity and achievement, and relations of power which are implicated in these actualities of living. The 'realities residing in life' can be manifest in sharp dissonances as well as harmonious intervals.

If this weakness stems from Dilthey's romanticism, another arises from his empiricist leanings. He remained too concerned, in the view of Gadamer, Habermas and subsequent critics, with the objectivism he sought to critique, for although he insisted on the differences between the human and physical sciences, he held to the belief that the former can produce results of comparable 'objective validity' to those of the latter (Outhwaite, 1994: 31; Giddens, 1977b: 55). For this reason, he did not 'draw the conclusions which would have brought into clear view his inherent opposition to a science free from value judgements' (Horkheimer, 1939: 431). At the same time, Dilthey's struggle to formulate a 'logic' for the *Geisteswissenschaften* proved instructive for Gadamer's own project of countering the assimilation of the mid-twentieth-century social sciences into objectivist cognitive models of enquiry and explanation. Carl Hempel's covering-law approach to history is an example of such a model in that it is based on 'the positivist claim of methodological unity between all the sciences, whether they study natural phenomena or human action' (Lloyd, 1986: 62; and see Hempel, 1942 and 1963; also Dray, 1966). This claim runs directly counter to the more idiographic approach of Dilthey who, even if he did not carry through certain insights as thoroughly as Gadamer may have wished, nevertheless represents a valiant attempt to establish the theoretical and methodological specificities of cultural and historical studies.

A definite limitation in Dilthey's work is that despite his anti-determinism, he never found a finally satisfactory way beyond an interactional pluralism, though he did believe that 'every social and cultural system contains the elements which will lead to its dissolution', and in this respect was close to Hegel despite his rejection of Hegel's *a priori* formalism (Hodges, 1969: 65). When he referred to the concept of 'objective mind', however, Dilthey was concerned with intersubjectivity, with sociality and cultural 'belonging', not with knowledge beyond history, with any absolutist form of knowledge. Gadamer indicts Dilthey for conceiving of historical knowledge as itself absolute, and attempting to ground it methodologically in a Cartesian certainty (Gadamer, 1979: 124). While there are instances of Dilthey being tempted into objectivist forms of thinking, this charge is exaggerated. I have already noted his critique of quests for unconditioned knowledge, and for all his respect for historians like Ranke, Dilthey understood clearly that 'what actually happened' in history cannot be reproduced in any original sense. The principle of replicability in the natural sciences was thus, for him, not applicable to the study of history in that historians inherit the cumulative knowledge acquired from the past experiences of others and their investigations are thereby transformed by it. In view of this condition of studying the past, what Gadamer himself overlooks is the multiple evidence of lives shipwrecked on the historical reefs of experience. His conception of the influence of the past and of tradition on contemporary life is complacently idealised, seeing neither as diverse rather than unified, and thus as the sites of conflicting intepretations. He fails to take into account the ways in which they can impose a direction without destination, or become an oppressive dead-weight on the minds of the living. For Dilthey, by contrast, the practical embeddedness of social understanding can itself be the ground for the 'tragedy of finitude'. As Warnke notes, while it is important to begin with 'agents' self-interpretations', it is sometimes necessary to go beyond them 'in order to grasp what they are actually doing in contrast to what they may think they are doing'. She then concludes:

To this extent Dilthey's attempt to extricate the *Geiste-swissenschaften* from the basis in life on which he originally founds them seems justified, if in the end self-contradictory. His problem is that viewing the human species as a continuation or refinement of the self-understanding developed in experience leaves them prey to the same self-deceptions to which ordinary life is subject. Gadamer does not seem to think this situation is as problematic as Dilthey does, but the question is why not? (1987: 34).

In the light of this, a further criticism is only partially tenable. Dilthey's early work has a marked tendency to methodological individualism, although he recognised the importance of referring to collective entities and collective experiences so long as these do not become hypostatised, as for example in the notion of a 'popular will', or mistaken for supra-individuals, as it was the case, classically, in German idealism: in true secular style, he dismissed the notions of a *Volksseele* or a *Volkgeist* as mystical and unusable. His later work, however, moved away from the earlier psychologism to an approach which recognised the need for a historically contextualised understanding of expressive forms; he came to feel that such forms can only be fully understood in relation to the social and cultural systems in which they are produced (Rickman, 1960: 316–17).[3] The emphasis was then much more on the 'social' in the individual: 'Every word or sentence, every gesture or form of civility, every work of art and every historical deed are only understandable because the person expressing himself and the person who understands him are connected by something they have in common; the individual always experiences, thinks, acts and understands in this sphere of what is common' (Outhwaite, 1975: 26–7). Methodologically, we can say that this requires moving to-and-fro between expressive forms and social life, and between that multiform life and its structural determinants. It is not as if signs, experiences and social structures are separate, isolable entities, entire unto themselves, though they are of course analytically distinct and cannot in that sense be collapsed into each other: hence the need to tack backwards and forwards between them. Yet Dilthey's attempts to grapple with these methodological requirements left various problems unresolved, and

I shall return to these in relation to the question of how a historical hermeneutics can best be conceived.

In attempting to assess the significance of experience as a key category in social history and cultural studies, I should perhaps stress that it is certainly not my aim to elevate it above all others or to argue for it as an *a priori* of language. When we strive to express the meanings of particular experiences, especially those for which there seems to be no inherited or readily available frame, then experiences attain meaning only through the ways in which, say in writing or talk, we wrestle with words. In those edgings out beyond the apparent limit of what is semantically possible, we seek to step a little beyond that which words stubbornly insist they are about. Yet even as we struggle to speak anew, what we inherit in the senses attached to words always constrains the possibilities for what can be said with them. In this sense language acts like a grid over the meanings that can be made of experience. Language mediates experience: it is the medium above all others in which experience is made meaningful. What exists for us does so because we have meanings for them; and language, along with other symbol systems, are means for codifying and classifying these meanings, for constructing reality. Language is also a social product, so reality is always socially constructed: 'all experience involves language and language is ineradically social' (Eagleton, 1983: 60). Echoing Wittgenstein, Alasdair MacIntyre takes this a step further in saying that 'the limits of action are the limits of description' and that we inhabit 'an interpreted world in which reinterpretation is the most fundamental form of change' (1976: 46). So experience is only possible because of the means for speaking of it, for expressing it, and 'expression' is never the utterance of an isolated self bringing meaning into the world in isolation from his or her social and cultural formation. In this respect it can be said that, despite my previous qualifications, Dilthey did place too much emphasis upon experience as a source of knowledge. More accurately, he could be said to have posited a relation between experience and symbolic structures which is too linear and unitary, and which in some ways errs towards voluntarism.

This is at times a tendency in his work, but as I have

tried to bring out, we should be wary of any facile designation of the negative label of voluntarism to his thinking about
the category of experience. If we are not we can easily miss
his particular approach to its historicality. So, for instance,
his conception of expression held to a dimension of utterance, communication and symbolic form which cannot be
subsumed into historically defiant 'cognitive structures'. What
is important in his conception of 'structures of experience'
is that they are at once cognitive, conative and affective –
their medium is not only that of thought or reason alone.
It is worth comparing Dilthey with Elias on this issue. For
Elias, the social sciences should deal not only with space
and time, but also with another, fifth dimension, that of
experience. In other words, the 'experiential' aspects have
to be included along with the directly visible 'behavioural'
aspects, and they include thought, affects and drives. While
these experiential aspects are 'not directly accessible to
people's observation in the same way as bodily movements',
they are, nevertheless, 'accessible to human observation . . .
through the examination of linguistic and other messages
from one person to another' (Elias, 1987: 116). This closely
parallels Dilthey's conceptualisation. His *lebens-philosophisch*
emphasis on 'lived experience' was an explicit reaction to
the excessive rationalism of Kant, among other philosophers;
it entailed a rejection of the 'absolutism' of the intellect
(Outhwaite, 1975: 25; Ortega y Gasset, 1963: 155–61, 175).
While Kant stressed the importance of experience in relation to empirical and synthetic propositions, knowledge for
him was still in large part not derived inductively from experience. Dilthey departed from his neo-Kantian heritage
where it strayed off into metaphysics, dealing, in the hands
of his younger rivals, Wilhelm Windelband (1848–1915) and
Heinrich Rickert (1863–1936), with absolute values and timeless meanings. He rejected any idea of a 'transcendental
self', and continued to insist that meanings and values are
lodged in social experience, which itself shows no definite
split between rationality and the irrational. Most importantly,
Dilthey critiqued the Kantian line for holding that 'behind
all cultural activity, transcendental analysis discloses *apriori*
forms' (Hodges, 1952: 27).

Again, the comparison with Elias is instructive. Elias has

spoken movingly of his breach with his revered teacher, Richard Hönigswald, over the question in Kant of *a priori* truth:

> I could no longer ignore the fact that all that Kant regarded as timeless and as given prior to all experience, whether it be the idea of causal connections or of time or of natural and moral laws, together with the words that went with them, had to be learned from other people in order to be present in the consciousness of the individual human being. As acquired knowledge they therefore formed part of a person's store of experiences (Elias, 1994: 91–2; see also Mennell, 1992: 8–9).

If Dilthey's work had at that time been more extensively published, it may be that a thorough engagement with him would have proved helpful to Elias at this stage in his career, for Dilthey's break with his Kantian heritage entailed a strikingly similar move. This involved the recognition that since there is only interaction between ourselves and the world, our experience must be understood in social and historical terms since it is, in these terms, that anyone's world is more or less defined. There is no essential or immutable 'human nature'; humans possess only 'historical nature', and their lived relations are social relations occurring in time and over time. 'What does historical movement mean? The work of one generation for the following, the merging of the individual into the significant social relations in which he serves' (Masur, 1952: 98).[4] It is important to add to this those aspects of historical movement which involve generational conflict, contestation, discontinuity and rupture, but the point at issue is Dilthey's rejection of the concept of transcendental consciousness as a metaphysical abstraction. This necessarily led to the question of how past experience can be understood, and of all the questions raised by Dilthey's work it is perhaps the most difficult.[5]

Knowing the Historical Other

In his biography of Schleiermacher, Dilthey considered Wilhelm Humboldt (1767–1835), the Prussian educationalist and philologist, to have proved 'that the reflective activity of the I cannot rest content with contrasting the representation and the represented purely and ideally but strives to perceive outside itself the idea visibly shaped in language' (Rickman, 1979: 121-2). As Dilthey put it elsewhere: 'understanding is the rediscovery of the I in the Thou' (Rickman, 1961: 67). This is quite different from the experiential sentimentalism of our Smiling Jack. Here Dilthey formulates for himself what Giddens calls 'the subject–subject relation' that is specific to the human sciences in that its analytic frames of meaning have to link up with those which already make up social life (Giddens, 1977b: 146). Dilthey is also quite explicitly anti-objectivist in his hermeneutic claim that any interpretation 'must take into account both the interpreter's point of view and that of the subject to be interpreted', though of course this still leaves open the question of how this methodological principle should be applied, how these different horizons of view can be 'taken into account'. Rickman offers a condensed response to this question in saying that 'we cannot understand Plato properly, either by treating him as if he were a contemporary or as if he were a historical phenomenon which has no relevance for us' (Rickman, 1979: 155). This is useful, and complements Simmel's dictum that one need not *be* Caesar in order to understand him, but it still begs the question as to how we may understand either Plato or Caesar, and the way that understanding can be characterised.

The gist of Dilthey's answer to this question lies in the historical nature of both interpreter and interpreted; both are historically produced, both possess historical sense, and live forwards as well as backwards: 'We are,' according to Dilthey, 'historical beings first, before we are students of history, and it is only because we are the first that we become the second' (Hodges, 1952: 154). The task of historical understanding is then to grasp what is characteristically historical in each. Yet the question remains. How are we to know that our interpretation is indeed the historical manifestation of *what* is interpreted if our interpretation is characterised by our historical mode of being? Following one main track of Dilthey's, 'the only answer we are likely to get is this: we know it when we feel that we can understand, and eventually grasp the meaning of what we see'. Knowing it when we see it is of course an intuitionist answer to the

question. As Bauman notes, this is a circular form of reasoning in which 'our effort to understand, and our satisfac-
tion with its results, obviates our concern with the question
itself' (1978: 36). It is, however, important not to attribute
to Dilthey the naive view that we can exactly replicate another's experience or the mental processes leading to expressions of it. Reconstructing or 'reliving' past experience
is not that experience but, necessarily, 'something generically different' (Hodges, 1952: 149). In discussing how historians reconstruct the historical world, Dilthey considered
the interrelations of experience, expression and understanding
to be methodologically central (Hughes, 1967: 197–8): 'The
human sciences are all founded in lived experience, in the
expressions of these experiences, and in the understanding
of these expressions' (Outhwaite, 1994: 30). Having firmly
rejected the idea of 'transcendental synthesis', Dilthey held
that interpretation should proceed by retracing the means
by which formal unity, order and coherence have been elic-
ited from lived experience. Historical understanding means
engaging with the ways in which people have experienced
their lives in terms of connections, relations, configurations
and, one should add, those 'reality disjunctures' which may
provide conditions for the politicisation of experience
(Rickman, 1961: 30; and see Pollner, 1987). Such engagement
must begin, at least, by interrogating the manifold expressions
which have given form to those experiences. Although something akin to close attentiveness is vital in the initial steps
towards any interpretive task, it is not simply enough to treat
the task of the cultural sciences as aimed at some sort of
inner understanding gained through sympathetic experience.
This is often the position Dilthey is alleged to have taken.[6]

   In focusing on the 'lived experience' of particular people
in the past, we cannot directly re-experience that experience. The view that we can may be described as dogmatic
empathy, and it was not Dilthey's. He recognised, clearly
enough, that no one is able to become disengaged at will
from their own social and historical being. This recognition
only provides a further starting-point, however, for it leaves
open the complementary point that we are not utterly locked
into such being, a point which is fundamental to the relation of conditionality and reflexivity in historical practice.

So again, in what sense can we build up knowledge of others' experiences, or establish any validity for our accounts of those experiences? We have already seen this as a difficulty in respect of evaluating the identification of different structures of feeling within a particular period. It is of course a tricky issue, and Dilthey's *verstehende* approach doesn't provide any sort of complete response to it, but what is at issue is that, in his later work at least, he did not simply adopt a romantic conception of the possibility of imaginatively climbing into other people's heads. He acknowledged the importance of combining general social theories and comparative empirical methods, and the *verstehende* approach then works, albeit problematically, in relation to what results from this combination when we situate particular cultural forms or practices in the broader context within which they have attained their meanings and values. It is then difficult not to disagree with the assertion that what has to be investigated is the relationship, as Dilthey put it, 'of all the forces which were combined in [any] historical conjuncture' (Outhwaite, 1975: 34).

This is different from comprehending all the separate details involved, which is out of the question 'if only because the historical process, being temporal, is like time itself infinitely divisible, and therefore infinitely rich in detail' (Hodges, 1952: 122–3). What it involves is an attempt to grasp its structured unity, its *Gestalt*, its intelligible order as opposed to its temporal order, as it gives shape to lived experience. The intelligible order of social and historical experience is more fully developed and integrated than, but nevertheless cognate with, 'the order which prevails in the smallest unit-experience'. There is, in other words, an 'inherent intelligibility' in lived experience, as it is made visible in language, and in its traces we should seek to discern not a neo-Kantian 'heaven of rational meaning-complexes' (ibid: 151–2) but the historical dynamic involved in processes where people, caught in social conditions and situations, confronted with ideological dilemmas, struggle to deal with them, and in their creative praxis to go beyond them as feeling, thinking and volitional actors. But again, how, across time, can we engage with time's traces? If historical understanding cannot, either empirically or logically, consist of a psychological re-enactment of past experience, how can it then arise when its only possibility of development is through the interaction of different cultural frames? In other words, how is dialogue through these different frames possible?

As I have said, in his orientation to this question, Dilthey did not hold to a naive or dogmatic empathy. His approach to interpretation was opposed to the dissolution, or bracketing, of questions of historical mediation, and in this sense is distinct from Husserl's method of 'eidetic' abstraction or Leavis's intuitive grasping of the vital stuff of life in poetry or literary fiction, which can only be asserted in the classic phrase 'this is so, isn't it?' Dilthey clearly recognised that empathetic 'projection of the self into the other can become an obstacle to understanding' (Makkreel, 1975: 252). Rudolf Makkreel usefully warns us against the mistranslation of Dilthey's concept of *Nacherleben* as 'empathy'. Rather, it refers to a mode of re-experiencing and re-orienting through the process of interpretation, that is reconsidering and re-evaluating ourselves and our *Erlebnisse* in relation to historical forms of experience or experience represented in works of art, social documentation or media texts. This does not claim an identification of subject and object except in a loose metaphorical sense. As Makkreel sharply notes: 'If understanding were really empathetic, then no one would be able to understand anything but other expressions of his own *Weltanschauung*.' The term *Nacherleben* is therefore quite different from empathy (*Einfühlen*), a term which Dilthey used very infrequently and certainly did not equate with *Verstehen* (Makkreel, 1975: 6–7, 252–3). Similarly, Rabinow and Sullivan insist that 'neither Weber nor the later Dilthey held the kind of "mystical" conception of human understanding often associated with the term "empathy"' (1979: 5). Dilthey's theory of understanding is a response to cultural and historical 'difference', and conceives of understanding as 'an indirect and reflective process' that is distinct from 'immediate knowing' but needs for that reason to root back into it. Nevertheless, although he overstates the criticism, Habermas is I think correct in judging that Dilthey never properly extricated himself from an empathetic model of understanding, despite its modification in the form of reconstructing acts of meaning-creation within a changed present and in relation to our historically specific *Erlebnisse*. In other words, he never worked through all the implications of accepting that 'the interpreter is as much a participant as the one he interprets', or as Habermas has deftly put it, that 'experience is mediated by the interaction of both participants; understanding is communicative experience' (Habermas, 1972: 180–1).

The statement that 'understanding penetrates into alien expressions of life through a transposition from the fullness of one's own experiences' remains characteristically Diltheyan, and for Habermas this psychology of understanding represents 'a monadological view of hermeneutics in the cultural sciences, *one that Dilthey never completely overcomes*' (ibid: 144–6, my emphasis). Any viable alternative to this requires working towards some sense of cultural translation or mediation as a process whereby the meanings of any expression, narrative or practice reside in what is always a contingent, mutable, unfinished relation. Since one cannot simply suspend the context of cultural experience and tradition in which one's subjectivity has been formed in order to become submerged 'in a subhistorical stream of life that allows the pleasurable identification of everyone with everyone', the hermeneutic point of departure must be to reflect on the object and oneself '*at the same time* as moments of an objective structure that likewise encompasses both and makes them possible' (ibid: 181). This dialogical engagement with past experience and its objectifications is aimed at understanding 'from the inside out', but is, at the same time, intersubjective in disposition and built on the recognition that any understanding of past experience is mediated by historical consciousness. The historical modality of our experience affects the meanings which past experience has for us. 'For what supports the construction of the historical world are not facts taken out of experience that then enter into a value-relation. Its basis is rather the inner historicity that experience itself owns' (Gadamer, 1975: 195). For Gadamer, the only objectivity which is possible is that achieved through what he calls the 'melting of horizons' which we only assume to exist by themselves. As Outhwaite has recently put it: 'The hermeneutic process is not the replacement of the interpreter's "horizon" by that of the object of study, but a dialogical process in which the two horizons are fused together' (Outhwaite, 1994: 25).

This is to go beyond the idea of 're-living' past experience towards the task of gaining some sense of the 'form of life', in Wittgenstein's term, which informed the meanings of any cultural expression or practice for a social group and 'speech community'. This task is dialogical in structure and scope. For Gadamer and others, it is the emphasis on language as constitutive of the meanings given to social experience, and 'being in the world', which enables analysis to move beyond the methodological individualism of the early Dilthey and of Weber, though as Outhwaite has suggested, 'much of what Dilthey wrote about the "objective mind" might today be cast in linguistic terms', a point which was perhaps prefigured in his reference to 'the idea visibly shaped in language' (Giddens, 1977b: 61; Outhwaite, 1975: 104; Hodges, 1952: 216). If by 'objective mind' we mean 'symbolic structures objectivated as cultural patterns and products', this speculation appears valid enough (Habermas, 1972: 338).

The particular emphasis Dilthey gave to hermeneutical understanding is that it is not confined to logical categories or to rules of procedure. As 'lived' experience 'involves cognition, feeling, and volition', so the process of engaging with past experience 'brings all these aspects of life into play'. Historical understanding is artful, but it works with materials yielded up from the past, with time's traces, which may be resistant to the interpretation we may initially want to advance, and because the traces it deals with are in this sense artfully recalcitrant its results can never have 'demonstrative certitude' (Hodges, 1952: 141). This is useful, both in itself and in more fully contextualising the objectivist twist in Dilthey. But there are still difficulties. Perhaps the most severe limitation of historical hermeneutics is that characteristically it neglects the ways in which social structures shape experience and the lifeworld 'from the outside in', or in other words 'in terms which go beyond those of actors situated in particular traditions, and which are of explanatory significance in relation to them' (Pusey, 1987: 64–5; Giddens, 1977b: 62). The limitation is in this sense germane to phenomenological approaches generally, and it is the converse of those associated with 'positivist' methodologies. 'The

central question, whether a full-blooded *verstehende* approach
can be combined with causal explanation . . . remains open'
(Outhwaite, 1975: 105). A second limitation is that it leaves
unresolved the grounds for evaluating past experience and
interpretations made of that experience, not to mention
varying expressions or accounts of that experience in the
past. At the least, dealing with this limitation requires amend-
ing Gadamer's conception of dialogue by recognising the
differences between attempting to understand, say, a past
cultural text for its contemporaries, 'and attempting to understand the significance of the text to our own present-day
circumstances' (Giddens, 1977b: 63–4). Any sense of such
significance has then to be seen as predicated upon a sense
of contrast and difference, precisely because people and
cultures do not remain invariant but change from one period in time to another. This means that the historical imagination is dependent on the realisation of difference, so that
'our delight in comparisons, in distance, in dissimilarity' is,
as Brecht put it, 'at the same time a delight in what is close
and proper to ourselves':

> We must drop our habit of taking the different social struc-
> tures of past periods, then stripping them of everything that
> makes them different, so that they all look more or less like
> our own, which then acquires from this process a certain air
> of having been there all along, in other words, of permanence
> pure and simple. Instead we must leave them their distinguish-
> ing marks and keep their impermanence always before our eyes,
> so that our own period can be seen to be impermanent too
> (Brecht, 1964: 190).

What does this entail for historical study, and for a historically oriented cultural studies? A brief response to this
question would be that all cultural expressions, forms and
practices are integral to historical process, are contingent,
definite and variable, and require historical explanation. This
involves, among other things, an imaginative interpretation
of cultural meanings and values in the society in which they
arose and attained a general circulation, but at the same
time 'experience' and 'expression' as time's traces can neither be taken as directly identical, nor as directly transmitted, across intervening time and into time present. Historical

reconstruction is inevitably incomplete, approximate, tel-escoped, and conditional. This is so because we are histori-cally bound and culturally located; hence the importance of reflexive practice, not in the interests of a deferred ob-jectivity but, instead, of a self-critical openness to our pre-suppositions in representing evidence and in making accounts, interpretations and claims about it. This reflexive quality was in the end exactly the importance for Dilthey of *Erlebnis* (Outhwaite, 1975: 25–6). What he held to was that people find their experiences meaningful, or at least those experi-ences they make count; they use these as material for thinking and talking; they strive to express – to press out – their meaning and significance culturally, in the broadest sense of that word; and potentially at least, these historically spe-cific 'expressions' can be meaningfully interpreted by others who, in interrogating them, may thereby be changed. From this we have then to take into account that language in particular is not just a means of expression mediating expe-rience of the world, since it is already that common sphere in which expressions circulate and out of which they are spun. It is the only way in which, over time, the meanings attached to experience can be transmitted. It is what makes experience social and historical, rather than 'private', 'in-ner' or manifest of some putative essence of being. Lan-guage also, being social, is a medium of domination and power. Historical enquiry and cultural analysis are not, of course, immune to the politics of experience but immersed in them. Recognising this involves asking which experiences are to be regarded as meaningful and which are to be taken as contributing to meaningful social arrangements. The politics of experience involve questions of choice. This is, finally, the relevance of sympathy in Dilthey's conception of historical understanding. What it entails is trying to grasp, along with structural and institutional forces, the points of view of the various people involved in any historical con-juncture, their ways of seeing and experiencing things, a point supported by Alan Ryan in stating that 'the import-ant definition of the situation so far as the validity of the explanation is concerned turns out to be the definition ac-cepted by the people concerned' (Ryan, 1973: 6). In other words we cannot, without detriment to what we study, ignore

the ways in which individuals and groups have already interpreted their world. Our task is, among other things,
making interpretations of these interpretations, and we need
in this view to begin by studying the social and cultural forms
for the meanings self-attributed to particular formative experiences, actions and counteractions, social ruptures and
changes, and the patchwork character of the histories of
lives within and across particular social categories.

Experience from Below

The principle of taking into account the viewpoints of those
people involved in any social or historical situation, their
ways of seeing and understanding their world, and the expressive forms and practices through which their experiences
are or have been mediated, was central both to the practice
of early cultural studies and of the postwar social history
that was concerned most particularly with the lives and cultures of the 'rude commons'. Both these areas of inquiry
were distinguished for taking the side of 'ordinary', often
exploited people and, for particular cases, of socially
marginalised or stigmatised groups; hence, for instance,
McGuigan's reference to 'underdog' sentiments (1992: 32).[7]
There were various aims involved in this general affiliation,
in particular those of making visible hitherto unrecognised
contributions to, or participations within, human history; of
undoing the discursive constructions which have 'fixed' subordinate groups into the position of victim, deviant, 'enemy
within' or stereotypical inferior beyond the ideological
boundaries of civility, enterprise and social progress; and of
revealing the structures and relations of power which have
underpinned such symbolic labelling, cultural demonisation
and historical sidelining or erasure. These aims were realised in a range of innovative and significant studies. Among
other things, it is important to highlight the real steps forward in disclosing and attempting to interpret what was
experientially hidden from mainstream disciplinary scholarship and mainstream cultural representations; in disturbing
fixed theoretical premises or over-neat theoretical coherences
with the culturally manifold, untidy, heteroglossic character
of articulated experience; in revealing the elaborate and

diverse ways in which cultural ordinariness is enacted; and in challenging conceptions of collective experiential unity or homogeneity, whether in mass society theory or in left-romantic projections of working-class solidarity and revolutionary promise.

The rich and distinctive work in postwar social history, beginning in Britain shortly after the Second World War with the Communist Party Historians Group, and continuing most significantly in the History Workshop movement, has been styled as 'an experiential view of the past, and particularly the past of the "people"' (Easton *et. al.*, 1988: 9). Since it began to blossom in the 1960s, the tags under which such history has been produced are various, and often overlap, as for instance with certain versions of oral and feminist history. But what has linked much of the work, along with the defining interest in social and cultural experience, has been the twin emphasis on developing the perspective of 'history from below' and – in a crucial link to the interest of early cultural studies in democratic education – on de-professionalising the practice of producing history. Too much of the 'new' social history was perhaps microscopic in focus, erring in the opposite direction to, say, *Annales* scholarship or nineteenth-century German cultural history. This does not mean that all such work failed to take into account broader social determinations and long-term historical developments; indeed, it is the achievement of the best of this work that it has revealed such factors and processes in a new light, and showed them to be in certain ways more complex than was previously supposed. In any event, after suffering school history lessons which were confined to the 'great historical figures' (usually male) and 'great historical events' (invariably European), to come across work which either attended closely to the specific, localised details of everyday life, or exposed the human costs of state-repression, nationalism, militarism, colonial expansionism, and male-domination in the commanding sectors of social life, seemed then to be a real opening up, a real argument begun, as the seams of the official national, imperial and patriarchal record were picked at and unravelled.

It is perhaps worth remembering, since it is now often left out of the record, that for a considerable number of

people various research interests in popular culture, subjectivity and experience as historically 'lived', in their diverse
and changing forms, were initially generated by an encounter with social and feminist history, rather than cultural studies. Getting stuck there, and becoming dogmatically
hidebound by certain disciplinary preoccupations or precepts,
was then of course another matter; traversing instead between social and feminist history and cultural studies seemed
at the time to be one resolution of this problem of perspectival
fixity, even though the movement concealed other problems
and was at the same time frustrating precisely because of
the experience of shuttling back and forth, and always anx-
iously looking back over one's shoulder. The anxieties were
located in both directions: a sense of perturbation about
being 'correct' in theory while also being continuously wor-
ried about 'getting the facts straight'. Yet, despite these difficulties and the various divergences that were otherwise in
some ways apparent, the interest in cultural ordinariness,
in 'lived' experience, in the 'cultural' as the *sine qua non* of
intersubjective exchange, and in the urgent yet difficult
questions raised by the politics of culture, seemed then to
bring people's history and cultural studies into the same
intellectual orbit. In the rest of this, as well as in the subsequent chapter, I want to explore some of these points of
convergence, which unfortunately seem in many ways subsequently to have become lost, and I want to begin by connecting them with some of the issues raised by hermeneutics
as applied to the study of cultures, past and present.

For Raphael Samuel, writing in the early 1980s, the 'main
thrust of people's history in recent years has been towards
the recovery of subjective experience'. He went on: 'As in
hermeneutics, the major effort is to present historical issues
as they appeared to the actors at the time; to personalise
the workings of large historical forces; to draw on contemporary vocabularies; to identify the faces in the crowd' (Samuel,
1981a: xviii). This comparison of the concerns of radical
social history with those of hermeneutics unfortunately went
unexamined at the time. I have felt nevertheless that it remains instructive, and it is for this reason that I have spent
some time sketching Dilthey's adaptation of Schleiermacher's
extension of hermeneutics into an early mode of interpre-

tive cultural and historical study. At the very least it is helpful to be aware of certain intellectual parallels of interest
and concern. It may therefore be useful to underline some
of the affinities between, on the one hand, the hermeneutics
coming out of the later Dilthey and the work of Gadamer
and early Habermas, which Dilthey's own work presaged, in
various important ways, and what can for the sake of con-
venience be lumped together as people's history and early
cultural studies.

In particular, there are common elements in a hostility
to positivism in its treatment of social subjects as objective,
externalised material for study; a stress on human agency
and cultural praxis, albeit one subject to various theoretical
difficulties and caveats; and a recognition that social science
data is never 'raw' but necessarily constituted as already
existing interpretations which have to be communicatively
engaged with from what is inevitably some other vantage.
In addition, there are parallel interests in intersubjectively
generated and reproduced meanings as central to the 'practical' character of expressive forms. These can be instanced
by positioning Habermas's conception of historical-
hermeneutic studies as 'governed by a "practical" interest
in intersubjective understanding', alongside 'Williams's long-
held claim that culture is the practical expression of socially
organised experience', and then by connecting both with
Richard Johnson's definitional approach to cultural studies:
'For me cultural studies is about the historical forms of
consciousness or subjectivity, or the subjective forms we live
by, or, in a rather perilous compression, perhaps a reduction, the subjective side of social relations' (Outhwaite, 1994:
27; McGuigan, 1993: 169; Johnson, 1986/7: 43). The
hesitancies and qualifications in Johnson's definition are
indicative of the minefield of problems that are involved in
any attempt to characterise the diverse connections that
cultural studies tries, in its most challenging moments, to
bring about. Yet, despite the dangers of triggering explosions
between the various differences of position and approach
which are brought into relation, what still in important ways
comes together here is a general acceptance of the need to
focus on intersubjective understandings and 'practical' historical consciousness through the expressive forms in which

experience is made to make sense for participants, to have, in a crucial emphasis, multiple meaning and value. Expressive forms are of course not taken as autonomous or free-floating, nor is any creative practice associated with them regarded as unbound by the material constraints and discursive conventions which provide the conditions of its realised possibilities. Cultural studies could then be said to triangulate around the interrelated questions of how social relations and identities are subjectively lived and experienced, how consciousness is social, and how the social is symbolically constructed, with this last question including the ways in which different social groups and categories are publicly represented. What counts is not only how cultural studies tackles these questions through its dual focus, with relations of power and subordination constituting its 'unifying' frame, but also how it attempts to deal with them through the inter-mapping of experience and theory.

Denying Disinterested Knowledge

In this regard, the particular relevance of hermeneutics is in keeping the researcher within the analytic frame as much as the historical or social subject, for social and historical enquiry is always informed, in greater or lesser degree, by the researcher's own identity, values and beliefs, which are rooted in and coloured by personal experience, as well as by his or her methods and pre-constituted knowledge of a topic. The acknowledgement that 'research is often an expression of personal interests and values' is of course precisely what has been 'long denied within the positivist paradigm' (Wilkinson, 1988: 494). The important shift of epistemological perspective which this involves is, however, not simply a matter of self-indulgently dwelling upon aspects of your own social experience, or simply elevating your involvement in certain forms of popular culture to an academic status, though of course these are always dangers. For this reason it may in some ways be advantageous, and more challenging, to engage critically with cultural forms or social practices outside of your own experience and time. The challenge of this does not mean that researchers thereby ensure a negation of influence from their own personal values and concerns, but rather that it alters the stakes of their involvement in the topic and method of research, and consequently of the ways in which this involvement has to be confronted. Tackling research topics which are outside your own 'lived' experience or historical time may then modify the perspectives adopted on that experience and time. Yet the topics that most of us deal with in social or historical enquiry often in some degree require our looking 'in' from 'outside', and this is then precisely the importance of self-consciously raising into view the relative shifts between involvement and detachment, the relative continuities and discontinuities between researcher and researched, which this entails.

One impetus for the development of cultural studies has obviously been the indifference of academic disciplines to popular culture itself, but any attempt to carry personal enthusiasm into the study of popular culture in a way which, as Richard Johnson remarks, 'is divorced from the analysis of power and of social possibilities' is clearly inadequate (cited in Turner, 1990: 5). In Norbert Elias's mature judgement: 'Without defining and explaining the power relationships of groups, macro- and microsociological studies remain incomplete and vague, and ultimately sterile' (Elias, 1994: 141). Similar points concerning both mainstream academic scholarship and the institutional pressures exerted by existing structures of power apply to the development of feminist research. The immediate issue here, though, is that the researcher does not occupy a position which is outside of, or immune to, the power/knowledge nexus. This is then the virtue of recognising that your values and beliefs are brought to the work of social and historical inquiry, and inform that work not necessarily in a negative or narrowly partisan way, but in a way that inevitably entails both involvement and detachment. Social research should not function simply to affirm existing forms of experience, but rather to gain a critical perspective on them. A key point arising from the discussion of Dilthey, however, was that we cannot divorce ourselves at will from our own social and historical experience, our own ways of experiencing the world we live in and have inherited. This impossibility can be turned to good account through the recognition that such experience

provides social research with a particular resource as well
as influencing or inflecting the manner in which the researcher perceives a topic. Again, the significance of this
has been most recently elaborated by feminism as well as
by cultural studies. The crucial upshot following from both
areas of work is that this impossibility is not something to
be regretted or denied, as it would be from an empiricist
epistemological stance, but on the contrary, that it must be
acknowledged as unavoidable and worked with instead of
against, in attempts to make it a methodological asset rather
than obstacle. As Norman Fairclough has remarked in connection with critical discourse analysis:

> It is widely acknowledged that people researching and writing
> about social matters are inevitably influenced in the way they
> perceive them, by their own social experiences and values and
> political commitments. I think it is important not only to ac-
> knowledge these influences rather than affecting a spurious
> neutrality about social issues, but also to be open with one's
> readers about where one stands (Fairclough, 1989: 5)

Although this presupposes that you understand clearly
enough where it is you stand on particular social issues, and
are happy with an unqualified allegiance to any one position, the point is well made and consistent with the critique
of objectivism. Given that social experience and values inevitably affect the interpretations made and the always provisional knowledges built up, these should be woven into
the work rather than suppressed in favour of some 'spuri-
ous neutrality'. To say otherwise is, as we have seen, to believe in the possibility either of direct, empathetic
identification and an elimination of your own existential self
and historicality, or of objectivist accounts generating knowledge divorced from particular motivating interests and practical concerns. Academic pursuits in the human sciences
cannot be isolated like that, cannot be taken as producing
through abstract disciplinary objectives some pure distilla-
tion of knowledge from the murky waters of social living,
with all its conflicts and contrarieties. This is perhaps still
more of a critical issue in social history than in feminist
research and cultural studies, where the role of representation is more explicitly built into the conceptualisation of

problems and issues, but the challenge of reflexivity to monologically represented accounts is applicable to all these areas of work.

In Sue Wilkinson's useful summary, such reflexivity needs to be seen both in terms of the individual conduct and experience of research, the research process, and the forms, assumptions and legitimating functions of particular disciplines which provide the research model. This involves, firstly, a disciplined self-reflection not only on your own personal stake in particular topics of inquiry, on the uses of experience as a resource, and on the social, cultural and historical grounding of knowledge, but also on the dialectical relationship between life-experience and social science research. Secondly, it involves thinking critically about the paradigmatic terms of specific areas of social and historical inquiry, the specific constellations of 'values and beliefs, cognitions, rules of order and techniques of procedure' which are germane to them, and the ways in which these inform and support existing social relations (Hughes, 1990: 73). As Wilkinson puts it, before going on to document the means by which the traditional paradigm within British psychology has protected itself against the impact of feminist psychology: 'Experiences are not only created but legitimised by institutional practices, and all members of a scientific community do not have equal power in deciding what is legitimate knowledge . . .' The critical impulse of reflexivity can therefore, in working against the grain of established paradigms, act as an agent of change at a disciplinary level (Wilkinson, 1988: 496 *et passim*).

As Wilkinson herself recognises, though, this impulse can lead to academic navel-gazing rather than an 'informed deviance' from disciplinary legitimations and constraints in the construction of knowledge, and cultural studies has at times been particularly guilty of this. The result at a quasi-disciplinary level is a fearful absorption into the endless permutations of discussion about the conditions and consequences of doing research, rather than actively getting on with the pressing research tasks themselves. At a textual level, the proliferation of various self-reflexive devices – as for instance in the work of Ashmore (1989), Mulkay (1985), and Woolgar (1989) – can at times undermine the 'readability

and persuasive power' of their argument even as they are
designed to draw attention to the rhetorical constructedness
of the writing which is the central theme of the argument.
'Indeed, the deliberate attempt is often made to undermine
their own textual authority until they reach the contradictory position of privileging the non-privileged nature of their
text' (Hopper, 1995: 63). At a more personal level, reflexivity can result in specious forms of almost congratulatory self-
reference, or more problematically, in the attitude that work
informed by the researcher's own positionality is critically
unassailable. The difficult question there is whether, and if
so where, one should draw a line in the sand. Yet these
dangers and difficulties should not inhibit the reciprocity
that is needed between a self-conscious, theoretically informed
perspective and the manifold quiddities of experience. An
important pressure deriving from the practice of reflexivity
is that of thinking critically of experience, of how it is constituted and of how its expressive forms are either ideologically placed or valorised as essentialist. On the other hand,
the counter-pressure deriving from an insistence on the
centrality of experience for social and historical inquiry is
that of challenging theoretical orthodoxies or shaking us
out of our critical self-absorptions. What is wonderfully awk-
ward about experience is that it can exceed the interpretations that may both encapsulate and distort it.

A further relevance of the hermeneutic emphasis concerns
the question of 'mutual knowledge'. As we have seen, historical and cultural analysis is concerned with evidence which
derives from a pre-interpreted social world. This is what
Giddens calls the 'double hermeneutic' of the human sciences, which involves us in interpreting, in narratives, accounts and theories, what has already been interpreted in
some way in the intersubjectivity of practical social life. The
concepts and ideas of the social sciences can then, in what
is always an interesting historical step, be taken up and absorbed into the world of 'lay' meanings and values. So, therefore, the 'necessary intersubjectivity of the social world makes
it "our world" in a way that has no parallel in the relation
of human beings to nature' (Giddens, 1977a: 12, 27). This
characteristic of the 'double hermeneutic' is in turn derived
from a key feature of the modern sensibility, which is the

conception that social experience is itself 'deeply reflexive', in the ironic sense 'that any particular order or structure can be destabilised by being seen from a different perspective' (Chaney, 1994: 96). This peculiarly modern characteristic of experience provides a resource for thinking, in that it enables us to subvert, to contradict, and to argue, against convention, against orthodoxy, and against belief, or in relation to whatever is advanced one-sidedly or in absolute terms, as 'brute facts' or 'brass tacks'. It is perhaps important to emphasise again that the received and unqualified Diltheyan idea of the relationship linking analytic frames of meaning to everyday frames of meaning in terms of some form of empathetic process of 're-experiencing' or 're-enactment' is inadequate on several counts. To the extent that the notion did go unqualified at certain times in Dilthey's thinking, this was because of the traces derived from the contemporary empiricist framework in which it was first developed, and the relative neglect of structures of difference in historical and cultural understanding. Yet among the other important contributions, what remains instructive about Dilthey's work are firstly, the attempt to develop an alternative approach to empiricism in historical practice, one component of which was the refusal to separate off reason from the emotional involvement of our lives, and thus to recognise the affectivity of knowledge; and secondly, to think through the problems of subject-position and mode of interest associated with the critical analysis of culture and society relations. The first of these features is what makes for a pertinent connection forwards to the concept of structure of feeling in its anti-dualistic implications, with the emphasis on structure *and* feeling, feeling *and* structure, distinguishing it from the irrationalism of appeals to 'raw intuition' or transcendentalism. The second gives it a reflexive twist. In view of this, 'the dismissal of *Verstehen* as a mere propadeutic writes off major elements of the *Geisteswissenschaften* tradition', a step that is unfortunate for a number of reasons, one of the most significant being that 'the preoccupation with the "meaningful" character of human conduct and culture that characterises that tradition is abandoned in positivistic philosophy, which attempts to reduce this to the content of "empirical observation"' (Giddens, 1977a: 82).

This is important in at least two ways. The first of these is connected to Gadamer's reformulation of *Verstehen* in ways that move beyond the notion of 're-experiencing' or 're-enacting' other people's experiences. For Gadamer, *Verstehen* is not to be regarded as a special procedure of enquiry appropriate only to the study of social conduct, but as the basis of intersubjectivity and as 'the ontological condition of human society as it is produced and reproduced by its members'. Historical and cultural hermeneutics in this way becomes not so much a matter of empathetic identification as of engagement with natural language, or the various forms of communication more generally, which constitute acts and events as 'meaningful' (Giddens, 1977b: 151).[8] Secondly, as noted above, the 'cultural sciences' tradition from Dilthey onward has been concerned with questions associated with the establishment and operation of critique: the standpoint from which it can be conducted, the ideas that will allow you to develop alternative perspectives to that of a dominant culture, or to exceed the limits of its horizons of seeing (Brantlinger, 1990: 30). Both these points need pursuing a little further.

In Gadamer's view, *Verstehen* involves an engagement with semiotic distance, an attempt to reduce the communicative gap between interpretion and its object. So, for instance, while a 'text' has a certain generic and discursive identity, its meanings go beyond any single author and are co-determined by the historical situation of the interpreter. 'That is why understanding is not merely reproductive but always a productive attitude as well' (Gadamer, 1975: 264). Understanding in historical and cultural analysis is always 'understanding otherwise' rather than a process of becoming locked into an original, fixed, stable 'meaning' in the Hirschean sense of its distinction from 'significance' (see Hirsch, 1976). In seeking to regain the 'meaning' which is the authorial intention, Hirsch is anti-historicist and in this sense close to Husserl and opposed to Dilthey, Heidegger and Gadamer. His objective is disinterested knowledge. We are back here via another route with the Kantian aesthetic of 'experience' abstracted from its historical conditions and circumstances, with the conception of *an* experience as timeless, and so antithetical to the time-bound nature of experiences in general, or of the disparate elements of experience in flux. These anti-historical distinctions also bring us back to the problem of historical and sociological reconstruction.

Such reconstruction builds on the texts, the documents and accounts, which constitute, at least in part, the evidential traces of a time, episode or circumstantial set. As we have seen, this process can never yield complete understanding of a pristine situation-in-itself; it involves an interpretation 'which was already partly but crucially constituted by the interpretations of their own situation of the actors participating in it' (MacIntyre, 1976: 45), and which is never independent of the accretions of interpretations already built up around a particular time or situation, or of our own historically conditioned frames of meaning and understanding.[9] Interpretation in historical and cultural analysis is thus serial reinterpretation, entailing 'a mutuality of question and answer' that is also a mutability: we begin 'with what is always already interpreted' and end with 'interpretations that remain always open to further interpretation precisely because human understanding is historically affected and as such is and remains finite' (Wright, 1990: 1–2). This usefully extends the critique of Romantic notions of understanding the 'authentic' meaning of a text, event or practice, but Gadamer's dialogical conception of historical understanding errs in its uncritical rehabiliation of prejudice and tradition. His argument against the Enlightenment 'prejudice against prejudice' is well made, and he notes that 'the historicity of our existence entails that prejudices, in the literal sense of the word, constitute the inner directedness of our whole ability to experience' (1975: 9). Yet this leaves open the question that vexed Dilthey. How can we distinguish between adequate understanding and that which is merely subjective, or between understanding that is transformative and that which is opportunist or reactionary? If understanding is situated, what criteria do we have for saying this analysis illuminates while that one distorts? Gadamer answers this by reference to tradition, for it is this which enables and constrains the variability of interpretation: 'it is not chance and not arbitrary who we ourselves are and what we can hear from the past' (Warnke, 1987: 81).

This is reasonable enough in itself, but as mentioned earlier,

Gadamer falls back on an uncritical ideal of tradition in the canonical or authoritative singular, and on 'good' prejudice in favour of it and of judicious engagement with it. The conception of historical understanding as dialogical then becomes diluted into that of a mutually open and harmonious conversation not dissimilar from our Smiling Jack's notion of communication, with its associated experiential sentimentalism. This removes from view the politics of consensus which are entailed in the imagining or inventing of traditions, and renders the concept of *Verstehen* incompatible with ideological critique, as for instance where traditionality is used to naturalise a repressive configuration of unequal social relations. This is not to say that traditions function as a matter of course to ratify a contemporary order; minority groups in particular have drawn on alternative sources and celebrations of pastness, in custom, legend and myth, to contest specific practices or institutions, and these have been integral to their own characteristic *habitus*.[10] It is precisely the attempt to develop a dialogical understanding of such alternative forms of traditionality which socialist and feminist history have, among other things, sought to achieve (Pickering and Green, 1987b: 17–18). For this reason, MacIntyre distinguishes between Burkean conceptions of tradition and tradition as 'a historically extended, socially embodied argument' about public goods and future possibilities: 'Living traditions, just because they continue a not-yet-completed narrative, confront a future whose determinate and determinable character, so far as it possesses any, derives from the past' (1985: 222–3). It is exactly these kinds of distinctions which are missing in Gadamer's conception of tradition which, for him, has 'a justification that is outside the arguments of reason'. In Eagleton's judgement: 'History for Gadamer is not a place of struggle, discontinuity and exclusion but a "continuing chain", an ever-flowing river, almost, one might say, a club of the like-minded' (1983: 73).

For Habermas, this is an illusion which misapprehends the ways in which modernity makes any notion of cultural tradition problematic. It is in this spirit that he considers the dynamics of knowledge as dialogue and communication to be Dilthey's central problem, though one whose interrogation is marred by a tendency to become prey to objectivism

(Hohendahl, 1983: 140–1). Habermas moves forward from this to extend questions concerning the grounding of hermeneutic activity into an argument for interpretive reflexivity and critical theory that hinges on its possibilities for the generation of emancipatory knowledge and action. Janet Wolff neatly summarises his critique by saying that 'all forms of knowledge originate in relations of domination and repression, though these relations are heavily disguised or concealed in the objectivism of both empiricism and interpretivism' (Wolff, 1983: 54). If we are to build from this then we need to see that social science stands, root and branch, in 'an inherently critical relation to its "field of study"':

> The status of social science as critique has to be elucidated through relating normative implications of social research and theory to reflexivity as the rational basis of freedom. Rejection of the dogma of the absolute logical separation of statements of fact and judgement of value does not compromise the possibility of sustaining such critique objectively; on the contrary, it is the very condition of its realisation (Giddens, 1977a: 28).

It is in light of this that past and present need to be brought into confrontation, so that we may be surprised, may reassess our initiating premises and assumptions, and expand our understanding 'in the joint production of meaning which is achieved in the fusion of horizons' (Wolff, 1981: 101). The point of this should be to avoid the uncritical reproduction of past prejudices, hidebound traditions and national myths. The weakness of Gadamer's hermeneutics is then targeted for the way it 'comes up against walls of traditional frameworks from the inside, as it were' (Habermas, 1977: 360). Such walls contain understanding from within just as much as they obstruct it from without.

This needs some qualification. For Gadamer, the hermeneutic situation is located 'between strangeness and familiarity . . . between the historically intended distant objectivity and the belongingness to a tradition' (Dostal, 1990: 70). 'The true home of hermeneutics is in this "between"' (ibid). This returns us to the question raised at the start of this chapter concerning the relations between formation and transformation. In this connection, Robert Dostal usefully

situates this sense of 'betweenness' with Gadamer's understanding of the experience of temporality, of proceeding
'constantly through the coexistence of past and future'. As
he neatly glosses it, 'the past gives us our future, and the
future gives us our past':

> To endorse the former at the cost of the latter would be pre-
> cisely the position of nostalgia for which Gadamer has some-
> times been criticised. To endorse the latter at the cost of the
> former, would deny the obvious fixity of the past as it has been
> given to us. Insofar as the future is what we look to and will in
> our present engagements, such a simple assignment of priority
> to the future would make the past a mere function of our sub-
> jective will – individual or collective (Dostal, 1990: 71).

This understanding of experience in time and of time is
therefore situated *between* nostalgia and historicism, so that
past and future are conceived not as being structurally isomorphic, but as coexisting reciprocally within the present,
where the past is gone and the future not yet come, but
lies open before us as the realm of possibility. It does so of
course only incompletely, for the past conditions it, in a
range of varying ways according to case and context. In this
sense, Gadamer refers to 'transition' as 'the true being of
time, insofar as everything is at the same time in it and
thereby past and future are together' (ibid: 73–4). This is
useful, and yet 'a mutuality of question and answer' is still
an inadequate way of conceiving Dilthey's central problem.
We remain with the difficulty of reconciling this mutuality
and its mutability with the organising power of tradition as
incorporated within a dominant culture. It is for this reason that Habermas distinguishes between the historical-
hermeneutical and the critical (ibid: 75).

This is an important distinction precisely because we are
today more conscious of the hazards of cultural and historical horizons than ever before, more sensitive to the historical as conditioned and contingent, and of the everyday as a
provisional, practical, situated accomplishment. This induces
a heightened awareness of the perils involved in reconstructing
the experiences of others who are placed outside the boundaries of our time and place. The processes whereby this is
done are now subject to a deepening suspicion and hesi-

tancy. At the same time, we are also increasingly conscious of the mediations of experience, by distinct yet ever-changing languages and by the texts and representations of the information and culture industries, with their characteristic time–space compressions. If the dimensions of time and space are shrinking, how does this affect understanding? Horizons assume cultural and historical difference as well as semiotic distance, and negotiating them means engaging with 'the deep, the profoundly perturbed and perturbing question of our relationship to others – other cultures, other states, other histories, other experiences, other traditions, peoples, and destinies' (Said, 1989: 216). This is what is entailed in the hermeneutic conception of understanding as the fusion of horizons, yet the opposition of terms in this conception encapsulates the paradox of its objective: the apparent moment of fusion realigns the boundaries of difference. Communication is not the melting of subjectivities into each other, and does not deal unequivocally with the 'truth' of the matter, despite the claims of our putative Smiling Jack. Instead, it conceptually focuses 'the matter at hand' and despite our best efforts, will always involve some degree of 'understanding otherwise'. Our perturbation in the face of historical forms of experience will never be completely overcome. In the movement from cultural elements in their 'lived' solution to their subsequent change into time's precipitate traces, there will always be certain things that don't translate, that drop away beyond the horizon and in this sense determine the limits of contemporary expression and of the cultural formation in which we live (Angus, 1994: 92–4). This is exactly the critical point. The weakness of Gadamer's figuration of understanding as a fusion of our own horizon of historical meanings and values with those of the past is that it is conceived as 'coming home', a safe returning to a familiar harbour. The challenge of historical understanding is the opposite of this, and its aim should be to 'erode the exclusivist biases we so often ascribe to cultures, our own not least' (Said, 1989: 225). What this entails is the recognition of cultural and historical limits by bringing them into experience through 'some other medium whose limit is different':

Artists and critics who engage in translations that point cultural productions to their horizontal context can uncover limits within the cultural field. Expressing these limits begins to engage a civilising effect. In a similar fashion, we can define reactionary cultural practice as the attempt to seal borders and prohibit translations . . . Our task is not to rescue tradition, but to embrace the horizon (Angus, 1994: 95–8).

Notes

1 Ortega y Gasset goes so far as to say that such 'having gone beyond is the presupposition as well as the imperative of all history' (1963: 140–1). From a quite different political perspective, Eagleton supports this claim in saying that 'a certain open-endedness and transformability is part of our natures, built into what we are; that the human animal is able to "go beyond", make something creative and unpredictable of what makes it, is the condition of historicity and the consequence of a "lack" in our biological structure which culture, if we are to survive at all, has at all costs to fill'. He is, however, careful to note that 'such creative self-making is carried out within given limits, which are finally those of the body itself' (1990: 409–10).

2 For further comparison of Dilthey and Bergson, see Makkreel, 1975: 209–15.

3 Reiner Wiehl notes that both Gadamer and Dilthey agree on the 'one-sided overemphasis of psychological interpretation compared to other forms of interpretation' (1990: 39). In this sense, and contrary to the impression given by Horkheimer, the later Dilthey moved beyond the psychological orientation of Schleiermacher's hermeneutics, and did so in the sense suggested by Swingewood in the previous chapter. Horkheimer does suggestively point to the relevance of psychoanalysis to the Diltheyan conception of experience in that, for Freud, experiences derive their meanings from the ways in which they are interwoven with the whole life-structure, though this in itself requires for Dilthey a historical and not solely a psychological understanding (Horkheimer, 1939: 440–3). It is, however, Habermas who takes up Freud directly for his relevance to experience and the lack of its expression in cases where experience is repressed. His interest is then focused on systematically distorted communication, or disruptions to dialogue, as well as on the process of the therapeutic relationship.

4 Gerhard Masur attributes to Dilthey the introduction of the idea of the historical generation (1952: 104). Generation as a non-biological concept actually dates from the early nineteenth century when it was first used to denote a structural feature of society and history. Dilthey derived his use of the term in this sense from Comte and Mill, and used it to refer to a temporal duration, an internalised feature of social and cultural identity, and a historically specific relation of individuals and groups to each other. 'Structure of feeling' likewise has reference to these three dimensions of generation as a structured process.

5 It is worth noting that although Collingwood was deeply influenced by Dilthey, his treatment of Dilthey's response to this question is generally disappointing. Holborn's verdict that it is unsympathetic and partly misleading is accurate (Holborn, 1950: 96; and see Collingwood, 1973: 171–5). It is perhaps also worth noting that although Georg Iggers sets Dilthey in a broad historiographical context, his account of Dilthey's ideas is even more misleading (Iggers, 1968: 133–44).

6 See, for instance, Gerhard Masur's *Prophets of Yesterday* (1963: 166) where he characterises Dilthey's conceptualisation of *Verstehen* as 'sympathetic intuition', or Terry Eagleton's *Literary Theory* (1983: 73) where he speaks of Dilthey's belief in the 'need to strive to surmount temporal distance by projecting oneself empathetically into the past'.

7 It is instructive to relate this connecting feature to the contemporaneous debate in mainstream sociology between Becker, Gouldner and Riley, which focused around the issues of objectivity and partisanship, relativism and the sociology of knowledge. For example, the commitment to viewing things from the point of view of subordinate groups and categories can be seen, in the terms of the debate, to have been taken in challenge to what Becker called the hierarchy of credibility in a stratified and unequal society. (See Becker, 1967 and 1974; Gouldner, 1975, chapters 1 and 2; and Riley, 1974a.)

8 As with Williams and others who have both induced and endorsed the turn to ordinariness, there remain unresolved allegiances to 'high' culture in Gadamer's acceptance of 'eminent', that is, classic literary texts, as those which 'most markedly bear authority' and which may therefore be deemed the most 'meaningful' (Dostal, 1990: 75). The problems of canonicity which this raises are self-evident. Needless to say, these problems also apply to Dilthey's conception of a national Germanic

literature in a way that was relatively orthodox for its time. 'Literary history is enlisted in the service of the Second Empire and becomes in the final analysis a science of legitimation' (Hohendahl, 1983: 136–7).

9 In a discussion of cognitive archaeology, Nicholas J. Saunders makes a similar set of points: 'In the ebb and flow of intellectual fashion, one point remains fixed – we can never discover a pristine world of universal truths or unassailable facts, never capture the exactness or totality of meaning. In other words, archaeology deals with approximations, semblances of past realities rooted in the inconstant "present"' (1995: 23).

10 'The *habitus* – embodied history, internalised as a second nature and so forgotten as history – is the active presence of the whole past of which it is the product' (Bourdieu, 1990: 56).

Chapter 6

Relations of Mutual Constitution

> But cultural studies is not just about theories or texts: it deals with lived experiences, and with the intersections of social structures, systems of representation, and subjectivities – intersections which are, of course, relations of mutual constitution. Here it *does* matter if the interpretation does not fit experience.
>
> (Janet Wolff)

Culturalism and Structuralism

It is a truism that experience is both what people make happen and what happens to them, and yet many of the problems in social and historical theory, in cultural studies and in sociological analysis, stem from this differentiation. In his entry on the term in the revised edition of *Keywords*, Williams notes that the direct and engaged participatory sense of experience contrasts most of all with the idea of experience as 'the product of social conditions or of systems of belief'; experience in this contrasting sense constitutes 'evidence of conditions or systems which by definition it cannot itself explain' (1987: 128). The opposition this sets up to the active sense of the term involved in the generation of structures of feeling, or the Diltheyan emphasis on the dynamic of experience pressing out through existing structures to a new defining expressive form or social figuration as part of the process of cultural innovation and change, could hardly be more striking. While in practice analysis has often taken intermediate positions, such opposition has

161

reinforced the polarised distinctions made between culture and ideology, individual and society, expression and the commodification of expressive forms, or creative possibility in the face of economic forces and constraints, with the greater stress on one or the other side of these oppositions then contributing to breaks and demarcations between different theoretical approaches and positions. For example, this applies very clearly to the two dominant paradigms of culturalism and structuralism identified by Stuart Hall in the early 1980s as defining the field of cultural studies. Though the relations between key theoretical problematics shifted during the 1980s, the underlying issues remained in tension. Historically reviewing the field in 1990, Graeme Turner noted: 'While the culturalism/structuralism split may have now dissolved, the three-way split of economic versus cultural determination versus individual agency still dominates, in one form or another, arguments about the formation of culture and the role of ideology' (1990: 210). Since these opposed orientations inform distinct currents of work in feminist scholarship and social history as well, it may be worthwhile beginning the discussion of this chapter by recapitulating their main lines of differentiation, and pointing up the conflicting understandings of experience which they entail.

These can be summarised readily enough. On the one hand, culture is seen to consist of those practices through which people construct and reconstruct signifying expressions and forms of significance which in various ways are articulated to the material and structural conditions of their social lives, and actively shape the social relationships into which they enter. Culture is viewed as a collective assemblage of particular symbolic and ideological resources which are used and configured in the process of making sense of social life, and of developing a distinctive form of collective identity. Culture is both this process and its objectified results; it involves the making and remaking of meanings and values – and at times the creation of new cultural forms for doing so – within inherited and imposed structures. The starting point for so-called culturalism is social experience, and involves examining the interactive relations between such experience and its signifying practices. Experience may then be seen as a site in which structures are reproduced, but there is no *a priori* guarantee of this outcome because experience is worked on, worked with, and at times worked against in order to transform it into something alternative, to bring about a qualitative shift in the conditions it provides and the possibilities it permits. Human agency is the crucial pivot in these negotiations, accommodations and transformations, and its material is cultural at every level. Now if we look at the practices that constitute culture in this paradigm, the key question is how much power any specific individual or social group has in determining or challenging their nature and outcome. While the issues involved in this question concern social, economic, political and ideological factors, which can be identified and described in their different alignments and different combinations according to place and time, we need also to ask what implications these factors have for this way of understanding culture. Does culture as the expression and realisation of social experience stand irredeemably compromised by the question of conditions not of people's own choosing?

On the other hand, culture can be seen to consist of the differentiated structures of signifying practices which mould and give direction to processes and relations of cultural exchange and transmission. The active and mediating role that is assigned to agency in the culturalist paradigm is, in this alternative approach, invested in these differentiated formal and generic characteristics of cultural texts and practices. Following from this, it is ideology rather than culture which counts within the structuralist paradigm; indeed, in many cases, the latter tends to become subsumed under the former. The classic instance of the structuralist approach is in Lévi-Strauss's concern to show 'not how men think in myths, but how myths operate in men's minds without their being aware of the fact' (1969:12). It is this kind of emphasis in structuralism which led Althusser to his characterisation of history as a process without a subject. If the concern in the cultural paradigm is with showing the active making of culture in everyday social interaction, in cultural forms as objectifications of everyday experience, the emphasis in structuralism is on the production of human subjects within ideology as a result of unconscious rules and logics, categories and classifications at work in the underlying structures of cultural forms. Structuralists, in other words, 'have contended that cultural forms are not the products but the producers of experience':

> Structuralism views experience not as the ground of culture but as its effect, the product of the ways in which individuals are transformed into thinking, feeling and perceiving subjects of different kinds in the context of differently structured relations of symbolic exchange ... For the structuralist, the diverse forms of human agency – the forms in which men and women think, feel and act out their lives – are the product of cultural determinations, not the other way round (Bennett *et al.*, 1981: 12).

In this de-centering of experience, the key question is how much power any specific set of structural principles or categories has over the men and women who are positioned as its vehicle and product. If experience, intentionality and rationality are 'the *effects* of representations and signifying systems, not their unproblematic origins' (Poovey, 1990: 618), can individuals or groups ever actively influence, critically discriminate between or challenge such representations and signifying systems? If they can't, why do the meanings of signs and representations change over time?

Culturalism and structuralism are catch-all labels which cover many variations on certain major themes. Both should be understood in a plural sense, though it is also important to note that culturalism is by contrast with its theoretical antinomy an externally imposed term of condescension. It has been disavowed by many of those whose work has been so tagged, partly because there is a good deal in such work which cannot be squeezed into the relatively tight confines represented by the term, and partly because of the common use of the term to damn with faint praises. After its earlier use by Anthony Barnett in his rejoinder to Eagleton's intemperate critical assault on Williams (Barnett, 1976; Eagleton, 1976), it was taken up in the late 1970s at the Birmingham CCCS, in particular by Richard Johnson and Stuart Hall, as a means of inferiorising it as an antecedent to structuralism.[1] In 1969, Hall had defined cultural studies as focusing on 'lived experience ... that peculiar order, pattern, configuration of valued experience, expressed now in imaginative art of the highest order, now in the most popular and proverbial of forms, in gesture and language, in myth and ideology, in modes of communication and in forms of social relationship and organisation' (Hewison, 1995: 185). By 1980, his distance from this position was marked by the extent to which his work had become influenced by the 'impact of the structuralisms', particularly those of Lévi-Strauss, Barthes and Althusser, and the linguistic paradigm on which they were based. It should be remembered that his work and that of the 'Birmingham School' collectively was far more eclectic than his famous 'two paradigm' scenario suggests, and inevitably other influences, such as poststructuralism and feminism (the first of these sketched by Hall in relation to Foucauldian discourse analysis and Lacanian psychoanalysis) have subsequently loomed much larger in cultural studies as a field and practice. Hall's division of the field in 1980 into two major informing paradigms appears to be an even-handed appraisal of their relative strengths, brought together in a neo-Gramscian synthesis. It was this synthesis which gave the field its relative coherence at this time; it formed the basis, for example, of the Open University's significant Popular Culture programme (U203), and in the view of one its main organisers, Tony Bennett, it entailed the transcendence of the two earlier paradigms. Hall explicitly counsels against falsely dichotomising the principal positions and developments in cultural studies around the two 'master paradigms' (Hall, 1980a: 67), and while in many ways the initial impression of being a balanced survey is borne out, Hall's essay has to be understood in relation to his own intellectual trajectory which had led him, by the 1980s, more or less to reverse his earlier position on the category of experience.

In this, Hall took his cue directly from structuralism. Structuralism turned the 'culturalist' approach upside down by recasting experience as the product of systems of signification and representation 'which by definition it cannot itself explain'. The position from which people are viewed as active agents in cultural production, as participants in the 'unmastered human practice' of historical process (Thompson, 1978: 295), was diametrically inverted into a position from which people were seen as bearers of ideology, 'spoken' by categories, positioned by structures, and from which history was conceived as these structures on the move, a process without subjects. As we have noted, these binary conceptions are present in the etymology of the term 'experience' itself: 'experience' as a process of becoming intermediary between conditions and consciousness, in what is an expanded and active sense, as opposed to its passive sense as referring to determinate conditions or structures which produce an always-already foregiven experience. In other words, as a term 'experience' is itself indicative of an entrenched dualism which has been recurrently manifest in the human sciences in contrasting schools and traditions of social thought, either where the action of individuals or groups has primacy over constraining structures (mode of production, social formation, ideology, language and discourse, psychic forces), or where these structures are paramount in ways which delimit or deny the human capacity to create and change. These various dualisms stem from the difficulties of reconciling conscious action and what are seen in one guise or other as determining mechanisms or forces, and were axiomatic to each side of the theoretical divide which marked the debilitating stand-off between cultural studies and social history in the late 1970s and early 1980s. Since then, this unfortunate situation has changed only to the extent that certain social historians such as Gareth Stedman Jones, Patrick Joyce and Joan Scott have taken the linguistic turn, while much cultural studies work of the past fifteen years registers the drastic loss of historical imagination noted earlier. The earlier impasse within cultural studies, mapped (and arguably rendered more intractable) by Johnson, has now been paralleled within social history with, to take just two examples, Elton's reactionary, empiricist call for a 'return to essentials' on one side being matched on the other by Jenkins's preferable, but opportunistic, interpretivist subsumption of history into historiography on the other.[2] In view of these opposed positions, I want to turn first to some of the problems associated with the structuralist tradition. I shall then go on to examine further some of the problems associated with the analytical use of experience as a resource and concept.

Shortcomings of Structuralism

The application of the concepts of Saussurian linguistics to cultural phenomena of all descriptions is methodologically characteristic of structuralism and its successors. A major shortcoming of the 'linguistic turn' conceived in this sense is that the structures and rules of language are decontextualised from their actual social usages, while the agents of language in forms of social communication are negated by these structures and rules or by the unconscious processes which produce them. The concept of experience is an important counter to this tendency in the sense that having experience of the appropriate contexts of appropriate language use is vital to functioning consciously in the medium of language, and to being a competent social actor in a variety of situations and milieux. The judgemental ambivalence of reference to someone as an 'experienced operator' is an example of the way this sense is taken up in a specific inflection. In this sense, the linguistic paradigm does not subsume experience since experience is required in the effective and discriminating application of speech or writing, as in other forms of expression. This is quite different from positing experience as antecedent to language, for experience goes hand-in-hand with learning from others to associate particular modes and manners of language use with particular social circumstances. Rather, the point is directed against the assertion of the extra-social primacy of language.

This implies an important switch towards examining practices of signification in terms of their social import and ground as well as their structuring principles and logics. We return here to the relation between resources of meaning and conditions of expression. It is doubtful whether structuralist and poststructuralist procedures are able to contribute much in overcoming the neglect of the question of how to move analytically between 'emic' and 'etic' approaches to experience which we have already noted as an unresolved difficulty of hermeneutics.[3] The methodology of Dilthey's hermeneutic circle requires an interactive movement between the parts and the whole of the object of study. This means that in studying a cultural text or practice we hop 'back and forth between the whole conceived through the parts

that actualise it and the parts conceived through the whole
that motivates them'. We 'seek to turn them, by a sort of
intellectual perpetual motion, into explications of one another' (Geertz, 1993: 69). Structuralist linguistics and its
semiotic application to quasi-linguistic objects provided the
valuable insight that the mutual definition of 'parts' and
'whole' operates through difference. This adds an important analytical distinction to the task of interpretation, yet
the constitution of signification in differentiation is conceived
as internal to the organisation of the language system or
text. The referent and the question of referentiality are
characteristically bracketed off without ever being given the
conceptual explication singularly afforded to the components
of the sign and the structuring principles of *langue* (Giddens,
1987: 84–5).

Structuralism, as for instance through its notion of the
arbitrary or unmotivated signifier, was always an assault on
the idea of language as reference to external reality, and
with Derrida's declarations that 'there is nothing outside of
the text', and 'every signified is also in the position of a
signifier' (1976: 158; 1981: 20), the sense of language having any identifiable relation to referents outside its own
domain is well nigh absolute. The domain of language becomes itself the only reality. To feel deep unease with this
does not mean denying that language is generally constitutive of what is taken as social reality, but it does register the
sense that without some conception of the correspondence
of language to extra-linguistic phenomena, however problematic this may be, the status of any evidence of the social
world, and of experience within it, is negated. The relationship of intellectual concepts, historical processes and social
institutions has then to be conceived as random. The particular conditions under which relations of social domination and subordination are 'lived' and reproduced, which
historical enquiry may provide evidence of, become lost from
view, and the dissolution of human agency is, in attempts
to challenge them, complete. The dissolution of agency may
have been Lévi-Strauss's ultimate goal for the human sciences (1972: 254), but 'experience' only attains conceptual
weight when we assert the opposite: the constitution of agency
under determinate historical conditions. The bracketing of

parole is the bracketing of social process, for *parole* occurs within that process and not in the dehistoricised limbo postulated for *langue*. It is worthwhile remembering Marx's comment on the absurdity of conceiving of 'the development of language without individuals *living* together and talking to each other'. For him any linguistic designation 'expresses as an idea what repeated corroboration in experience has accomplished' (cited in Corrigan and Sayer, 1978: 197).

While the synchronic mode of structuralist analysis supplements the hermeneutic task by identifying the relations of difference which constitute the parts of a cultural text in respect to each other and to their totality, its major drawback has always been that it offers no means of explanation for the contingent, processual nature of interpretation. What then gets neglected is the historicality of the experience of cultural process, and what this entails are the historically definite ways in which agents – subjects acting in conscious, intentional and reflexive ways – instantiate, adapt and modify language and 'textual practices' in particular social circumstances and settings. This is where the emphasis on *langue* becomes obstructive, for the problem with an emphasis on the constraints of linguistic structures is that it cannot handle the creative uses of language, 'the volatile liberty of *parole*' (Anderson, 1983: 44). Of course we should be cautious in our use of the idea of cultural creativity and the role it plays in social practices; it should be neither symbolically aggrandised nor subjectively romanticised. Structuralism was right to criticise the idea of language as a transparent medium which simply gives form to an intention to speak, to express experience, to press it out into meaningful constructions. But language operates interdependently with practical consciousness and social relations: we are both scripted in our social interactions and able to shape the meanings of what we say in our communication with others. 'The real communicative "products" which are usuable signs are . . . living evidence of a continuing social process, into which individuals are born and within which they are shaped, but to which they then also actively contribute, in a continuing process' (Williams, 1977: 37). From the objectivist displacement of the subject in the dialectic of structure and subject, and the rejection of the referent in the interaction of

signs and world, the move to poststructuralism was then to
'subjectivism without a subject' (Anderson, 1983: 54), the
endless deferral of cultural meanings, and the reduction of
the concept of 'context' to a sort of rhetorical trope of sociological and historiographical discourse. Goodbye, we might
say, to all that history, and to any viable forms of historical
explanation, for the direct repercussion of structuralism's
assault on the idea of referentiality – its denial of the referent which the sign denotes – was that historical change
became 'as mysteriously inexplicable as the Romantic symbol' (Eagleton, 1983: 111). The supreme irony here is that
the negotiation of 'difference' is a key historiographical
problematic in that change over time and in our understanding of time's traces constitutes the very possibility of
history itself. I have suggested that hermeneutics presents
us with a fruitful starting-point – pointing to a set of tentative directions rather than providing a definitive map – for
thinking through the issues involved in this problematic,
and I have done so to the extent that its emphases seem to
me preferable both to the putative scientific certitude of
early structuralism, and the relativistic equivocations of its
poststructuralist progeny.

The danger of the 'linguistic turn', then, is that language
becomes reified, seen as static and self-sufficient, while social,
economic and political relations in human history are downgraded or wholly absorbed into the ahistorial play of signifiers
or the overarching epistemic structure of discourse. It is a
danger which Marx referred to as the 'mentalisation of language' (Corrigan and Sayer, 1978: 197). The specific issues
involved in horizonal translations across time fade into in-
significance. Of course it need not have happened like
that. Volosinov's linguistics, had they been more widely disseminated at an earlier period, would have provided a salutary counter to Saussure's. What counted for Volosinov was
the contextual and changing meanings of language, and these
for him were the products of social conflict and struggle: as
he put it, 'differently oriented accents intersect in every
ideological sign' (1986: 23). Social reality is handled through
signs and language in an ongoing and changing society, and
the variable social accents which intersect in the sign-system
are neither equal nor do they provide any guarantee of agreed

meanings and values. For Volosinov, it is this which maintains the vitality and dynamism of particular signs, rather
than some historically invariant sense or structure. This
approach is quite at odds with both normative conceptions
of language and the formalist closure of structuralism. It
brings to the forefront the ways in which interactions of
signs, texts and discourses occur in the context of historically contingent social relationships which are part of broader
social and economic inequalities, broader conflicts of interests and values, and broader structures of power and authority.

The Experiential Pull

In his 'two paradigms' topography of cultural studies, Hall
distinguishes structuralism from so-called culturalism through
the latter's emphasis on creativity and historical agency and
through what he calls its experiential pull. Hall treats the
category of experience in a negative light, largely because
he regards it as conceptually 'uninspected', as obscuring the
determinate conditions of what is 'lived', as having produced
'the quite unsatisfactory concept of "a structure of feeling"',
and as encouraging an expressive correlation of structures
– 'simultaneous in effect and determinacy because they are
simultaneous in our experience' (1989: 62). These objections have been highly influential, and I would hope that
my attempt to 'inspect' the concept of experience, which
began with a critical examination of 'structure of feeling',
will at least help to counter the 'uninspected' reiteration of
such objections in accounts which simply flow with the fashionable tide. I would also hope that my treatment of 'expressive form' is distinct enough from romantic notions of
spontaneous creative efflorescence and of self-authenticating 'voices' even as I have opposed the easy contemporary
reference to 'expression' as a boo-word. My general approach
runs against the tendencies both to pit experience conceptually against structural conditions or such conditions conceptually against experience. It is in this light that I take
Marx's famous statement that people make their own history but not under conditions of their own choosing as
embracing both agency and structure and entailing the need
to integrate them in cultural and historical analysis. What I

have been exploring in my whole argument are, in short, the manifold implications of Dilthey's admirable formula: to be consciously a conditioned being.[4]

In taking my immediate cues in this book from socialist and feminist history, historical hermeneutics and variants of cultural studies, I have not intended my argument to be an endorsement of every use of experience as a concept within these different fields. In view of this, and as a complement to the previous section, it is now appropriate to spotlight some of the major shortcomings of the analytical use of experience, and I shall begin this by returning to the question of historical recovery. In trying to point up other aspects of this question, I have deliberately not brought into full view one of the key founding texts of cultural studies which is associated with it. Edward Thompson's *The Making of the English Working Class* (1968b) is undoubtedly a landmark text, and I will be able to deal with it here only in summary fashion. Thompson's main concerns in this study were to show class formation as a historical process, as a pattern of relations that can only be understood in its temporal duration; to show class consciousness as emerging out of the dense and contradictory experience of various kinds of workers which is felt and articulated in terms of common identities and interests defined in opposition to those of other social classes; to show that the development of class-for-itself is an active process of cultural self-making; to gain some sense of working-class history as experienced and constructed 'from the inside' by its participants, during the turbulent times of late-eighteenth-centry and early-nineteenth-century England; and finally 'to rescue the poor stockinger, the Luddite cropper, the "obsolete" hand-loom weaver, the "utopian" artisan, and even the deluded follower of Joanna Southcott, from the enormous condescension of posterity' (Thompson 1968b: 13). Following from this, the massive effort that has gone into the recovery of a sense of the sufferings, anxieties, confinements, deprivations, resilience, resourcefulness, struggles and aspirations of ordinary people represents a major reconfiguration of the landscape of the past. Those who were hidden from history – the working class, women, ethnic minorities, social outcasts, grassroots political activists, etc. – those who had sunk beneath the 'enormous condescension of posterity', were brought back into the frame, their social conditions, political activities and cultural practices recuperated, in what amounted to a newly constituted recognition of respect for what 'common people' did and had done to them. What all this has amounted to could well be called a turn to experience, but it is not now this turn – among all the turns and twists that historiography is ravelled into – which is given much respect. Indeed its leading motivations, criteria and principles are openly called into question, and derided as epistemologically naive when set against the latest last pronouncement in the Senior Common Room.

Unsurprisingly, some of this work has romantically evoked popular traditions and treated 'people's history' too much in isolation from the broader political struggle for socialism. The unexplicated notion of 'experience' has then served as 'a kind of theoretical warrant' for such historical populism (Meiskins Wood, 1982: 47). Indeed, it has sometimes been assumed that the problems of social and historical invisibility or stereotypicality can be overcome simply by recovering or revealing the 'actual, lived experiences' of subordinated groups, which are regarded as self-evidently authentic. This assumption and the approach that goes with it have been fiercely condemned as resurrectionism, and the naivity of it stems from a failure to acknowledge and work with the historiographical issues discussed earlier, as for instance those involved in reinterpreting the already interpreted traces of past events and experiences across time in the light of the horizons of historical change which in themselves mandate the act of reinterpretation. Yet the dismissive attitude evident in this castigation of simplistic historical practice should be equally condemned, for it carries the implication that exactly this project of dialogical engagement with time's traces is foolhardy, and doomed to the perpetuation of a peculiar illusion. An even more cutting indictment of 'radical history' is that the experiences of the exploited and downtrodden in the past are deemed worthy of reverence simply because this burnishes the self-regarding socialist or feminist credentials of those involved in the research. No doubt this motivation, if that is the word to describe it, has underlaid certain examples of research into the history of working-class life and struggle, but the hostility of the attack should neither distract us from what are the real interpretive difficulties, nor allow back-door entrance under the camouflage of an indictment of socialist or feminist commitment to notions of value-neutrality in historical research and cultural analysis. This leads on to the quite different use of the past as a resource for challenging the constructed forms of relations of subordination.

Past experience in this sense is taken as a point of reference in efforts to contest negativised aspects of the historical record or is drawn on in order to reinterpret the lives of subaltern groups affirmatively. The project involved in this is often to galvanise particular identity categories around a celebrated sense of their own distinctive and unique characteristics and heritage. This is fine in itself, yet at the same time the same issues of authenticity and self-involvement arise. In the 'Negritude' and 'Black is Beautiful' movements, for example, as well as in various forms of contemporary feminism, the desperate need to challenge patriarchal and racist assumptions and pressures has at times depended on an essentialised black or female identity as a means of assertive differentiation. This has been evident in historical as well as other forms of discourse. Being black, or being female, has then been advanced as a privileged source of experience and subjectivity. As Laura Lee Downs observes, a limitation of identity politics advanced in this fashion is that it considerably restricts the possibility of untying the chains of race or gender by making knowledge discontinuous across the boundaries of category-specific experience. The relativist denial of any 'Archimedean standpoint' renders 'the experiential content of these categories . . . the sole source of authority':

> Each experiential territory is hermetically sealed off from the others, in order to protect the authority of one's experience from challenge or scrutiny, and no illusion of universal truth stands over and above, binding (however coercively) the subjective truths of our experience into some kind of coherent social whole (Downs, 1993a: 6–7).

This leads Downs to conclude that 'identity politics has merely inverted the hierarchy of categories and identities handed down by the very conservative politics it seeks to subvert' (1993a: 7–8). Understandably, the claim that a common experience of 'womanhood' should constitute the basis for women's studies, as well as for the critique of methods and theory in established disciplines of the human sciences, has at times been made in staking out this new area of feminist scholarship (see, for example, Smith, 1979; Westcott, 1979; and Eisenstein and Jardine, 1980). The crux of the problem here is that if you cannot lay claim to the difference of your shared experience, feelings and desires, then on what grounds can you assert the distinctiveness of your common identity? This is a difficult question. There would now seem to be a widening agreement that the assumption of such common experience is inadequate for feminist intellectual work and politics, particularly in respect of the view that the argument for a separate treatment of women carries the danger of confirming 'their marginal and particularised relationship to those (male) subjects already established as dominant and universal' (Scott, 1988: 3). It may well be that the problem with reversing male-defined conceptions of 'objective knowledge' by formulating knowledge in terms of the exclusive experiences of women as seen by women is that it then arrives at the same reductive and fragmentative position and so refuses to see, as Oshadi Mangena has put it, 'the interrelatedness and interconnectedness of male and female experience in society'. Equally, gender is not an absolute condition of experience, and cannot be separated from other significant categories and determinants: 'It is not the case that we all have a common experience as a consequence of our gender with differences of race, class and nationality simply added on' (Mangena, 1994: 277 and 281).

In seeking the redemption of experience as a conceptual unit of analysis, I have emphasised one caveat in particular. This is that the category of experience does not belong on a pedestal. It should not be elevated to some point beyond the reach of social, economic and political conditions, for these always delimit even if they do not causally determine the experiences of particular collectivities. Nor can experience be validly conceived as an abstract universality outside of the discourses which frame its leading possibilities of meaning in specific instances and contexts. My argument has moved from a critique of transcendent aesthetic notions to considerations of the social hermeneutics of experience in order to stress that experience cannot be taken in itself and only in itself as a validating source of knowledge. To take up Janet Wolff's point in the epigraph to this chapter, lived experiences need to be approached in terms of the mutually constituting intersections of social structures, systems of representation and subjectivities. This is crucial, for privileging any one of these is likely to lead to sociologistic forms of explanation, self-enclosed textualist readings, or radical forms of essentialism and relativism.

Yet it is important to be clear about other, more specific dangers of using experience as a sole ontological alibi of knowledge or identity. Firstly, where 'experience' is taken as conceptually self-evident, its application tends to be over-subjectivised, reified or confused in indiscriminately running together several different dimensions of, say, female experience (the biological and social, for instance). Secondly, it renders certain binary oppositions – those of objectivity and subjectivity, rationality and emotion, being and consciousness being examples – that much more entrenched. This would then, among other things, underwrite scientistic approaches to knowledge in that emotions and feelings are seen as separate from the intellect and the faculty of reasoning. Oshadi Mangena refers to the knowledge resulting from these approaches as 'tainted objectivity' and argues that 'when such knowledge is used for social organisation it fosters oppression on the part of those whose experiences and knowledge were subordinated in the process of analysis' (1994: 277; cf. Harding and Hintikka, 1983). This is all well and good, but where research methods become too exclusively focused on experience, what of the error of 'tainted subjectivity'? For example, this would seem potentially to be a danger with Shulamit Reinharz's 'experiential analysis' (1983), with its appeal to what she calls a 'feminine cognitive style', in that it inverts the claims of positivistic research models rather than examining, say, the epistemological relations between objectivity and subjectivity, and the implications which these have for institutionalised structures of power. 'By opposing one to the other', feminist critiques of such research models and feminist methodologies proposed as alternatives, may 'implicitly reinforce the very dichotomy they aim at over-coming' (Lazreg, 1994a: 50). Despite the many values of the accent on women's experience in feminist history and cultural studies, the very accent in itself may have the effect of endorsing the relegation of the sign of the feminine to the realm of subjectivity, feelings and experience to which historically it has been subordinated. To the extent that this is true, it is unfortunate for both women and men in that it constitutes a latent endorsement of patriarchal assumptions and values, and reinforces the obstacles facing men in their attempts to confront their inherited alienation from this realm. Thirdly, and perhaps most importantly, the privileging of experience begs the very difficult questions of understand-ing the experiences of others, even where this is women's understanding of other women or black people's understand-ing of other black people, in other cultural locations or in other cultural histories.

In discussing feminist scholarship which deals with women's experiences in different cultures from that of the researcher, the Algerian writer Marnia Lazreg mentions the ethical dan-gers of appropriating 'other' women's voices by objectifying them, turning them into *objects* of study, and of construct-ing for these 'other' women a new subjectivity which may or may not 'intersect with the one experienced by the women in question'. As she points out, there is no guarantee that this intersection will occur because there is no obvious mechanism for moving from one type of experience to an-other (1994a: 53). This is a valuable observation, but inevi-tably it leads us to ask why there should be a need for such guarantees. Such a need could be taken to suggest the ob-jectivism which historical-hermeneutics, cultural studies and feminism have cogently refuted. In taking up David Chaney's recent question 'what have we learnt from cultural studies?' (1994), one lesson is surely the impossibility of 'demonstrative certitude'. Cultural studies in this sense is consistent with the hermeneutic principle that because the analysis of culture always occurs within culture the problem of relativism becomes central to the process of understand-ing. As Ben Agger puts it, 'all versions of cultural studies are fundamentally pluralist about what "counts" as legitimate cultural expression and evaluation', though he carefully distances himself from the poststructuralist promotion of 'end-less readings ungrounded in more substantial notions of truth and justice':

> All of us who do cultural studies, including neo-Frankfurters, reject the arrogance of the Enlightenment's subject philoso-phy. But that does not mean that we can thus dispense with a concept and practice of subjectivity and intersubjectivity; the subject's decentring by poststructuralists offers neither axiological nor strategic guidance (Agger, 1992: 20–3).

Lazreg sees intersubjectivity as 'a necessary requirement for the understanding of difference within and between gen-der', and in view of her generally sound objections to epis-temological claims based on an assumption of the privileged or immutable nature of women's experience, would presum-ably accept the rejection of absolute values. She is never-theless forced to pose the need for analytical guarantees because she regards experience as intrinsically individualistic (1994a: 53 and 59). This is a common assumption, and given the association of experience with subjectivity and personal expression, an understandable one. It is, nevertheless, mis-taken, for it denies the possibility of experiences *as* inter-subjectively constructed and understood, and without this possibility even identity politics, not to mention, indeed, any collectivity, formation or movement, would be unviable. As Roy Bhaskar has noted, while experience is 'susceptible to a purely individidualistic analysis', the fact that 'knowledge is not analysable in terms of individual experiences does not imply that it is not analysable in terms of experience' (1975: 187).

This objection is not intended as an endorsement of the faddish shibboleth of a 'criticism without guarantees', but rather as part of the effort at establishing the groundwork of critique in a pluralised cultural world. In this context, 'experience' remains analytically important because misin-terpretations of the experiences of others abound, and be-cause constructions of the otherness of the experiences of subordinated groups are intimately wrought up in social and and ideological conflict. It is in part against such strategic distortion and symbolic violence that social critique needs to be directed. Following the earlier part of her statement, this is what is equally vital in Wolff's rider that 'it *does* matter if the interpretation does not fit experience' (1995: 35). Carolyn Steedman's *Landscape for a Good Woman* (1986) stands as eloquent testimony to that. It is then precisely because representations *are* representations and 'embedded first in the language and then in the culture, institutions, and political ambience of the representer' that we 'should remember that the study of man [*sic*] in society is based on concrete human history and experience, not on donnish abstractions, or on obscure laws or arbitrary systems'. The problem then, in Said's view, 'is to make the study fit and in some way be shaped by the experience, which would be illuminated and perhaps changed by the study' (1978: 272, 327–8). Experience may then expose the cracks in the wall of explanation which orthodoxy has papered over, or render problematic what has become theoretically entrenched. This in turn suggests a mode of procedure which is 'contextually grounded and specific' in its attention to competing and conflicting accounts of experience, events and situations, to 'interpretive asymmetries' and 'reality disjunctures' which bring into focus, in any given confrontation, the experience itself, the method of observation, and the form of reportage (Stanley and Wise, 1993: 142–4). The general current of this kind of approach runs counter to the objectivist paradigm: 'we fail to report or discuss the contradictions between experience, consciousness and theory, because the paradigm we work within tells us that these are unimportant or non-existent' (ibid: 153). For Liz Stanley and Sue Wise, such contradictions are grounded in their distinctive ontological sense of being female and fractured. Hence their focus on 'the multiple and continual fractures that occur between experience and categories', for the 'ontological jolts' that occur 'when events constrain by bringing women back into being "a woman" rather than a person are crucial to the processes by which an explicit feminist analysis comes into being' (ibid: 206).

This account is highly compressed, but its general virtues are summed up by Eagleton in marking as a key achievement of the women's movement its redemption of 'lived experience' from the 'empiricist connotations with which much literary theory has invested' in it : '"Experience" need now no longer signify an appeal away from power-systems and social relations to the privileged certainties of the private, for feminism recognises no such distinction between questions of the human subject and questions of political struggle' (Eagleton, 1983: 215). One of the lessons that emerges from this is that experience 'which is not theorised has a way of dissolving and slipping out of view'. This returns us to what Dilthey described as 'the tragedy of finitude' where people become stuck in 'defending entrenched feelings' (Rowbottom: 1979: 43–4). To quote Stanley and Wise again, without 'subjecting experience to analysis, then "experience", even our own, is *not* something we already know about' (1993: 170). In ways all too easily forgotten, especially by intellectuals, what we know is always partly derived from experience, in the direct, 'lived' sense of the word, and this knowledge is both practical and interpretive as we use it to ground our ongoing existence. Of course knowledge is not limited to experience in this sense, and what we make of our social and historical experience is more than experience, again in this sense, can be expected to deliver. The ways in which we interpret and understand forms of social experience are not dependent only on what we ourselves experience, or on what members of our own or previous generations may narrate directly to us of their own specific experiences.

Yet the general point following from Janet Wolff's observation insistently remains, for the danger to which she points stems not only from right-wing condemnations of 'victimology' and 'victim studies' but also from a radical-left 'self-generating conceptual universe which imposes its own ideality upon the phenomena of material and social existence, rather than engaging in continual dialogue with these' (Thompson, cited in Palmer, 1994: 119). Historically, it is a tragic irony of the organised Left that it has so often failed women in this way, 'refusing to absorb their lived experience, pushing them out to the fringes, denying their insights in the name of a pure Marxism or Leninism, forcing the separation of the personal from the political and then bewailing the falling-away of the faithful' (Tweedie, 1980: 8). While questions of gender and women's experience were too often downgraded in the work of both Williams and Thompson, their general 'appeal to experience' in historical and cultural analysis was directly

opposed to intellectual currents and political practices which
deny the significance of popular culture, initiative and creativity. It is to some of the problems associated with this experiential appeal in their work that I now want to turn.

Experience in the Williams–Thompson Axis

Raymond Williams and Edward Thompson have been among
the most important socialist writers in Britain during the
postwar period. While their importance has been recognised
and celebrated, the centrality of the concept of experience
in their work has been severely criticised. Much of this criticism has derived from the problems associated with understanding experience in the polarised senses distinguished
at the start of this chapter, and in what follows I want to
take up at least some of the issues that are involved. As far
as Williams is concerned, his focus on how people experience the conditions of their existence, and render them up
in symbolic responses that then characterise their collective
identity, has been considered at times to meld into a rather
amorphously described 'way of living' and a later somewhat
vague 'whole social process' where the distinctions between
different social and cultural practices become blurred. Secondly, and with reference to his oxymoronic conception of
the 'long revolution' – the famous titular encapsulation of
his argument for the democratisation of cultural production and exchange – Williams has been criticised for valor-
ising cultural change and innovation over and above industrial
and political struggle, and to have underplayed the question of state power (see, for example, Barnett, 1976). This
tendency was connected to his alleged 'political gradualism',
which was said to be manifest in his advocacy of the extension of popular participation in education, industry, politics, culture and communications (Eagleton, 1976, ch. 1).
In so far as this claim is valid, it is so only for the earlier
work, and even then it is exaggerated in order to contrast
weakly with Eagleton's impatience at this time for a grandi-
osely unspecific revolutionary rupture.

A third point of criticism by Eagleton dismissed as 'a form
of romantic populism' Williams's 'culture is ordinary' dictum and his 'deep-seated trust' in the capacity of ordinary

people actively to challenge and create 'meanings and values' in these interrelated institutional contexts. In one aspect of this, Eagleton claimed that it was as if Williams considered the transformation of meanings and values as the source and generation of all social change. This brings us finally round to Williams's 'insistence on experience', his 'passionate premium upon the "lived"', which 'supplies at once the formidable power and drastic limitation of his work'. Eagleton did not confront this apparent paradox. Rather, instead of elaborating on the analytical and theoretical strengths of this work, he dwelt obsessively on the limitation of what he identified as early Williams's 'left-Leavisism', the 'drastically limiting' residue of humanism which could only be eradicated by 'a science of the text'. The structuralist limitations of Eagleton's critique here have already been dealt with, but these need also to be underscored by reference back to Dilthey's dissociation of the social from the natural sciences, the point of this being that Eagleton's pietistic scientism entailed a failure, firstly to recognise the implications for analysis of that tripartite structure of beliefs, feelings and desires with which for Dilthey conceptually approached the experience of historical subjects, and secondly the need to engage with the connection between social experience and imaginative grasp, which was always Williams's subject (Inglis, 1995: 248).

Connections of this kind are integral to what historical and cultural interpretation are about, which is why I have dwelt so much on questions associated with the hermeneutic 'recovery of meaning'. These are not reducible to straw humanist targets, and in any case, the risk of stirring up the sediments of humanism seems to me preferable to the analytical impossibility, in the Althusserian Orrery, of working with, as well as critically challenging, the self-accounts and interpretations of historically located agents. Unless we are willing to listen to what historical 'voices' have to say in their own terms, so to speak, then our own assumptions and expectations will tend simply to bask in their self-confirmation. One of the values of attending sympathetically to people's social experiences in the Williams–Thompson axis is that it provides a check to the tendency towards an authoritarianism of intellectual authority. This is true for historical practice as well as for social theory. The ways in which we establish 'relations between phenomena which could never be seen, felt or experienced' by people in the past, and the ways in which we organise our findings 'according to concepts and within categories which were unknown to men and women who make up the object of the study', is characteristic of our relationship to time's traces (Thompson, 1978: 211). Following from this, it has been central to my argument that our relationship to time's traces must be two-way. It must be a dialogue *with* difference if we are not to absorb the traces of time past utterly into the dense epistemological tissue of time present. Of course, even as we open our ears to other historical voices, we hear them within the horizon of our own historical range. This is why recognising their historicality does not necessarily entail stepping on to an ever-descending spiral of relativism. Our understanding is culturally and linguistically embedded, and yet is equally characterised by the ability to 'understand otherwise' and to recognise the distinctiveness or quality of other forms of consideration, other premises and perspectives. This ability is known as rationality.

When we speak of being experienced, it is the possession and exercise of this ability which we partly have in mind. It involves being open to the challenge of new experiences, or the experiences of others, and drawing on these to revise one's own conceptual schema of understanding or to extend their warrant. It is to learn by example of difference. Returning to Eagleton's critique of Williams's use of the category of experience, it is not as though analysis of the transformation of meanings and values provides us with a master key for explaining all historical process and change – there isn't one anyway. But sympathy and respect for the experiences of others are certainly preferable to the intellectual sterility and arrogance of Eagleton's theoretical position at the time of his 'patricidal' attack on Williams.[5] Such sympathy and respect carry their dangers, as we have acknowledged. Thompson severely criticised 'the sentimentalists with their vapid portrait of the all-holy-common-people, touched up with real heroic instances, but with every interesting wart and wrinkle erased' (cited Palmer, 1981: 68), though he had himself to some extent overplayed the heroic

qualities of the first English working class. It may be that
these risks have sometimes to be run in the interests of
broadening our understanding. More importantly, though,
once this approach is tempered into the steel of 'a discipline
of attentive disbelief' (Thompson, 1978: 220–1) – attentive
because willing to listen and anxious to learn, but sceptical
because unwilling to take anything on trust and anxious to
interrogate – it may facilitate dialogue with the 'foreign-
ness' of history. It is precisely this kind of dialogue which
cultivates the growth of rationality. To quote Georgia Warnke
again: 'The awareness that one's knowledge is always open
to refutation or modification from the vantage point of
another perspective is not a basis for suspending confidence
in the idea of reason but rather represents the very possibility of rational progress' (1987: 173).

It is of course true that at times Williams's political optimism ran away with him and he could speak as if ideological infiltration in the understanding of experience was
irregular in occurrence and readily countered: 'the meanings of a particular form of life of a people, at a particular
time, seem to come from the whole of their common experience, and from its complicated general articulation' (Williams,
1968: 28). This statement does indeed seem epistemologically
idealist and romantically populist. It is as if undesirable
meanings and values (such as racism) do not arise, and as
if experience is not hierarchically stratified or never the site
of social conflict. But nothing is easier in critique than singling out a lazy sentence and claiming that it has a general
bearing on the whole *oeuvre*. Needless to say, it is hardly as
if this was Williams's last word on the question of experience. It is also important to stress the heuristic value of
Williams's attempt, from a relatively early stage, to conceive
of experience and culture in relation to an entire structure
of social and cultural organisation. 'The analysis of culture,'
he wrote, in a now famous formulation, 'is the attempt to
discover the nature of the organisation which is the complex' of relationships 'between elements in a whole way of
life' (1961: 63). In the early work this rested on a theoretically weak and idealised sense of social totality, but in general terms this way of conceiving of the task of cultural analysis
was useful, not least because of its insistence on thinking

relationally about cultural elements within a whole social process as a means for attempting to offset more selective and partial modes of representation and comprehension. The 'way of life' formulation was of course static and homogenising. Thompson's alternative emphasis on culture as a 'whole way of struggle' gave open recognition to the antagonisms of interests and values that are continually played out within culture. Williams's different early preoccupation with the existence of commonalities in cultural life, despite class difference and conflicts over whose interests, practices, meanings and values will prevail, meant that this was an emphasis he could not initially espouse. Thompson's reformulation of the so-called anthropological term for culture was therefore a salutary counter to the more holistic method of analysis in Williams, and yet retrospectively, given the ways in which it became conjoined with Gramsci's idea of cultural hegemony, Thompson's critique underplayed the analytic potential and directional force of Williams's concept of structure of feeling, not to mention the more materialist inflection later given to the kind of sociological analysis developed in Williams's *The Long Revolution*.

The charge that Williams in his early work subscribed to a notion of unmediated experience is in some ways valid (see, for example, Radhakrishnan, 1993: 286); he did speak, for instance, of being able to find, in the art-forms of a past period, 'a particular sense of life, a particular community of experience *hardly needing expression*' (Williams, 1961: 64; my emphasis). What is equally important to note, however, is that he did this in respect to a sense of 'difference': the sense of a past nexus of experience is gained precisely because it is different from any such sense available to us in our own time and place, and indeed each emergent structure of feeling is generated through a new generation's sense of difference in its whole life. It is then precisely this which requires expression (ibid: 65). All cultural history, regardless of its particular object of study, needs to attend to people's experience, for it is often through their experience that support for or challenges to the doxa are made. This does not mean that, as one of Williams's *New Left Review* interviewers put it, experience provides 'a kind of pristine contact between the subject and the reality in which this subject is immersed' (Williams, 1979: 167). In response, Williams was adamant in his refusal of the notion of any 'natural seeing': 'there cannot be a direct and unmediated contact with reality' (ibid). Yet he remained sceptical of the concept of mediation when it offers little more than a sophistication of reflection theory, with its dualisms of social reality and art, social process and language, base and superstructure.

The error of reflectionist theory is to assume that social reality can be 'read off' from a cultural text; the denial of this in idealist aesthetics simply swings to the opposite pole by removing cultural texts and practices from their determinate social and historical contexts. To see mediation as constitutive is to conceive it in a different sense, as not distinct from or not acting as (in Adorno's words) 'something between the object and that to which it is brought' (cited in Williams, 1977: 98). Cultural reproduction is then not simply a relay or complement of social production: 'The problem is different, from the beginning, if we see language and signification as indissoluble elements of the material social process itself, involved all the time both in production and reproduction' (ibid: 99). Giddens has put the same point more emphatically in saying that: 'There are no signifying practices. Signification should rather be understood as an integral element of social practices in general' (Giddens, 1979: 39). Social experience cannot be known outside of the variable expressive forms and interpretations in which its meanings are realised; it cannot be captured in any raw, unmediated state. On the other hand, the signification of experience does not occur in isolation from the social frames which enable experience to become manifest in its regularities and then in any departures from those regularities; without such constitutive frames experience reverts to an ontological convulsion. This can of course, at one extreme, lead to agency's sociologistic point of disappearance. Here again we confront the opposite dangers of metaphysical and reductionist approaches to experience.

Eagleton's indictment of Williams's deep-seated respect for 'common experience' was based on the line taken by Althusser, who collapsed all social experience into ideology, which he defined as an 'imaginary relationship of individuals to their real conditions of existence'. For Althusser, 'ideology has always-already interpellated individuals as subjects'; individual subjects can then only be envisioned as the unwitting bearers of ideological structures which pervade 'all human activity'. Ideology is 'identical with the "lived" experience of human existence itself' (Althusser, 1977: 160–4; 204–5; for one instance of Williams's opposition to this, see Williams, 1980: 241). This conceptualisation of ideology is incompatible with the active sense of both culture and experience, it constructs 'subjects' as incapable of learning from experience, and it cannot explain cultural change and conflict. Most of all, it polarises the moments of 'making' and 'being made', instead of seeing them as interdependent. We have arrived, as Williams put it, at 'the last stage of formalism' (1979: 172). For Eagleton at this time, to put any premium on cultural or historical experience was to be narrowly phenomenological and naively empiricist in approach, but this could only be squared with an assimilation of Gramsci's concept of hegemony in Williams's reaffiliation with Marxism, happening at precisely this time, by indicting Williams for placing the concept of hegemony on an experiential footing, and 'over-subjectivising' the social formation.

Both Williams and Thompson were interested in investigating the points at which resistances and challenges to cultural hegemony emerge, and in rediscovering instances of this in the radical democratic tradition in Britain, a tradition which runs counter to a conservative and reactionary line of cultural and social criticism. Williams's interrogation of this produced *Culture and Society* (1958), whereas Thompson's classic study of the formation of the English working class showed how that formation drew on the radical tradition of 'the free-born Englishman'. Williams and Thompson were concerned with popular experiences and practices which are not incorporated into effectively dominant institutions and values, with alternative cultural forms to those within an apparent 'hegemony' which constitute 'an ever present threat to official descriptions of reality' (Thompson, 1978: 164). They both refused to reduce lived everyday culture entirely to those dominant pressures and limits, or indeed to anything as mechanical and monolithic as Althusser's ideological state apparatuses. Although Thompson viewed hegemony as a useful concept, he did not regard it as referring to 'an all-embracing domination upon the ruled – or upon all those who are not intellectuals – reaching down to the very threshold of their experience, and implanting in their minds at birth categories of subordination which they are powerless to shed and which their experience is powerless to correct' (cited Palmer, 1981: 95). Similarly, it is in the light of Williams's insistence that 'no mode of production and therefore no dominant social order and therefore no dominant culture ever in reality includes or exhausts all human practice, human energy, and human intention' (1977: 125) that he stressed the importance of distinguishing, as we have seen, between alternative and oppositional, residual and emergent elements of culture. This is an important point in that experience is sometimes regarded as necessarily involved in nothing other than social and cultural reproduction, as for example is the case with Parsons's conception of socialisation as an integrating process in which dominant values are internalised through learning experiences.

Eagleton's criticism relies on the mistaken assumption, noted earlier, that experience is intrinsically individualistic, and elides the problems involved in attempting to be open to forms of life outside of the horizons of one's culture or historical generation. If hermeneutics is politically weak, its compensating strength lies in its opposition to dogmatism. This relies most of all in its willing towards the confrontation between interpretive horizons, for it is this confrontation which creates the possibility of thinking critically of time's traces and of our own temporal being at one and the same time, and of extending the reflexive monitoring of our own experience by contrasting it, culturally and ethically, with what others, in other periods and other cultures, have done with what they have taken from their own historically and culturally filtered experience. To do this is to contest the idea of any definitive horizon of cultural outlook or belonging, and it is this which may initiate the process of dogmatic corrosion. The critical question which then follows is whether such a conception of ethical and cultural reflexivity simply reproduces a humanist voluntarism.

As we have seen, the appeal to 'lived' experience may at times be taken to presuppose experience as a source of subjective knowing outside of existing ideology and culture, in the life as historically lived, so that where this source provides contradictory evidence to that otherwise available, in dominant or residual forms, political contestation and resistance appear to emerge spontaneously. Any approach which stresses the importance of experience will always be potentially inclined to the tendency to assign it too great a role in the organisation of knowledge, and to subjectivise the social. Yet as Fred Inglis has noted, Williams always 'sought to correct the over-individualising of social explanation in English-speaking thought, and to insist upon the inclusively social formation of lives and selves and histories' (1995: 50). Further, the tendency I have called experiential sentimentalism is not necessarily synonymous with normative voluntarism. In this quite distinct tendency, the conduct of agents becomes functionally determinist when taken to manifest an internalisation of the ideological structures which make for the continuities of social order. While the former conception of experience may exaggerate the capacity of individuals to promote community cohesion or to initiate a change of outlook, the latter undermines any attempt to explain transformations in social values and their institutional structures.

This is a central problem with Parsons's attempt to broach the question of 'how purposiveness or a diversity of wills is compatible with "order"'; what remains unaccounted for is the reflexive monitoring of conduct on the basis of an understanding of past experience and the circumstantial frameworks in which conduct takes shape (Giddens, 1979: 254). Although Parsons's action theory was based on a critique of nineteenth-century positivism in attempting to analyse the subjective dimension of social life, the privileged term (particularly in his later work) became system rather than subject, with an assumption of a harmonious integration between them (Swingewood, 1984: 254–9). Hence the parallels that have been drawn between Parsons's functionalism and Althusser's structuralist Marxism, the most important being that 'each reaches a position in which subject is controlled by object. Parsons's actors are cultural dopes, but Althusser's agents are structural dopes of even more stunning mediocrity' (Giddens, 1979: 52). As Barnett pointed out, the analytical force of Williams's concept of structure of feeling was to break with Leavis's metaphysical conception of experience as 'a single paradigmatic criterion of subjective judgement' and to restore the category of experience as socially located and historically contingent, its changing textures being understood as part of a 'mutable and various social history' (Barnett, 1976: 62). 'For all that is not fully articulated, all that comes through as disturbance, tension, blockage, emotional trouble seems to me precisely a source of major changes' in signification, discourse, culture and social practice (Williams, 1979: 168). Yet the force of it goes beyond this in its relations to emergence and resistance on a collective basis rather than in terms of voluntaristic individualism, so to see it as both addressing an inadequacy in available theories of ideology and as commensurate with the weak conceptual status of 'pattern' is not only to take away with one hand what is given with the other, but also peremptorily to dismiss the productive tensions of the project that lay behind it (Eagleton, 1976: 33–4).

For me at least, these tensions are consistent with a central dimension of cultural studies as a project, which as well as being concerned with the study of cultural production, distribution, consumption and exchange, and the analysis of cultural texts and practices, explores 'lived' experience in everyday cultures. This involves examining how such experiences in everyday life are woven into webs of meaning and significance, and how ideological meanings are woven into experiential encounters and understandings. This two-way analysis involves coming to terms not only with how people connect their social experience to cultural and political representations, but also with how that experience is mediated by representations which become integrated into the meanings that attain legitimate currency in everyday life. Attention to cultural self-making and the experience of culture must also be concerned with the ideological structures in which cultural creativities operate and which they have to negotiate, with how, in other words, we are able 'to understand the texture of hegemony/subalternity, the interlacing of resistance and submission, opposition and complicity' (Martin-Barbero, 1988: 462). In cultural analysis, this simultaneously moves away from conceptions of 'mass culture' passivity and a simplistic 'dominant ideology' thesis, although as we have seen, certain media theorists such as Fiske have taken the move to the point where media audiences and popular consumers are assumed to resist and subvert the encodings of dominant meanings and values as a matter of daily cultural routine. If any theoretical approach to popular culture deserves the term 'voluntarism', it is Fiske's. The problem with this approach is that it swings over to the opposite pole from the positions taken by cultural critics like Adorno and Horkheimer, Schiller and Mattelart. It replicates Adorno's ideas about mass culture in voluntarist reverse, and it threatens to induce a 'complacent relativism, by which the interpretive contribution of the audience is perceived to be of such a scale and range as to render the very idea of media power naive' (Corner, 1991: 281). Ultimately, Fiske's idealisation of consumer resistances colludes with the marginalisation and exclusion of certain cultural identities and 'voices'. The idea of 'semiotic democracy' does not make much sense to those whose social experience is systematically misrepresented by legitimated institutions, whose characteristic cultural forms and practices are neglected by mainstream media, or whose voices are relegated to the ghettoes of minority programming. Media texts are polysemic, but at the same time structured by power and difference; the activeness of cultural consumption is not equivalent to the power of cultural production in contemporary capitalism. The representation of social experience and the social experience of representation only make sense as distinguishable processes in the light of this structural asymmetry.

Questions concerning the cultural relations of domination and subordination have always been central to the idea of 'history from below'. Such history seeks to recover the experiences of subordinate social groups in the context of these relations. Yet in Edward Thompson's seminal contribution to this approach in English history, his use of the concept of experience is inconsistent and unbalanced. The particular emphasis is evident enough: 'experience' forms the junction between social being and consciousness, and it is taken most of all in its active sense as the means by which 'structure is transmuted into process, and the subject re-enters into history' (Thompson, 1978: 362). Yet what is not

clear is where experience is specifically located, for his analytical use of 'experience' slides in its reference between
conditions, consciousness and the 'lived' itself (Hall, 1980a:
63), and it is then difficult to see how it performs the mediating role he assigns to it. Further, the radical historicality
of the way he conceives of experience drains any consideration of its structured and determined qualities of explanatory power, except of course in terms of the productive
relations that mark his residual adherence to a classically
Marxist model of causation. Thompson used the category
of experience as a means of polemically countering his theoretical and methodological bogies – rigid economism, economic historicism, structural-functionalist sociology, structuralist
philosophy and the rest – without giving it any satisfactory
theoretical grounding in itself. Indeed, given its centrality
in 'culturalism', the lack of any sustained attention to the
concept of experience was a definite weakness, as numerous critics have pointed out.

Yet it is important to stress that the 'culturalist' stress on
experience, agency and consciousness was not made in opposition to theory, as it has sometimes been taken, nor did
it stem from an unwillingness to deal in abstractions. There
is an obvious need for abstract concepts and systematic theoretical formulations as ways of understanding the many complex, wide-ranging, increasingly global structures and relations
in the contemporary world, and it is clear that 'culturalism'
goes with this and is not empiricism under another name.
The resistance was rather to the aggrandisement of science
above all other forms of observation and enquiry, along with
the mythologising of scientific method; to the methodological habit of squeezing human life into boxes, tables, charts
and diagrams, or what in statistical analysis might be called
painting society by numbers; and to the preening elaboration of abstract 'theoretical practice', to upper-case Theory
as a self-sustaining, smoothly interlocking, highly schematised
intellectual apparatus which need not be troubled by application to specific, concrete cases. The intention was at the
least to register a need for wariness in the use of abstract,
reificatory concepts, and to question the claim that theory-
building is superior to historical enquiry and knowledge.

Thompson's strictures on the constraints of available factual evidence should be readily familiar to anyone who has tried to produce a concrete historical account. He did not of course conceive of such evidence as raw or unmediated; it often carries with it a particular ideological freight, and it is this which historians must interrogate even as they try to 'get the facts straight', as the saying unproblematically has it. Historical evidence is often of such complexity in what it apparently does and does not say that, as historians, we need to be as mindful of the risk of reducing its interpretation to a horizonally bound theoretical perspective as of the dangers of allowing our imagination free rein. This point is quite compatible with recognising the importance of concepts as critical tools and imagination as an interpretive resource in the face of the supple, fluid contours of past experience and action. I would agree that Thompson did not adequately theorise the interaction of concepts and historical evidence, but this error is in my view relatively minor when placed against the enormous condescension of its opposite in the thoroughgoing epistemological relativism of Hindess and Hirst, who denied any validity to historical knowledge by claiming it to be entirely dependent on the given theoretical paradigm which permits it. For them, the study of history is, in a breathtaking assertion, 'not only scientifically but also politically valueless' (1975: 312).

For Thompson, experience was the stuff of history. Through time's traces we can reconstruct that experience, though this always involves an element of 'understanding otherwise' because of the distance and difference intrinsic to history's successively receding horizons. The turn to ordinariness here involved attention to the underprivileged, to mundane experience and popular cultural forms and practices. Thompson's study of the emergence and development of the English working class, the crystallisation of its class consciousness out of a specifically working-class structure of feeling, was in many ways concordant with Williams's expansion of the range of what 'culture' could be held to cover, including what he called 'the basic collective idea' in working-class culture, and 'the institutions, manners, habits of thought, and intentions which proceed from this' (1958: 313). The appeal of this attention to the cultural values and meanings, beliefs and institutions of 'ordinary' people was its basic anti-elitism, its hostility to Stalinist 'iron laws', its suspicion of Fabian social engineering, and its opposition to the orthodoxies of economic history ('steam power plus the factory system equals the working class'). There is also, as for Williams, the connection to be made with Dilthey's recognition of 'experience as feeling' and thus of the affectivity of knowledge as people 'handle' such experience culturally through obligations and reciprocities, desires and aspirations, value-systems and beliefs, and 'through more elaborated forms, within art or religious beliefs' (Thompson, 1978: 363). It is this process which grounds the possibility of ethical evaluation and critique, and it is in the end facile to use the straw target of humanism as a means of dismissing the effort to chart its occurrence in historical cases. The objectivist appeal to (material) interests is not to be counterposed to a subjectivist appeal to (idealist) values: 'every contradiction is a conflict of value as well as a conflict of interest' (ibid). This is powerfully borne out in Thompson's extrapolation of the value of historical practice in *Whigs and Hunters* (1977b). In dealing with the infamous Black Act of 1723, he shows that it cannot be adequately explained in the reductive terms of a tightly determining economic base, for while the law in this case was set up as an instrument in defence of the property rights of the ruling class, to see it solely in these terms is an example of one-dimensional Marxism. As Thompson put it:

> The essential precondition for the effectiveness of law, in its function as ideology, is that it shall display an independence from gross manipulation and shall seem to be just. It cannot seem to be so without upholding its own logic and criteria of equity; indeed, on occasion, by actually *being* just (1977b: 263).

Thus the constitution of the law cannot be conceived simply and solely as a reflection of the economic interests of a dominant class, for otherwise it would have no hegemonic efficacy. This has been achieved historically by embodying certain universal principles of equality of treatment, and these are values which can at times be used to contest the partial and unjust exercise of the rule of law. 'The law may be rhetoric, but it need not be empty rhetoric. Blackstone's

Commentaries represent an intellectual exercise far more rigorous than could have come from an apologist's pen' (ibid).

Duality of Structure

The attempt to understand political and ethical considerations in terms of each other is not equivalent to moralism, as Anderson has supposed. Rather it is one of the strengths of Thompson's work that he did not dissociate the socialist tradition from questions of moral economy, social justice and ethical conduct, for such questions historically have been a debilitating blind-spot of Marxism, particularly in its more 'scientific' modes. A more difficult point is whether his concern for values, and the choices and meanings they imply, led Thompson to underplay the structural determinants of experience. It is difficult because he vacillated, even in the same text, as is evident for instance in comparing his statement that 'experience is valid and effective but within determined limits' with the later claim that for 'any living generation, in any "now", the ways in which they "handle" experience defies prediction and escapes from any narrow definition of determination' (1978: 199 and 363). Where I think Thompson's attempt to realign Marxism with the Romantic critique of industrial capitalism that is part of the English historical experience foundered theoretically was on the insistence of his separation of experience and structure. This is a key point in Anderson's (1980) critical re-evaluation of Thompson's work. As we have noted, Thompson's emphasis was on the active process of cultural self-making in the formation of the English working class: 'The working class did not rise like the sun at an appointed time. It was present at its own making' (1968b: 9). Although he argued that this involved a dialectic of experience and social being, not only are the terms themselves under-conceptualised, but also the ways in which social being and experience interact dialectically in the historical process are under-analysed. In theoretical terms, this reveals the major weakness of the 'culturalist' perspective. In Thompson's epic study, the weakness is manifest as an insufficient attention to the 'being-made' of classes, or to that which in contingent circumstances prevents practice from being 'mastered'. In

Giddens's words: 'The spectrum of conditions which actually led to the formation of the English working class are
collapsed into an opposition between protest and resistance
largely internal to the ideas and behaviour of the members
of the working class themselves' (1987: 212). Yet in advancing this same point, Anderson fell back on an economistic
definition of class formation: 'It is, and must be, the dominant *mode of production* that confers fundamental unity on a
social formation, allocating their objective positions to the
classes within it, and distributing the agents within each class'
(1980: 55). It was precisely the functionalist undertones (not
to mention condescension) of this kind of analytical position which Thompson sought to redress in his emphasis on
experience and agency in the historical process, though ironi-
cally it was his profound mistrust and relative neglect of
structural factors which weakened the force of his efforts at
doing so.

Beyond this there remains the problem of historical outcome, for as already noted in relation to the example of
Archduke Ferdinand's assassination, this is not necessarily
willed, intended or anticipated by social agents, and not only
as a result of their actions being uncoordinated or failing
to operate in concert. Thompson's acknowledgment of history as 'the record of unintended consequences' therefore
has important implications for the category of agency, which
is of course central to all his writings. Such acknowledgement means that conscious human agency is limited by historical eventuation and outcome occurring as processes
'behind the backs' of social agents, which should have in
some ways qualified Thompson's sense of the centrality of
agency in history (Benton, 1984: 212; cf. Trimberger, 1984:
225). In response to the at times vague and muddled conceptual use of the term 'agency' by Thompson, Anderson
defines it in a rather utilitarian manner as 'conscious, goal-
directed activity'. He then goes on to discriminate between
different goals, ranging all the way from mundane aims to
revolutionary praxis, and this lends weight to his charge that
Thompson's use of the term 'experience' is analytically variable. There is a sense in which such variability occurs sensitively in response to its manifold historical and cultural
qualities, but the limitations for Thompson's historical analysis

of his inadequate conceptual elaboration of the term is the point where criticism cuts in. This is particularly so in regard to the relations of experience and agency. As we have seen, Dilthey's formulation of *Erlebnis* refers both to the subjective involvement and outlook of individuals who live through a variety of historically determinate situations, circumstances and events, and to what is actively and reflexively taken up from such participation as a guidance for future action. Giddens quite properly remarks that the 'first does not necessarily imply the second', and that 'Thompson's appeals to the significance of agency in history tend to assimilate them'. This then blurs the distinction between what is valid or useful experience and what is not, along with the historiographical problem of understanding how the distinction has applied in the lives of historical participants (Giddens, 1987: 211). But the far more stubborn problem is that of 'developing a standpoint able adequately to encompass both action and structural constraint', and 'a means of examining the intersection of the objective and subjective' (ibid: 213–15).

This has long been an abiding problem for the social sciences. In the confrontations between Thompson and Anderson, it is manifest in reverse emphases on one side of the equation at the expense of the other. These are similarly present in the antipathy of Thompson's position to Althusser's, so that an anti-structuralist antagonism connects with Thompson's failure to deal adequately with objective determinants, and an anti-humanist antagonism results in Althusser's failure to deal adequately with experience and agency. This way of isolating in stripped-down, abstract terms the theoretical oppositions at play gives little sense of why I have, in the past, generally found Thompson's writings so inspiring and Althusser's so enervating. The basic line of argument at issue, though, is not only that the position staked out by Althusser was debilitating for historical and cultural analysis and for the role which I believe the category of experience should perform within such analysis. It is also that, while Thompson's obstinate refusal to nod passively at sociological platitudes about 'social forces' has considerable justification in that these are 'always nothing more and nothing less than mixes of intended and unintended consequences of action in specifiable contexts' (Giddens, 1986: 220), his case for experience and agency as central units of analysis was undermined by diametrically opposing them to *La Structure*, to use his typically derisive term of reference.

Yet the alternatives that have subsequently been advanced, and which add further twists to the 'linguistic turn', are hardly preferable. For this reason I have been arguing that historical and cultural analysis needs to overcome the type of semiotic reductionism identified in Easthope's recipe for cultural studies. This kind of approach offers only a limited conception of the dynamic contextuality of social experience and agency. Yet, in the end, the earlier points of emphasis on bottom-up perspectives, on the ordinariness of cultural process, and on specificity and contingency, have proved insufficient for dealing with experience as a structured process. While experience will always require a heterodox set of concepts from which those appropriate to its empirical cases will need to be selected, I have suggested that this insufficiency derives primarily from the dualistic opposition of agency and structure. Giddens's emphasis on the duality of structure is designed to overcome such opposition by treating agency and structural constraints as integrally bound up in each other. Giddens conceives of structure as the medium of agency and agency as the medium of structure. Structures provide 'rules and resources implicated in the "forms" of collectivities of social systems, reproduced across space and time', while at the same time agency operates as the means by which individuals routinely reproduce such structures in the course of their everyday activities (1987: 220–1). It is this which gives social life its recursive quality. Agency occurs in relation to it through the reflexive monitoring and appropriation of *Erlebnis* and for this reason can be defined as 'the capability of acting otherwise' (ibid: 216).[6] Giddens's theory of structuration preserves Thompson's emphasis on knowledgeable and reflexive agents and avoids 'an imperialism of the social object', while at the same time overcoming the equation of structure with constraint: 'it is of the first importance to recognise that circumstances of social constraint in which individuals "have no choice" are not to be equated with the dissolution of action as such'

(1986: 2 and 15). Structure is then both constraining and enabling, and it is this which characterises its duality. Conceived in this manner, the term avoids not only the false opposition of hermeneutic voluntarism and sociological objectivism, but also the analytical inadequacies of the ways in which each of them treats the category of experience.[7]

Labouring to Learn

If strategic conduct is taken in this way as a chronic feature of the *durée* of everyday life whereby agents draw upon structural properties in the constitution of social relations, this still leaves open the question of how these relations may change or how new ways of understanding them may emerge. How, in other words, does a reconfigured experience of 'experience' develop in such a way that structural properties are not only produced and reproduced but also transformed? How, in short, does the 'otherwise' of 'the capability of acting otherwise' occur? This question, for it is the same in each formulation, is also pertinent to the study of postwar youth subcultures in British cultural studies.

Subcultures are by definition 'below' certain cultural formations whose institutionalised practices they at least threaten to subvert; for this reason they have long been associated in the sociological literature with deviance. As David Chaney reminds us, youth subcultural analysis of this period should be understood not only in relation to the characteristic interest of early cultural studies and post-1950s social history in social minorities and margins, which I have already emphasised, but also in relation to the broader context of work on the sociology of crime and 'delinquency'; on 'labelling' theory, deviancy amplification and the media creation of moral panics; and on the movements associated with Black Power, peace, and 1960s counter-culture. This work in turn provided a 'receptive intellectual climate' for the early studies of Foucault and the 'discovery' of Bakhtin (Chaney, 1994: 36–40). These are important connections, but the specific focus of studies of British youth subcultures in the 1970s was on the relations between deviant and transitory spectacular cultural forms and white, male working-class experience, concentrating partly on generational specificities and

partly on the use of expressive resources and practices derived from a subordinated working-class 'parent' culture. The
conceptual linkages made between experience and culture
in these studies are consistent enough with those so far traced.
The term 'culture' designates the ways in which social groups
'give *expressive form*' to their life-experience and collective
'way of life'; it consists of the particular 'forms in which
groups "handle" the raw material of their social and material existence', with this 'material' never being wholly of its
own making (Hall and Jefferson, 1977: 10).

What is especially interesting is the way this distinctively
'culturalist' approach was amalgamated with a more structural definition: 'Culture is the way the social relations of a
group are structured and shaped: but it is also the way those
shapes are experienced, understood and interpreted' (ibid:
10–11). It is notable that this attempt to forge a workable
connection between Hall's two paradigms is not subsequently
mentioned or developed by Hall. As already suggested, the
omission is explicable in terms of Hall's 'hidden agenda' in
that stage-setting piece, which was to evacuate the category
of experience from the conceptual repertory of cultural
studies. This also explains the lack of attention paid in his
'mapping of the terrain' of cultural studies, as also in similar
interventions by Richard Johnson, to the work of their
colleague Paul Willis. For among the practitioners of cultural
studies in the late 1970s, it was Willis who, above all,
represented a counter-current to the forceful drift towards
structuralism, not through the sort of outright opposition
to structural concepts taken by Thompson, but rather through
his attempt to embody in practice the double hermeneutic
of sociological enquiry by measuring such concepts against
the irreducible *livedness* of subcultural experience (McGuigan,
1992: 98). The point of this was not to use an ethnography
of experience as 'the authenticating test of cultural analysis', but instead to explore the methodological possibility of
'being surprised' by the ethnographic evidence, and so moving
to 'knowledge not prefigured in one's starting paradigm'
(Hall, 1989: 62; Willis, 1980: 90).

I want now to finish this chapter with a brief consideration of Willis's work at this time, firstly because, as Giddens
has shown, it is very much commensurate with his theory of

structuration, and secondly, because it does not fall neatly
into the two paradigm divide identified by Johnson and Hall
between culturalism and structuralism, which is perhaps
another reason why it does not figure on their cultural studies
map.[8] In what is nevertheless a renowned cultural studies
text, Paul Willis's *Learning to Labour* (1979) explored the
patterns of behaviour and forms of everyday language used
within a particular social and cultural context, showing how
the large-scale, abstract processes that shape contemporary
capitalist society are contingently manifest and lived through
in localised life-histories. The book shows how the social
experiences of his subjects – a group of twelve working-class
'lads' in a West Midlands English town – were handled in
cultural terms, given concrete shape and response in the
forms and resources available to them within their everyday
milieu. These generated acute insights into the rationale of
education, conformity and authority, yet it was precisely their
resistance to the imperatives of academic attainment which
then locked them into their disadvantaged class position,
and produced a subjective affirmation of manual labour.
Among other things, this shows the limitations of resistance
when it is lodged predominantly within the existing symbolic and explanatory terms of immediate social experience,
for these then entailed, in Dilthey's term, the tragedy of
their finitude. Their culturally mediated impulses produced
a counter-school mentality in what was a creative response
to the collision between their social experience, member-
ship and expectations on the one hand, and received
legitimations of the value of intellectual learning, deferred
gratifications and academic qualifications on the other. Yet
the unintended consequences of their resistance as it was
lived out were a distortion and displacement of their basic
insights and a reproduction of existing relations of production, as well as specifically working-class versions of sexism,
racism and homophobia. The creative impulses did not generate a structure of feeling in the sense conceptually outlined in Chapter 2 because they did not move significantly
beyond inherited forms of experiential understanding in the
parent working-class culture. Their subcultural insights did
not become transformative, were not converted into praxis
because – and this was the central paradox – the sense of

superiority and independence they provided remained rooted
in the affirmative meanings and values of the working-class
experience.

Learning to Labour was a sobering corrective to socialist
aspirations for the historically necessary political potential
of working-class consciousness. It was also an attempt to break
with other, more pessimistic accounts. Willis's study of the
relations between schooling, creative resistance and the structural demands of the labour market provided an alternative
to mechanistic explanations of schooling and the reproduction of class inequalities in terms of the inculcation of passive working-class youth, to lofty claims that the educational
system functions simply as an arm of state control, and to
fatalistic generalisations about ideological power. His alternative proposed a reverse emphasis giving due place to the
cultural field within which popular experience is articulated,
to the agency which is involved in economic and cultural
reproduction, and to the ways in which social structure is
contingently realised in the institutional frameworks of everyday social interaction. In Willis's account, social and cultural reproduction operates not only through the educational
transmission of dominant cultural values, but also, in what
is a tragic irony of self-damnation, through the cultural practices and subjectivities of working-class youth themselves in
their responses to the contradictions which they encounter
in their own experience. Conceptions of the social world
are produced within particular subordinate groups in the
course of their everyday lives, and it is their production on
the familiar ground of mundane experience which makes
for their effective internalisation. Willis's analysis of the effects of the double articulation of freedom and inequality
in counter-school culture was a decisive step beyond crudely
determinist accounts of social and cultural reproduction. It
was an important development in another way too. The
everyday culture of subordinate groups was not regarded as
a refractory obstacle to a discussion of social determination
but rather as the very ground upon which such discussion
must proceed. In Willis's text the theorised treatment of
questions concerning determination and reproduction is
wedded to an ethnographic presentation of what the 'lads'
have to say about their experience and their responses to

that experience. This then points up the limitations of macrosystems analysis. As Marcus and Fischer put it: 'Ethnography is thus the sensitive register of change at the level of experience, and it is this kind of understanding that seems critical when the concepts of systems perspectives are descriptively out of joint with the reality to which they are meant to refer' (Marcus and Fischer, 1986: 82). To go back to Willis's own words:

> The ethnographic account, for all its faults, records a crucial level of experience and through its very biases insists upon a level of human agency which is persistently overlooked or denied but which increases in importance all the time for other levels of the social whole. Although the world is never directly 'knowable', and cannot empirically present itself in the way that the ethnographic account seems sometimes to suggest, it must nevertheless be specifically registered somewhere in theory if theory pretends to any relevance at all (Willis, 1979: 194).

This is a crucial point. As we have seen, there are of course dangers in celebrating profane creativity in lived cultures. Among these, the tendency to romanticise instances of rebellion or challenge suggests, when it occurs, a projection of the researcher's desires or values on to those who are studied, and at times relies on a grossly generalised mode of description to underscore the contestation of institutional forms, as for example in this example from Willis:

> The piratical, often outrageous air of the bikeboys lives off, finds its meaning and clumsy grace from the ludicrous orderedness of the rest of us. They show just how easy it is to be a pirate when the rest of us wear grey. Our incorporated, bureaucratic, mindless existence is the air through which the motor-bike exhaust tears and crackles (Willis, 1978: 175).

The blanket reference to 'the rest of us' is in itself too easy a move, and we may ask whose existence is covered here, in this grandly dismissive sweep of the analytical hand. The question concerns not only the obvious absurdity of painting everyone apart from the spectacularly vivid bikeboys in monotonal grey, but also where Willis himself is placed in

this curious inversion of the 'them' in 'us' definition of ideology which he offers elsewhere (Willis, 1979: 169). The
ethnographic attention to small, telling detail can have a
reverse side in such rhetoric, and we might note two features of it in particular. On the one hand, the process of
identification encouraged in this kind of passage provides
implicit vindication of aggressive forms of masculinity, in so
far as they are sympathetically examined at the expense of
female and ethnic subcultures, and in so far as they limit
the attention paid to sexism, to racism, to other forms of
inequality and discrimination outside of class, and to the
ideological buttresses of the division of labour. On the other
hand, subcultural celebration over-radicalises transitory instances of style-revolt and does not balance its detailed analysis
of symbolic forms of contestation with analysis of their limits, as the 'grey orderedness' of organised power continues
unabated. (For more on such points, see McRobbie and
Garber, 1976; McRobbie, 1980; Gilroy, 1987: 12–13; Skeggs,
1992: 186–8.)

Despite such dangers in the analysis, the point is that
resistance, however mediated by custom, ritual or style, is
concretely there in the equation of culture and ideology.
The importance of this is twofold. Firstly, it shows that social and cultural reproduction do not inevitably require the
unwitting collusion of structurally subordinate groups. For
this reason, Willis rejected Althusser's structuralist account
of ideology and social reproduction, in which people are
only passively implicated, or rather 'interpellated' as subjects. Willis's study suggested a contrary account in revealing 'deep disjunctions and desperate tensions within social
and cultural reproduction'. As he put it: 'Social agents are
not passive bearers of ideology, but active appropriators who
reproduce existing structures only through struggle, contestation and a partial penetration of those structures' (Willis,
1979: 175). This supports the point made in Chapter 2 on
commonsense argumentation and ideology, and what is most
at issue in the interaction of existing structures and cultural process is 'the degree to which those at the centre
can appropriate for mere production the novel creations of
those on the margins versus the degree to which those si-
lenced on the margins can gain a voice at the centre in the

conduct of their own lives' (Shotter, 1992: 20). Secondly, a
particular social formation cannot be described and analysed only in terms of its structural features; what characterises it just as significantly are forms of 'contested settlement',
the always uneasy equilibrium between accommodation and
resistance. The contingent and mutable ground of that equilibrium is social and historical experience.

Yet we cannot simply leave it there. A key thread in my
argument has been that while the everyday world and the
dynamics of experience within it should be a central feature of both social history and cultural studies, these resources of enquiry cannot be taken as the complete basis
for any sociology or historiography for the demonstrable
reason that the lives of women and men are influenced by
factors and forces originating outside the everyday world in
which they are situated. This was a relevant consideration
for subcultural analyis in the 1970s: 'Subcultural strategies
cannot match, meet or answer the structuring dimensions
in this period for the class as a whole' (Hall and Jefferson,
1976: 47). In taking experience as a category for focusing
the historicality of the webs of meaning and significance in
which human lives are woven, we need always to bring into
account the imposed conditioning phenomena which are
beyond people's immediate control. If we then follow through
the implications of this, experience also becomes a category
for acknowledging the discontinuities between the researcher
and the researched, given that these 'constitute the initial
directedness of our whole ability to experience'. Dorothy
Smith has observed that through such concepts as class,
modernisation and so on a 'realm of theoretically constituted objects is created, freeing the discursive realm from
its ground in the lives and work of actual individuals and
liberating sociological inquiry to graze on the field of conceptual entities' (1979: 174; 1987: 130). It does not necessarily follow from this important comment that we can then
dispense with conceptual frameworks in favour of lifeworlds
themselves as the starting-points of social research, since we
shall of necessity always begin, in that way, with certain modes
of conceptualising experience in everyday life, and, as already suggested, it is better to elaborate these rather than
leave them implicit and unexamined. It is at the point of

interaction between concepts and evidence that the really critical questions apply, and it is at this point that the effectiveness of any conceptual tool is to be gauged by the way it is able to further the aim of cultural analysis in developing a contextualised understanding that takes into account the vocabularies of experience in the everyday world and at the same time loosens the hold of their tenacious usualness.

In the light of this we can say that there is every need in the world to realise and, on occasion, re-view the confines of our lived experience, and in practice we each of us do this to varying degrees at certain moments in our lives as we live them. But we can only do this satisfactorily when we have closely observed what it is we know to go beyond, and where it is that the shortfalls and deficiencies may lie, in what is allowed, presupposed or unelaborated within the usual frames in which our actions acquire meaning. Similarly, where we have set ourselves the task of representing the cultural and historical experience of a particular class, community or social category, we must develop ways of understanding that experience outside of its own declared or expressed terms, in different terms which enable us to get an analytical purchase on it from a different angle to the one preferred in the 'lived' point of view. But again we shall never accomplish satisfactory ethnography or history if we do not believe that those terms in themselves, in their own right and on their own home ground, should command our closest attention. 'Theories must be judged ultimately for the adequacy they display to the understanding of the phenomenon they purport to explain – not to themselves' (Willis, 1979: 194). When experience becomes an outlawed term, what is 'ordinary' in culture confronts once again the gates of paradigm-land, and analysis stands to lose what must be central to its rationale, which is turning the ordinary inside out so that we can see more clearly how it has attained its institutionalised and entrenched familiarities.

Notes

1 See in particular Johnson, 1978, 1979 a and b; and Hall 1980a and 1981. Eagleton's attack on Williams was first published in

1976 as 'Criticism and Politics: The Work of Raymond Williams', *New Left Review*, 95, Jan–Feb.

2 See Stedman Jones, 1983; Joyce, 1991; Scott, 1988; Elton, 1991; and Jenkins, 1991.

3 The distinction between 'emic' and 'etic' analyses derives from that in linguistics between phon*emics* and phon*etics*. Phonemics is concerned with the sounds selected and deployed in distinct languages, which are thus language-specific, while phonetics classifies sounds in terms of the broad acoustic range of which the human voice is capable. In cognitive anthropology, 'emic' and 'etic' have been used to refer to those forms and categories which are internal to a culture, as opposed to those which are allegedly universal. 'Etic terms were to provide the grid-language for objective cross-cultural comparison. The epistemological critique of this distinction showed the invalidity of the notion of purely etic categories that somehow stand completely outside any culture-bound context' (Marcus and Fischer, 1986: 180). Once relativised, the categories are better understood in terms of Geertz's distinction between experience-near and experience-far concepts (Geertz, 1993: 57–8).

4 This formula of Dilthey's is cited in Gadamer, 1979: 124, which unfortunately I came on too late to incorporate into my argument. It should however be clear that it relates directly to the need to grapple with what Edward Thompson called 'the crucial ambivalence of our human presence in our own history, part subjects, part objects, the voluntary agents of our involuntary determination' (1978: 280; cf. Thompson, 1957: 122 for an earlier formulation of this point and evidence of the continuity in his work).

5 See Inglis, 1995: 249–52 for more on Eagleton's attack. For Eagleton's subsequent reappraisal of Williams, see particularly the introduction to the collection of essays on or related to his work, which Eagleton edited (1989).

6 Giddens remarks elsewhere (1983: 63) that 'an agent who has no options whatsoever is no longer an agent'.

7 See also, in particular, Giddens, 1979, and 1986 chapter 1, for further elaboration of his theory of structuration.

8 Giddens shows how Willis's work of the late 1970s 'conforms closely to the main empirical implications of structuration theory'. He offers a more detailed treatment of Willis than I am able to give here (see 1986: 288–304).

Chapter 7

Against the Repudiation of Experience

I do not believe that language is the first cause, and I see nothing wrong in asserting that meaning derives from something we might call experience, as well as from immediate context.

(Deborah Cameron)

The Framing of Experience

From the poststructuralist viewpoint, experience is the bridge which only asses cross. It is a bridge which is regarded as far too rickety to be worthy of repair. The conceptual use of experience is criticised in particular for presupposing a mode of being which exists prior to its expression in words or images.[1] Linguistic or visual expression is then the product and transmission of what emerges out of experience, which is taken up uncritically because of the authority vested in it by its qualities of being concrete, immediate and lived. From this perspective, there are at least two serious faults with this use of experience, in social history or cultural ethnography. These are, firstly, that without critical attention to the linguistic and discursive terms in which experience has been cast, it reproduces the ways in which subordinate groups and their experiences in society and history have been rendered subordinate in the first place; and secondly, that it plays an academic game conventional in the human sciences of substituting new evidence for old without interrogating the epistemological basis of its referentiality as evidence. Poststructuralism takes the alternative position that social experience and subjectivity are constructed by categories of differentiation, such as those of class, gender, race and sexual orientation, and that the practices of representation associated with these categories of discourse operate in the interests of existing structures of power by assigning, fixing and naturalising various subordinate 'types' and identities.

The take-up of this position in recent approaches to historical and cultural analysis entails a rejection of the experiences of socially 'invisible' or relatively powerless groups as a grounding for analysis and as a source of interpretive guidance, for the more or less explicit reason that they have already been ineluctably shaped into a negative Otherness. Their experience, in other words, has been so deeply structured by categories of differentiation, which assign people into given subject-positions through the discursive practices of ascribing immutable characteristics of body, intellect and identity to them, that the attempt to make it culturally and historically visible inevitably reproduces the terms used in the ideological construction of its difference. The rejection of the experience of such groups on these terms appears then to have little to offer their need for social recognition, and little to contribute to their struggle culturally to develop a more positive sense of identity, or politically to challenge the social inequalities by which their own scope for experience is materially delimited. Indeed, its implications go further in calling into question the attempt to recover the subjective experience of those who have been 'hidden by history' as it has been written, to write out from or examine the experience of those at the social margins, or to develop an understanding of the symbolic strategies of resistance to the experience of exploitation and oppression. Such ventures may be acknowledged for their effort to draw on alternative material or to enlarge what is enacted on the historical stage, but the use of such experience as resource or evidence is compromised *ab initio* by that which has constituted it as *different.*

In the study of cultures past and present, interrogation of the ways in which certain forms of experience have been assigned certain meanings as a result of the discursive frames in which they have been placed is a vital step to take. Indeed, it is axiomatic that any serious analytical use of forms of experience should engage in such interrogation, that it should refuse to take on trust the accounts that are given of experience even as it takes such experience as its object of study. It is only when we do this that we can begin to see whether and to what extent experience has been constructed in ways which attest to the values, interests and desires of those who wield and deploy the orthodox discourses of power/ knowledge in history and society. While accepting these points, what I am concerned with here is a particular representation of how an analytical interest in experience is taken *ipso facto* as evidence of precisely such a naive taking on trust of the self-produced accounts of what has been experientially 'lived through' by the marginal or oppressed, or of the expressive forms and performances which 'press out' certain meanings from what is thus 'lived' through. It should by now be clear that certain versions of the idea of expressive form in relation to *Erlebnis* can indeed fall prey to forms of voluntarism, essentialism and functionalism. Quite different is the application of this striving to wrest the meaning out of experience, to make it signify and *have* significance, as a way of enhancing some sense of, some realised connection back to the ontological grounding of experience, even though this can only be fully achieved in language and discourse, in expressive form. This is not, I should add, an attempt to return to a conception of ontology as fixed, frozen or absolute, but rather to recognise it as always contingent, always in process and movement, and in that way connected to the historically located, historically knowing subject. In this sense, then, it is integrally bound up with social and historical process. In conceiving of it thus, I am concerned with the theoretical position against which it is opposed, which can be variously described but which usually amounts to a one-sided constructivism that reifies language and cannot satisfactorily handle the question of emergence, and thus of transformation and change.

Within its representation, naivity and gullibility is what much social history and 'culturalism' are desperately guilty of. As such, it is alleged that the work which is done under these titles remains within the epistemological frame of orthodox historiography or dominant ideological constructs, and so tacitly at least accedes to them. This is largely the representation constructed by Joan Scott, who indicts those in social history, feminism and cultural studies who use 'experience' as an analytical category.[2] Scott's position is that any attempt to grasp experience without closely attending to language is an illusion founded on the conception of experience as a self-authenticating truth. The way out of this illusion is to identify the privileged terms and categories by which experience is given identity, to reveal and subvert the hierarchy upon which such terms and categories are dependent, and then to displace them from their assumption of superiority. Scott's approach is to draw attention to the ways in which the subject within experience is produced by particular and contingent discursive strategies which assign the subject and her experience to positions of subordination, and attempt to make those positions and the values inscribed in them appear absolute and inevitable. This is consistent with other forms of ideological analysis in that Scott wishes to demystify these categories of differentiation by showing the radical oppositions upon which they are predicated.

The importance of this has already been acknowledged, and I would certainly agree with Scott that historians should, in Spivak's words, 'make visible the assignment of subject-positions' (Spivak, 1987: 241). As part of any historical or sociological enquiry into the constitution of social groups, we should try, as Scott puts it, to 'understand the operations of the complex and changing discursive processes by which identities are ascribed, resisted, or embraced' (Scott, 1991: 792). Attending analytically to symbolic forms of differentiation is valuable in revealing how alterity is contructed through various discursive oppositions and antagonisms, and in showing how, as Laura Lee Downs puts it, the 'truth' of dominant subject-positions 'has purchased its inner coherence at the cost of suppressing the heterogeneous voices of history's many others' (1993a: 419). What has also to be insisted upon is the importance of listening attentively to those voices, in whatever ways it is possible to 'recover' them, not because they themselves are more true than dominant subject-positions, but because they have the right to be heard,

and heard where possible in their own words. More significantly, we need to listen to such voices because they sometimes speak against the grain of subject-positions assigned
from 'outside', because they are then in some way resistant
to the dominant definition of those subject-positions, and
strain against the power-lines than run through identity and
experience.

It should be clear that what is then taken from such voices
is not the same as sentimentally taking on trust what they
say. Simply replicating what they say and relaying them in
that way is a characteristic feature of cultural populism. In
specifying intention as an indispensable concept for historians, Tim Mason noted quite rightly that 'we do not have to
take people in the past at their own words concerning their
intentions'. The 'realm of their self-consciousness as presented in historical sources is not trivial, but it does not
define the limits of our understanding. It is a starting point;
it constitutes a problem, not an answer' (Mason, 1995: 222).
This closely accords with my own argument. Yet in attempting to develop an analytical understanding of the cultural
and historical scope of people in the past, we should as an
initiating point of reference carefully attend to, and work
out from, what 'history's many others' say of their own experiences, some of which we ourselves will be fortunate not
to have endured. Before going on to deal more substantively
with Scott's critique of the category of experience, it may
be useful to give a particular example of the significance of
this way of 'listening' to the 'voices of history's many others'
at the same time as cross-examining what they say and
deconstructing the categories by which they have been
mediated.

In their account of interwar broadcasting in Britain, Paddy
Scannell and David Cardiff discuss certain formative documentary projects in what was still a relatively new medium
of public communications. One of the key figures in the
generation and production of these radio projects was Olive
Shapley (see Scannell and Cardiff, 1991: 344–9). During the
second half of the 1930s, Shapley worked for the BBC's North
region, where there was rather more scope for innovation
than there was with the National Programme in London,
which of course had a nationwide audience. Shapley

pioneered the use of mobile recording technology to document the details of people's lives in the North West of England. Her programmes broke new ground both with respect to content and technique. She put together documentary accounts about the lives of ordinary people – long-distance lorry drivers, for example, or the tramps then common on English highways and byways – and used 'actuality evidence' linked with narrative commentary recorded in the Manchester studio. Her approach was informal and intimate, and she attempted to set up a co-equal relationship between the presenter, those recorded speaking about their own lives, and the listening audience.

Shapley's documentary *The Classic Soil*, which Scannell regards as her masterpiece (Scannell, 1986: 21), compared working-class life in and around Manchester in the later 1930s with the social conditions and circumstances which prevailed in that area of the north of England a century previous. The details of this came from Frederick Engels's famous book, *The Condition of the Working Class in England* (Engels, 1969), while the contemporary testimonies were recorded from local men and women, young and old, including those working-class people who could be described as relatively well-off and those existing below the poverty line, who struggled desperately, on a regular daily basis, simply to make ends meet. This historical point of reference was chosen by Joan Littlewood, who wrote the commentary for the programme, while Olive Shapley produced it and 'made all the many recordings used to build up a richly textured account of contemporary working-class life and experience' (Scannell, 1986: 21).

Certain executives in the BBC took exception to the programme because it was in their view one-sided and unbalanced. What was meant by this was that the programme did not contain any commentary from officialdom, any voice of social authority, yet it was of course this departure from the usual mode of mediating working-class experience which in large part marked the innovative character of the programme, its attempt to cut through the 'dehumanising effects' of established modes of discourse on 'social issues of general public concern' (ibid: 9–10). This attempt was based on a democratic impulse to let people 'speak for themselves' and to exert a 'willingness to listen' to what they had to say. It was an example of what Mass Observation described as 'the breaking through of the ordinary past the official' (1939: 210). The irony of the charge of bias levelled against the programme was that the women and men who lived in the terraced streets that would later become nostalgically portrayed in the British TV series *Coronation Street* were precisely those whose 'voices' carried the greatest, or most direct, authority in relation to any evidence arising out of the experience of living in them, year in, year out.

While the comparative past/present framework for the programme showed that certain improvements in Mancunian working-class life had been made since Engels's classic survey, there was a much greater sense of historical continuity in the conditions experienced and endured by ordinary working people, and as Scannell puts it, the overwhelming impression of the programme which Shapley put together is 'of resilience in the face of enduring poverty'. Here is the 'voice' of the young woman whose words concluded the programme:

> I work in the cotton mill in the card room. I've had to work hard ever since I left school, and me mother and father before me. That's all there is for me – work, eat and sleep. What else is there? If you don't work you don't eat. I know when I was out of work for two years I walked the shoes off me feet, and if I hadn't found work when I did (*pause*) I'd've done away with meself. I'm thankful enough to be working now. Although it's hard I never grumble. All I ask is steady work to keep meself in bread and butter. I don't want money and plenty of luxuries. All I want is a comfortable living. But what's the good of looking into the future? I've enough to do to worry about tomorrow.

There seem to me all sorts of analytical issues that are raised by this compressed narrative, but the most immediate question I want to address is how it works as an account of working-class experience. In order to answer this question comprehensively, it would be important to set it back within the narrative composition and explanatory structure of the programme as a whole, and to relate it to the various broader discourses in which, and against which, it may have been apprehended at the time. These would include the framings of different social conceptions of poverty and the causes of poverty; of other contemporary accounts of the experience of being poor, or unemployed, in constant need of the necessities of life, existing from day to day in the absence of security and prospects; and of various traditions of representing such experience as they would have influenced audience perceptions and understandings of the broadcast account. These in turn would have to be related to the contemporary movement of documentarism that was prevalent in various media, such as film and photography, as well as in various forms of written reportage and print journalism, and considered also for their influence on a developing tradition of specifically radio documentary programming in the immediate postwar period.

That kind of historical contextualisation would perhaps only broaden rather than deepen our understanding of this account, though at the same time it would help to sensitise us to the sense that what this young woman had to say of her life in some ways conformed, fairly comfortably, with a conventional 'outside-in' pattern of observing and understanding the social and psychological consequences of poverty and proletarian labour. Among its stock heroic elements were endurance and the wresting of meagre hope out of an ample experience of adversity, which are exactly those glossed by Scannell. Often enough, though, such attributes are familiar enough from other autobiographical narratives, and in specific instances they are often salutary markers of what has been distinctive in class or generational experiences in the past. The poor-but-happy-with-little syndrome of autobiographical retrospect cannot be explained simply as an 'interpellation of the subject' by an 'ideological apparatus', for, among other things, internalised aspects of it may have been recoded in the interests of a more positive conception of self or self-achievement. This discursive syndrome has nevertheless to be examined for its contribution to particular value-systems and assessed for its over-typification of certain social groups and certain class structures of experience. Yet even as we do that, what is in one sense intriguing about Shapley's young informant is that she only seems to conform to that syndrome, and so to allow a lateral entry of those patronising 'outsider-in' attitudes to deep poverty and involuntary unemployment. I don't think she lets any sensible historical 'listener' off the hook in quite that way.

In Scannell's judgement, the words of this anonymous young woman 'sum up the experience, the circumstances and the expectations of a class and of a generation' (Scannell and Cardiff, 1991: 349). We are now so used to this kind of statement from publishers' blurbs on the back of paperback books that it is perhaps difficult to see past such hype and so to address the question as to why as a statement it simultaneously seems to illuminate and confound what is imparted in the passage. In many ways, when assessed against the weight of available historical evidence, the judgement would seem to be appropriate, and we could go to all sorts of other sources to substantiate it. But it is also appropriate to point to its omission of gender, for the 'voice' concluding *The Classic Soil* was a woman's, and it was not simply coincidental that two women, each signally important in the history of sound broadcasting, were involved in scripting and producing the programme. It is a gendered class subjectivity which is expressed in the passage, though it is important not to render this monolithically, and in the light of such a caveat, it is instructive to place Scannell's judgement alongside the differently gendered experience of another working-class woman of the same generation and region, which Carolyn Steedman discusses in recounting the life of her mother. The deliberate point of this is to rub the historiographical orthodoxy against its grain in order to show its tendency to make other experiences – of envy of those economically better-off, for instance – appear far too starkly peculiar and aberrant, freak features in the landscape of the past, and to overcome any celebration of 'psychological simplicity in the lives lived out' in those 'endless streets of little houses' (Steedman, 1986: 7 *et passim*).

But the question of how this particular account 'speaks for itself' – and then for a generation and a class – cannot be left at that. It does, I think, do both. It does succeed in encapsulating much of what other people in her position endured, but it does not do so in quite the conventional and straightforward way in which that experience of the northern working-class landscape has often been configured, and indeed, celebrated. This is why it is important to point up issues of pattern and variation, for otherwise we could easily neglect the peculiar quality which this sparse fragment from a life otherwise 'lost to history' has in its part-descriptive, part-evaluative articulation of working-class experience. This quality may then be said to reside in its initial accommodations to that conventional view, allied with its resistance to any attempt to position it in a more usual sentimental or heroic framework of interpretation. For it is about both endurance in the face of daily struggle and experience of that struggle driven to the very edge of despair. When I have read it and discussed it with students I have taught, they have generally found it as moving as I do, and have suggested that this is most of all a consequence of its overwhelming tone of matter-of-factness. It is perhaps this specific tone in the 'voice' which facilitates and fertilises the process of *Verstehen* for us, in our changed historical conditions and circumstances. Those with whom I have discussed this item of autobiographical flotsam heaved up out of the swirl of historical tides have then usually agreed that it is through this that we derive from it a sense of sorrow that while it is given us to die, it should not be anyone's fate to suffer in that way. It should perhaps be said that there are personal reasons of my own for this response in that I cannot help imagining my own grandparents, or aunts and uncles, listening to the programme as it was broadcast, in their terraced homes in Oldham and Stalybridge, particularly bearing in mind the distinctive characteristic of this form of regional documentary radio in foregrounding 'ordinary working people both within the programmes and as a major part of the audience' for whom they were made (Scannell, 1991: 349). Yet beyond these speculative resonances with a distinct family history, what is finally most striking about the account for me is its concentrated attention to the stark lineaments of experience, and the way it seems to convey a desperate equilibrium of feeling in its eloquent austerity of speech.

It could of course be said that such features of its description and its drawing of lessons from experience are themselves rhetorical, that it operates with a clearly defined rhetoric of being unrhetorical. In some ways this may seem to account for the way in which all that experience and

emotion is caught in so few words, impacted in such plain
diction: how in this sense its ordinariness is turned inside
out. Yet such an explanation of its narrative qualities would
presuppose a degree of calculation of which the account
itself leaves no traces. Instead, its quality of existential
'insiderness' inheres in its almost overwhelming sense of a
lack of contrivance. In this way, or so I would suggest, it
takes us to another place that is not portrayed in the familiar landscape, or, as often seems to happen, is effectively
hidden by the abstract sociological terms of material depri-
vation, subsistence living, the commodification of human
labour and so on, of which it speaks *in other terms*. Historically, an account such as this needs to be situated in more
structural forms of explanation if we are not to allow the
realm of this women's self-consciousness to define the limits of our understanding, but contrariwise such forms of
explanation also require such accounts if our understanding is not to be limited by lack of engagement with the
social tales of which they tell, and with the particular
subjectivities of which they speak. In this case, this is so
because of, and not in spite of, its stunning scarcity of detail. It is this scarcity that gives such bare-bone clarity to
her experience as a young woman – she would have been
in adolescence when the interview was recorded – in words
that were for her unrehearsed and not in need of contextual elaboration or additional explanation. As we try to grasp
this account historically, it is this quality which is both fetching
and frustrating, for the passage yields so much, and yet so
little, as it were in one and the same breath of air. It speaks
volumes, but it is the sheer volume of circumstantial finer
shading in her life which is lost, and at which the fragment
only hints. In the end it is not its style of utterance that
counts, but its powerful condensation of experience and the
denial of experience. There is in its printed version a slight
rendering of her local accent, which can in no way match
the colour and texture of its spoken version, but it would
nevertheless be somewhat trite to say that it is, in the end,
all the more eloquent for not being eloquent, in any conventional understanding of the term, for this belies the way
her account acutely transmits its sense both of despair and
resilience in the face of an endemic poverty, an enforced

unemployment, and when in work, a systematic grinding down
of life-experience by her daily round of mill-hand female
labour.

There is, I'm sure, much more that could be said of this
one short, unadorned narrative from one single, 1930s radio documentary, and not only in ways already indicated.
For instance, there is the question of her humility, if that is
the right word to express her desire only for a scant material sufficiency of goods and her apparent lack of envy for
the rich, whom she would have been taught in school or
church to regard catechistically as her 'betters'. Her tanta-
lisingly compact account also stands in need of a much
broader discussion of its relation to a bourgeois social imaginary of the poor or unemployed in her own or in other
historical periods, which Shapley's documentary, through its
own narrative and rhetorical strategies, sought to question
and in some ways to supersede. But an example can only
be an example, and in this context any example can only
be arbitrary. To go on further would be to run the risk of
chewing too much on her own bare bones. The point of
introducing this particular account here is simply to raise
one or two issues – for a single example cannot do much
more – about 'listening to' and questioning the 'voices of
history's many others', and to illustrate my point that somehow we must always *do both* as we move uneasily between
social history and cultural criticism. What these 'voices' are
able to say is, as Edward Thompson clearly recognised,
'determined by the questions which the historian proposes.
They cannot "speak" until they have been "asked"' (1978:
222–3). In making this recognition, Thompson 'implicitly
accepts Gadamer's point that the meaning of a historical
text does not reside in the communicative intent of its creator,
but in the mediation between the text and those who understand it from the context of a different tradition'
(Trimberger, 1984: 228–9). This is again to invoke the question of a historical imagination. As was recognised earlier,
this question is not incompatible with an examination of
the discursive and rhetorical forms in which experiences are
conveyed. Yet, equally, that kind of examination does not
of necessity require the stuff of experience, however theoretically problematic this is, to be treated with drastic and

peremptory suspicion. It is this suspicion which characterises Joan Scott's general approach, and it is often shared by
other historians who have arrived at such suspicion through
their own 'linguistic turn'. Principally, it leads Scott to identify
certain tendencies within social history, to take these to an
extreme, in what is a characteristic strategem of caricature,
and then to present them as typical practice.

The tendencies in question are appealing to experience
as 'uncontestable evidence and an originary point of explanation'; taking as 'self-evident the identities of those whose
experience is being documented', thus naturalising their
difference; locating 'resistance outside its discursive construction'; and reifying agency 'as an inherent attribute of individuals, thus decontextualising it'. For Scott, the project of
making hidden experience visible 'precludes critical examination of the workings of the ideological system itself, its
categories of representation . . . its premises about what these
categories mean and how they operate, and of its notions
of subjects, origin, and cause' (Scott, 1991: 777–8). It would
be pointless to deny these tendencies, for they certainly exist.
It would also not be difficult to find examples of them, in
various branches of enquiry. What is disappointing is that it
becomes difficult to share with Scott one's frustration with
these tendencies because of the polemical interest she has
in standing them on their head. Scott's error is to fix 'experience' as the negative 'other' of discourse.

The resort to caricature is evident in her criticism of notions
'that history can faithfully document lived reality, that ar-
chives are repositories of facts, and that categories like man
and woman are transparent' (Scott, 1988: 2). It is easy to
agree with such criticism because, as we have seen elsewhere,
it is directed at straw targets. There can be few social, cultural and feminist historians who would hold fast to such
simplistic assumptions. It would, however, be quite another
matter if we were to say that historians in the past have
tended to consider subjectivity and identity as an unmediated
relay of experience, to offer the social experience of historical 'actors' as the unproblematic evidence of referentiality,
and to use such evidence as a convenient shield for their
own narrative or analytical mediations in the construction
of historical accounts. There are few historians who have

not at times slipped into these tendencies, and in a persuasive essay, Scott (1988: 68–90) shows how E. P. Thompson, in his path-breaking account of the formation of the English working class (Thompson, 1968b), employed certain binary oppositions that endorse gendered categories, and render class itself a gendered construction.

Yet various things are underplayed in Scott's essay. The first is the problem of historically representing the institutional production of these oppositions at the time while also, in the production of history, analytically undermining them. Another is an appreciative sense of the historical conjuncture and theoretical arguments out of which Thompson's book emerged, though this is perhaps understandable in what is an attempt to show the subsequent difficulties faced by feminist socialists in their encounter with the discursive codes of class and gender. However, Scott is not the first to begin to untangle the tricky knot of these difficulties, and it is not as if the knot has been cut at the first fell swoop of the deconstructionist sword. This impression results from underplaying how the project of women's history has been collectively advanced. What also remains faintly acknowledged in the essay is a sense of the enormous influence of Thompson's book on feminist historians of the 1960s and 1970s, even as they struggled against it in trying to establish a different agenda. As Catherine Hall records, *The Making of the English Working Class* was 'a text on which many feminist historians cut their teeth' (Hall, 1992: 9).[3] These same historians then went on to build on the understanding of Thompson's masculine representation of class, as for instance in the 'massive delineation . . . of *middle-class* identity, described in gendered terms' (Steedman, 1994: 112; and see, for instance, Davidoff and Hall, 1987; Newton *et al.*, 1983; and Whitelegge *et al.*, 1984). Such dilutions and omissions of emphasis are telling ones, for they result from Scott's stronger sense of textual codings than of what Thompson called the discipline of historical context.

Experience as Ideology

Scott's approach draws directly on Foucault. Foucault's greatest historiographical contribution is to our understanding of changes in the social mechanisms of power and in the constitution of relations of power and knowledge. This contribution derives initially from his work on the emergence of the clinic, the asylum and the prison as institutions which centralise means of surveillance, classification and ordering, and which complement those forms of social domination based on technical or instrumental rationality that have been a central concern for sociologists such as Weber, Adorno, Horkheimer and Marcuse. The importance of Foucault's work extends beyond this in its implications for social management, for over time these new means of control have become, in his view, so widely generalised that they are morally interiorised by the individual, who as a result becomes a self-policing subject. Foucault's underlying argument is that in modernity there has developed a very pervasive normalisation and social discipline. The transition which he traced was from the exercise of sovereign power through external violence and violence as exemplary spectacle, to its realisation in administrative techniques, social engineering, abstract rules and self-discipline; although in relation to sexuality, which was the focus of his later work, he attacked the 'repressive hypothesis' of Victorianism which interprets the work-ethic and this-worldly asceticism as reliant on the subjugation of libidinal energies and discourses dealing with the topic of sexuality (see Foucault, 1990: part 2). This relates to his rejection of the liberal view of power as conceived in solely negative terms, as proscription or constraint.

Foucault attempted to move beyond seeing power solely in these conventional terms to recognising its productive and generative consequences for knowledge, for facilitating new objects of knowledge, new discourses and new truth-claims. In the same way, he took the view that 'the "will-to-knowledge" in our culture is simultaneously part of the danger and a tool to control that danger' (Rabinow, 1986: 7). Power 'produces reality', 'produces domains of objects and rituals of truth'. 'Conversely, knowledge induces effects of power. It is not possible for power to be exercised without knowledge, it is impossible for knowledge not to engender power' (Sarup, 1993: 74). Foucault sought to deal with knowledge and discourse in terms of power rather than meaning, power as 'a productive network which runs through the whole social body' (Foucault, 1980: 119; see also Sheridan, 1980: 139; and O'Brien, 1978: 513). In this view, power is not a force or capacity which is simply possessed and applied by those in positions of authority; rather, it is ubiquitous, running through every kind of social relation and spreading in filigree webs through all areas of everyday life (Foucault, 1980: 39). This sits with difficulty alongside Foucault's refusal of an ontology or telos of history, and of the notion of anything historically constant in the human subject, for what metaphysically remains as an invariant is his Nietzschean conception of the 'will-to-power'. Yet, given this sense of the ubiquity of power relations, it followed from his conception of social change that his work came to focus on local and specific struggles, on what he called the 'micro-physics of power', and in taking this focus he was similarly critical of grand theories and 'totalising discourses' like Marxism and psychoanalysis. The 'micro-physics of power' are realised in diverse and often contradictory subject-positions which encourage the internalisation of values and beliefs supportive of the power/knowledge nexus of the modern social order, and these subject-positions are produced within discourses manifesting such relations of power as the capacity to define, classify and categorise the social positions and identities of subordinate groups.

Scott's own resolution of the specific difficulties of gender construction, division and exclusion invokes Foucault's genealogical mode of analysis, which looks at the past for differences not continuities, for breaks and reversals in discourse rather than origins or causes; seeks to disrupt settled assumptions of what connects past and present; and turns to the singular and neglected in rejection of conceptions of history as involving linear forward movement and evolutionary progression. The aim of such analysis is, in short, to tear away the veil from the invisible operations of power by tracing the genealogies of modes of discipline, surveillance and control in institutional practices and categorisations (see, for example, Foucault, 1986). This kind of analytical approach can of course be singularly effective. It can be used, among other things, to problematise the location of 'women' in nature or in objectified collectivities such as social class, to show 'women' as 'synchronically and diachronically

erratic as a collectivity', and 'being a woman' as historically
inconstant (Riley, 1987: 35). Exploring how 'gender ideology and woman's position' are analytically related is important
if we are to understand, for example, 'why working-class men
and women invest shared experiences... with different
meanings', why both Samuel and Jemima Bamford went
together to Peterloo, 'shared the excitement... the horror
and the fear', but 'experienced it differently on account of
their sex' (Lewis, 1985: 120; Hall, 1992: 150; Bamford, 1893,
vol. II: chapter 25; and Marlow, 1970). Yet the diminution
of those experiences to a relatively minor level of consideration does not necessarily follow from the intellectual
heating up of the organisation of representations of difference in discourse, which then ascends as a theoretical mer-
cury to the top-level of the analytical thermometer. That,
however, is precisely Scott's preference in her displacement
of class consciousness as the cultural expression of shared
experiences, albeit predominantly male, wholly into the ideological representations of social class. Neither focus, in my
view, should be regarded as exclusive or sufficient; we need
to think of new ways of bringing them into productive synthesis. The 'deconstructive' move certainly offers new ways
of interpreting historical evidence and symbolic exchange,
and the opportunity for these in historical and cultural analysis
should always be welcomed, but in studying the historically
neglected or culturally discredited, we need to do so not
only against assumptions of a unitary conception of collective experience and consciousness, but also against the relegation of experience and consciousness as mere effects of
linguistic representations and discursive strategies.

Effectively, it is this relegation which Scott seeks to accomplish: discourses 'position subjects and produce their
experiences', so that it is 'not individuals who have experience, but subjects who are constituted through experience'
(1991: 779). This implies a conception of experience and
of the experiencing subject as vectors of determining structures of which the subject is always and ever unaware, and
it leads her dogmatically to assert that 'experience' is *intrinsically* empiricist and essentialist, rather than being so posited in certain usages and applications. She claims that for
social, cultural and feminist historians, 'experience' is a

foundational category, 'an "irreducible" ground for history' (ibid:781), and this results in even 'professed anti-empiricists' allowing an implicit endorsement of empiricism. Scott's baby-with-the-bathwater denunciations of the value of 'experience' as an analytical category stem directly from this claim. Faced with her linguistic idealism, it is tempting to tilt the balance back the other way and insist on 'the irreducible material determinants of the social process of symbolic exchange' (Garnham, 1983: 321). This is of course too crude, for discursive processes cannot be reduced to these material determinants, but nor should the reverse reduction apply, as it does for Scott: 'Language,' she peremptorily announces, 'is the site of history's enactment' (1991: 793). And if we conceive of language in Derridean terms of the 'irreducible heterogeneity of *différance*', as Scott does, what we have, again, is 'the randomisation of history', history as 'legislated accident' (Anderson, 1983: 48–50; Said, 1978: 311). This is, and not by accident, close to Foucault's view that history has no rational course, no general purpose, no constants: 'history is both uncontrolled and directionless' (Philp, 1990: 78).

That 'experience' has on numerous occasions been used foundationally does not mean that this is an inevitable corollary of its use, nor does its use necessarily provide an epistemological alibi for categories such as man, woman, black or white and so on in terms of the ways in which they have been ideologically constructed in discourse as absolute and opposed. This is exactly what Scott assumes in quoting Teresa de Lauretis's redefinition of experience as the

> process by which, for all social beings, subjectivity is constructed. Through that process one places oneself or is placed in social reality, and so perceives and comprehends as subjective (referring to, originating in, oneself) those relations – material, economic, and interpersonal – which are in fact social and, in a larger perspective, historical (de Lauretis, 1984: 159).

This can be taken in one sense as a handy reminder of the danger of over-subjectivising social relations, or of conceiving social experience in the atomistic terms of individualistic orthodoxy. There is of course the opposite shortcoming, which has had insidious consequences far beyond those of moral liberalism, of conceiving of collectivities as an undifferentiated 'mass', thus sweeping aside the subjects who are 'concurrently and often contradictorily engaged in a plurality of heterogeneous experiences, practices, and discourses' (ibid: 171–2). But the more important sense is of experience as the compound, changing sum of a subject's interaction with the world, which is why de Lauretis chooses the word 'experience' rather than 'ideology' (ibid: 211). Her project of elaborating the notion of experience in relation to semiotic theory and a feminist conception of subjectivity entails an attempt to re-embody the 'ghostly presence' of the subject in semiotics. This means that in one way Scott accurately assimilates de Lauretis to her position in that de Lauretis speaks of 'experience' as the 'continuous engagement of a self or subject in social reality', both of which are semiotically conceived: 'semiosis names the process of their reciprocally constitutive effects' (ibid: 182). But in another sense, her position diverges from Scott's in that feminist theory is for her a practice based on experience, which in another formulation is defined as 'one's personal subjective engagement in the practices, discourses, and institutions that lend significance (value, meaning, and affect) to the events of the world' (ibid: 159). It is through such engagement that feminist theory and analysis is 'aimed at confronting that experience and changing women's lives concretely, materially, and through consciousness' (ibid: 184) – all terms from which Scott would now fight shy. For de Lauretis, the specificity of feminist theory may be sought 'in that political, theoretical, self-analysing practice by which the relations of the subject in social reality can be rearticulated from the historical experience of women'. This is to speak of a social and historical subject who is an 'acting', 'creative' being, able to intervene, induce habit-change and change in consciousness, and it involves attempting to refigure the notion of experience rather than, as with Scott, ditching it as utterly and irrevocably specious.

Yet neither de Lauretis nor Scott provides a satisfactory response to 'the most central theoretical issue in historical interpretation: what causes change in history'. By 'discounting the role of material circumstances in shaping reality', Scott in particular 'implies that a change in "discourse" about woman and man can transform the position of real women'. This is to deny 'the possibility of any but contingent and relativist conclusions' (Koonz, 1989: 19–20). Experience is inevitably contaminated by ideology, but it is not equivalent to it. To claim that it is bound to naturalise existing, oppressive subject-positions is the reverse of the claim that direct access to the real is to be gained through a subject's experience; it is these notions which are specious, rather than 'experience' itself. Scott's position is locked utterly into the former, for as she puts it: 'Experience' is 'an ideological construction that not only makes individuals the starting point of knowledge, but that also naturalises categories . . . by treating them as given characteristics of individuals' (1991: 782). This dismisses any sense of experience as collective, and is quite different from conceiving of experience as the sites of construction of concrete, social subjects in an ongoing engagement with the social and historical world.

The degree to which such construction is 'internally' managed or 'externally' imposed is always relative to case and context, and thus a question of historical understanding. Yet 'experience', in a form of reference that imperatively requires the use of scare quotes, has somehow taken on the active function of reproducing what used to be described, in the consciousness-raising days of feminism, as stereotypicality. How could this be? Scott champions her own method as a guard against presentism in that, for her, an examination of the category of woman rehistoricises it, contests the essentialist notion of womanhood as making for shared attitudes, feelings and interests among women across place and time. In this respect, she takes Downs to task for universalising the condition of women as being afraid. In contesting this, Scott attributes such fear among women as 'the effect of a certain feminist discourse'. This causally displaces social violence, the violence of rape, wife-beating and the brutal assault of old women in the course of robbery, to forms of discourse about it. In Scott's view, feminism simply reflects what she calls the 'ideology of violence', and both then 'produce' social violence, naturalise it, and reproduce its terms, so that they are together identified as the cause of women's fear, rather than, or as well as, the experience, perception and anticipation of violence itself. Downs, in her reply, has little trouble in showing that that which Scott purports to historicise is historically very much abbreviated, indeed almost collapsed into the contemporary period (so much for the guard against presentism), for there are numerous examples, slavery being the one cited by Downs (1993b), which could be adduced to show how the fear and experience of male violence have centrally shaped and delimited women's lives in other times, other places. This should not of course be taken the other way as meaning that women's fear of men is historically invariant. Yet what quite rightly disturbs Downs even more than the 'representation of fear as a postmodern condition', is Scott's view that women's experience can only be attributed to naturalised representations of it, and to their amplification in feminist contestations of such representations and the values on which they rest. Feminism, in this view, simply reproduces existing structures of power when it invokes women's experience, since that experience cannot be invoked outside the terms in which it has been discursively cast. This is a circular and closed system of understanding.

In claiming that identities are mediated by the experiences which ground them in a particular social, cultural and historical matrix, I fully recognise that the realisation of such experiences intersects pivotally with language, for how else can we have any mutual recognition of them? Language, but also visual imagery and dramatic performance in all its guises, is what experience is 'pressed out' into, the communicative forms in which they attain cultural meanings. My point is rather that rape or domestic male violence, to take the cases at issue, are not phenomena which can be characterised as concerned solely with a struggle of discourses. This may be seen as advancing limit cases, but limit cases often serve to illuminate the 'normal' and taken-for-granted modes of everyday social conduct. Obviously, in order to talk of certain acts we need to have recourse to a particular range and structure of expression, utterance and reference, and entry into these at the point of speech or other forms of communication necessarily conditions and makes possible the ways in which we think of certain acts. At the same time we should not forget that language use (language in the hurly-burly of social use, the bracketed *parole*) occurs in, and is shaped by, particular situations and contexts which cannot be subsumed within language as system (the epistemologically privileged *langue*):

> Contexts form 'settings' of action, the qualities of which agents routinely draw upon in the course of orienting what they do and what they say to one another. Common awareness of these settings of action forms an anchoring element in the 'mutual knowledge' whereby agents make sense of what others say and do (Giddens, 1987: 99; see also Giddens, 1986).

These settings work to regulate and configure events, actions and discourses; they are the particularised sites in which the social is relationally constituted. The structures of social relations in this sense provide, as Roy Bhaskar puts it, the means, the 'rules and resources for everything we do', and form 'the unmotivated condition for all our motivated productions':

> We do not create society – the error of voluntarism. But these structures which pre-exist us are only reproduced or transformed in our everyday activities; thus society does not exist independently of human agency – the error of reification. The social world is reproduced or transformed in daily life (Bhaskar, 1989: 4).

In the light of this it could be said that it is the socially organised production of culture that needs to be emphasised, not the decoding of cultural texts. Any act of signification or representation is always embedded in the social fields in which it is made and assimilated, in ways which involve cultural practices at work upon as well as within the social relations in which they occur. Cultural texts, in the extended sense of this term, cannot be taken as offering a direct and transparent relay of social relations or historical conditions which may then be 'read off' from the text, which, as we have noted, is precisely the error of reflectionist theory in assuming that texts, or natural language, are the neutral, transparent means for mirroring 'reality'. An analytical attention to the social fields of cultural production should act as a restraint on impulses towards the abstraction of signifying practices. It should raise suspicions of the claim that structuralist linguistics can be applied to all forms of human culture. To say that cultural production and social practices operate in ways which are analogous to language is heuristically useful in respect of the principle of identifying the construction of relations through difference, but the claim is finally permissible only by a bracketing of the referent and a withdrawal into the signifier. This move then results in the tendency to textualise social relations and institutions, and to destabilise the very possibility of resisting existing structures of power or choosing between different social arrangements, different modes of conduct and different lines of action: 'the fragmentation of both subject and knowledge, and the concomitant collapse of social relations into textual ones, diverts attention from the operation of power in the social sphere, fixing our gaze upon its metaphorical manifestations in the text' (Downs, 1993a: 420). That is precisely where Roger Chartier's gaze is fixed when he asserts that the 'representations of the social world themselves are the constituents of social reality' (1982: 30).

Reflexivity Reprised

At one point in her diatribe against the historical and ethnographic use of experience, Scott makes the point that for historians, as well as for other students of the human sciences, the subject in question should be conceived as 'both the object of enquiry' *and* 'the historian who produces knowledge of the past based on "experience"' derived from archival sources or from fieldwork (1991: 782–3). This is an important point, and it is one which I have emphasised in outlining certain connections between cultural studies and the hermeneutic tradition. A key point underpinning this emphasis has been that adding to or refining the already vast number of definitions of culture or cultural fractions is not really what counts. That kind of activity is only a starting point in any piece of cultural analysis – a way of orienting oneself or sharpening one's sense of direction in any particular case. What is of greater significance is the recognition that any writing about cultural texts, processes and institutions is itself a cultural act: a product of culture which produces culture in the very act of attempting to grasp it. The study of cultures can never be simply a matter of observing and describing – if this was the case, then ethnography could

kiss many of its more fraught methodological problems goodbye in an instant. Cultural hermeneutics encourages a reflexive form of critique which tries to follow through the
implications of the necessarily participatory nature within
culture of intellectual work upon culture. Hence the importance of critical attention to the ways theoretical position and method of analysis inform, enable and constrain
our acts of interpretation. Any such act inevitably constitutes an intervention within theory, within knowledge, within
culture – for it has its own stake in how knowledge is conceived and how culture should be conceived, reproduced
or changed.

Joan Scott calls for a similar reflexivity in historical study.
She stresses the need within social history, and more specifically within women's history, to question the categories on
which historical accounts are based, to think critically about
the assumptions, conventions and practices of the discipline.
This is obviously commensurate with the kind of benefit I
hope would ensue from a greater cross-fertilisation of cultural studies, hermeneutics and social history, for it is now,
I think, clearer than ever before that historians should attend more closely to the frames in which their narratives
and analyses are produced, and in the interests of reflexivity, should generate, to a greater degree than is commonly
the case, second-order symbols, more layered forms of historical interpretation and understanding, and significations
which twist around to take in analytically the processes of
engaged signification itself (Myerhoff and Ruby, 1982: 2).
Reflexivity in historical and cultural analysis involves being
open about the means of our practice, and necessarily follows from 'any method which demands scrutiny of its own
terms and procedures' (Nathanson, 1974: 243). As I have
suggested elsewhere, adopting and applying a reflexive attitude does not guarantee any ready-made solutions to the
difficulties involved in thinking about the culture/society
nexus. All it will do is guard against interpretive sophism or
ideological collusion by helping us question our questions
(Pickering and Green, 1987a: 174–5). It is in this way that
reflexivity relates to cultural studies, for one of its key principles of approach is to ask questions about the rules of
asking questions; hence the resistance to attempts to codify,

unify or systematise it. It exists in critical relation to institutionalised maps of knowledge, and thus questions the historical construction of disciplines in the human sciences,
critically examines their first principles, their omissions and
exclusions, and perhaps most particularly the forms of their
separation (Green, 1982: 88). In this way, cultural studies
acts as the grit in the academic oyster.

Object and Interpretation

It will have been noticed that this is not that far from
Foucault's abiding attention to the ways in which academic
methods impart legitimacy to the interpretations based upon
them, to the ways in which the range of criteria in play,
and the grounds upon which such criteria are said to be
based, allow the assessment of the truth or falsity of statements. There is much to be learned from this kind of approach, though it does contain the potential danger of
becoming obsessive about the methodological and theoretical apparatus to the neglect of that which it is supposed to
support, and of encouraging an ever-anxious epistemological patrolling of the boundaries of social and historical knowledge rather than generating their expansion. It would of
course be well if historians were to work more openly than
they usually do with the recognition that the knowledge they
produce is not objective and value-free, but always implicated in the politics of cultural practice. However, they do
at least operate with the principle that in constructing meanings from the past, events and experiences, evidence and
concepts, first-hand accounts and subsequent interpretations,
are not interchangeable, not susceptible to abandonment
on an open sea of signification where every wave of the
signified slides under its signifier and any dry land of extra-
linguistic reference remains forever out of sight on some
lost ontological horizon. It is this diminution of analytic
distinctions and groundings which inhere in the tendencies
that follow from the textualisation of historical processes
and relations. This was, as already noted, always the problem with structuralism as a formal mode of analysis, rather
than its binding synchronic purview, and while the poststructuralist insistence on the undecidability of textual meaning

develops an important critique of claims for interpretive finality or for absolute determinants of meaning, it leaves us ineluctably locked inside texts upon texts upon texts, as we sit surrounded by the detritus of both subject and knowledge. This is considerably at variance with the hermeneutic emphasis on humility and a willingness to *listen* to others which was preferred in an earlier chapter, and it provides an enormously beguiling distraction from the heart-searching question of whose interpretation is being constructed in cultural analysis, whose meanings are being accredited and given authority, those of the investigator or those of the participants in social and historical experience? In structuralism's case, it was a universal meaning that could be fathomed only by the structuralist. In discussing his treatment of kinship systems, Tim Dant suggests that Lévi-Strauss's own form of discourse analysis 'both attempts to articulate the rules governing the formation of the type of discourse and interpret the "meanings" of utterances within the particular discourse'. Again, the same questions arise: whose meanings, and whence reflexivity?

> These meanings are analytically generated, constructed from outside the discursive contexts under analysis, that is they are not meanings as used by participants. While the methods of structuralist linguistics seem to have some role to play in studying the structure of meaningful systems, they have nothing directly to offer the unravelling of meaning (Dant, 1991: 107).

The denial of experience as a building block in cultural and historical analysis is central to this shortcoming in structuralism and its successors, for what it allows, or at least gives easy passage to, is the construction of meanings which are alternative to, and indeed, may take no heed of, those of the experiencing participants. For Lévi-Strauss, what had to be avoided are what he derisively called the 'shop-girl's web of subjectivity' and the 'swamps of experience' (Rabinow and Sullivan, 1979: 10–11). While, as I have stressed, it would be naive to suggest that the meanings of experiences are transparently revealed in the utterances of participants, 'there is a critical difference between approaches which attempt to assimilate indigenous understandings to their analytical procedures, and those which . . . superimpose their own

interpretations on whatever may be locally current ... [As]
soon as we start to historicise not only our data but also
our own practice, we are inevitably led back to the local
and particular' (Pickering and Green, 1987b: 6–7). Oral
history, as a form of enquiry which attempts to recuperate
evidence of the local and particular, has at times been guilty
of assuming an effectively linear relationship between in-
formants' accounts of the past and a historical reality which
they reveal, as if what is reconstructed on the basis of experience and memory has some unproblematic reference to a
given 'then and there'. But oral history has at least turned
its ears towards the experiences of participants, and declared
itself ready to listen to what those experiences have been
made to mean on their own home ground, before 'working
them up' in secondary forms of narrative and analysis. 'Oral
history gives social history a human face ... It gives history
back to the people in their own words and in giving a past
it also helps them towards a future of their own making'
(Tosh, 1984: 176). What is transmitted in material gathered
through interviews, focused group discussions or participant
observation is not holy writ; such material needs to be critically interrogated, and even where it is it will quite rightly
become subject itself to critical interrogation, as we have
seen, for example, in the point that work on working-class
subcultures in the 1970s valorised the masculinity of public
space, and reproduced the terms of subordination and abuse
prevalent among male subcultural participants. But the separate question of whether experience is a reliable source of
knowledge is not inherent in the category of experience
itself, and claims that this is the case can, most easily, be
falsified by citing instances where experience is a limited,
distortive or indeed fallacious source of knowledge. The more
critical point, which is the one at issue, lies in the relations
between the cultural meanings that are 'pressed out' of experiences and the subsequent interpretations of those meanings in cultural analysis:

> More defined and explicit hermeneutic tasks have to be under-
> taken in order to forge the communicative link between the
> cultural object and its interpretator ... If a hermeneutic ele-
> ment has never been particularly pronounced in structuralism
> or post-structuralism, it is because signification has been pri-

marily dealt with in terms of the internal organisation of codes, or as the play of signifiers, rather than as the 'recovery of meaning' (Giddens, 1987: 102).

Experience is culturally 'handled', but its cultural and historical significance lies in the way it occasions social reality and, through events, situations or sequences of events and situations, grounds the interactive tension between expressive forms and social determinants out of which meanings are configured. What is experienced can have a subjective and an objective take, even as these aspects exist in an uneasy, uneven but nevertheless reciprocal relation, and may already be more or less sewn into existing expressive forms or be relatively unarticulated and yet to be fashioned into a collectively recognisable cultural form or figure. Williams's categories of dominant, residual and emergent are again directly relevant here, but the emphasis on experience brings back into the analytic frame, as he well knew, the dynamic of feeling alongside thought, thought alongside feeling. This dynamic is closely akin to what Suzanne Langer called 'significant form', in which 'the factor of significance is not logically discriminated, but is felt as a quality rather than recognised as a function' (1953: 32). The functionalist view inclines us to regard affective form as a 'sign' pointing to social rules, rather than in itself a sphere of meaning that is public and socially significant (Rosaldo, 1980: 35). The fact that

> thought is always culturally patterned and infused with feelings, which themselves reflect a culturally ordered past, suggests that just as thought does not exist in isolation from affective life, so affect is culturally ordered and does not exist apart from thought (Rosaldo, 1984: 137).

In Grossberg's characterisation, affect 'is closely tied to what we often describe as the feeling of life'; it is 'what gives "colour", "tone" or "texture" to our experiences' (1992: 56–7). Yet it is in relation to both thought and feeling that experience passes imperceptibly into culture and vice versa, though not inevitably of course in an untroubled way: 'Il y a des gens qui n'auraient jamais été amoureux s'ils n'avient jamais entendu parler de l'amour' (La Rochefoucauld, 1931: 83). It is in this sense that the subjective modalities of experience blend in with, and are in many ways only made possible by, broader cultural forms and performances which constitute the webs in which we are historically suspended.

It is instructive here to remember that for Dilthey, neither the 'subjective' nor 'objective mind' are reducible to each other. Dilthey talks of both the 'individual slant' which distinguishes the personal knowledge of life, and collective experience which enlarges and checks that slant according to shared beliefs, value-systems, rites, rules of conduct, definitions of public goals and public good, and so on, which have a greater weight of authority and power over lives because conceived as 'common knowledge'. Every individual is 'a point where webs of relationships intersect; these relationships go through individuals, exist within them, but also reach beyond their life and possess an independent existence and development of their own through the content, value and purpose which they realise' (Rickman, 1976: 180–1). It is in this sense that people are culturally shaped, and yet also culturally creative as they operate within the related structures of experience, expression and understanding. So, for Dilthey, what was important was the principle that cultural forms and practices have to be understood in terms of human experience, and experience understood in terms of how particular, historically located people think, feel, act and desire: these threads run through experience in one interwoven strand (Hodges, 1969: 91). It is part of my argument that we have not yet fully grasped how we should operationalise this principle, and that cultural analysis must overcome the temptation to separate these strands out and consider them in isolation from each other, even as it plays to its current strengths in dealing with the relations between narrative composition and thematisations of experience and the realisation of experiences in particular social arrangements and particular forms of social participation and interaction.

The Poststructuralist Hat

Yet, returning to the initial point of the poststructuralist critique, Dilthey did not regard experience as 'a subjective process of becoming conscious of fundamental organic states'.

Experience is organised by symbolic structures and 'always mediated by an act of understanding meaning' : 'the objective structure of valid symbols in which we find ourselves embedded can be understood only through experiential reconstruction such that we revert to the process in which meaning is generated' (Habermas, 1972: 147). Social and historical experience is not an autonomous *object* that exists apart from what social analysts or historians may make of it in the meanings they produce in writing about it. When it is conceived in that way it can of course support claims for the objectivity of social or historical knowledge in which the role of the analyst in producing that knowledge is occluded by virtue of such claims. But accepting this does not mean that the opposite is true. What is made of social and historical experience, by the actor or analyst, is at the same time subject to what that experience can be made to yield by reverting to the process in which meaning is generated, and in any particular case the discursive meanings that are made of experience do not have an infinitely free range since they must be shown to be in some way grounded in the experience out of which meanings are made if they are to be held to make cultural or analytical sense in relation to such experience. This is not to say that that there is any objective meaning in any experience since, obviously enough, any experience is open to a considerable number of varying interpretations. But not any interpretation whatsoever. Although experiences are relative they cannot in themselves be endlessly relativised, for they would then become an indistinguishable welter in which anything that happens would be equivalent to everything that happens, and the only remaining position left to us would be ethical and political nihilism.

The poststructuralist dissolution of social experience, along with its collapse of 'reality' into 'representation', makes it difficult to see how historically constituted social relations and identities can be changed. This is Downs's difficulty: 'the weapons forged in the contest against the totalising aims of truth – aporia, discontinuity, and indeterminacy – offer scant ground for any constructive political and intellectual projects . . . There is no room for change . . . for in the course of exposing unstable fictions like woman, deconstruction forecloses altogether on the possibility of an authentic, meaningful subjectivity' or 'meaningful intersubjective encounter' (1993a: 423, 425–6). Deconstruction is certainly an advance on structuralism's endorsement of binary oppositions as absolute and closed, for it shows how systematically ordered categories are, despite themselves, unstable and contradictory, and with reference to signification and representation it provides a useful tool for levering open the ways in which subject-positions are produced, naturalised and reproduced. But what else is this, in the end, but 'a sort of patient, probing reformism of the text'? (Sarup, 1993: 56). And if subjects are co-opted by discourses, where does one locate 'the emancipatory impulse to free people from the cultural forms which it is implied by the theory are "responsible" for their cooption ?' (Soper, 1990: 152). We cannot go back and simply substitute the anti-Cartesian, multiply fractured sense of the subject advanced by poststructuralism and postmodernism with the older, humanist sense of self (Lévi-Strauss's 'spoilt brat') which exists antecedently in a position rationally choosing between different moral options and alternative cultural routes. There is every need to uncover the power relations in categories of ethnic, sexual and national identities where these are based on essentialist conceptions of a 'true' and fixed 'self', impervious to change, just as there is to rework 'difference' against the grain of monolithic and negative definitions of 'otherness'. But how is this to be done when identity has no stable centre, no place from which to begin the struggle? The poststructuralist subject is radically dispersed: wherever its hat is laid, that's its home. Unless we allow that we are not so impossibly scattered and dispaced in our social and cultural identities, in our sense of who we are or can become, that we cannot make intelligent and informed allegiances, discriminations, and choices among contending discourses, how are we going to move, how are we going to make ourselves, culturally and historically, as fit human beings for the future?

This takes us back to Foucault. As did Kuhn on scientific paradigms and paradigm-shifts, Foucault provided a new historical mode of procedure and a new historical perspective on the workings of discursive practices and on changes

in formations of discourse over time. Each discursive practice sets up a framework of rules and procedures (as, for
example, those of regulation and exclusion) which govern
what is written or said, and what is thought, within given
areas of experience, which pattern otherwise disparate experiences and in this way bring them fully into consciousness. One role for the historian then becomes that of
surveying the grounds for the constitution and dissolution
of this framework. Aside from the tendency in this to
hypostatise language as an autonomous system beyond human undertaking, it also raises the problem of appropriate
point of vantage and assessment. For Foucault, as for
Nietzsche, it is not possible to establish any objective knowledge of history; instead, there are only more or less powerful versions of what is taken as historical in discourses about
the past. It is because writing and practices of representation generally are so conditioned by their discursive rules
and imperatives that there can be no absolute truth or falsity in any discourse. However, we do not need to invoke
the possibility of absolute truth in asking how it is we discriminate between truth-claims:

> Foucault's claim that truth is merely what counts as true within
> a discourse is not easy to accept. If what Foucault says is true,
> then truth is always relative to discourse; there cannot be any
> statements which are true in all discourses, nor can there be
> any statements which are true *for* all discourses – so that, on
> Foucault's own account, what he says cannot be true! (Philp,
> 1990: 70; cf. Dilthey in Rickman, 1979: 50).

If, as Eagleton has put it, 'objects are entirely internal to
the discourses which constitute them', how can we ever 'judge
that a discourse had constructed its object validly'? (1991:
205). On what basis could one say, or come to realise, that
a particular form of historical experience had been misrepresented or that the weight of certain constructions of experience is oppressive? The final Foucauldian response that
discourse manifests the ubiquitous will to power/knowledge
and that this has resulted in the modern self-policing subject does not provide an adequate answer because in this
conception power is so pervasive and dispersed across all
social relations it is impossible to specify any particular

locations for it. 'Once hypostatised as a new First Principle, Zarathustra-style, power loses any historical determination: there are no longer specific holders of power, nor any specific goals which its exercise serves' (Anderson, 1983: 51).

The same problem arises from Foucault's formulation of resistance in that no cultural or historical grounds for it are identified: power is said to presuppose resistance, but the forces or mechanisms for its generation were not analytically dealt with by Foucault; 'where there is power, there is resistance' remains at the level of an assertion of the contrary: 'Power relationships are "reversible" – as Foucault puts it – in the same sense and for the same theoretical reasons as textual significations are "undecidable" for Derrida' (ibid). Despite this problem, however, Foucault's work has been suggestively applied in studies which proceed from and attempt to keep interpretive faith with the concrete, local experience of particular social groups. A fine example is Lila Abu-Lughod's study of the symbolic forms through which Bedouin women resist the social power of men, where she argues for the analytical use of resistance as a diagnostic of power. Taking her cue from Foucault's hyperbolic assertion, she inverts this to show 'how in the rich and sometimes contradictory details of resistance the complex workings of social power can be traced', and how these contradictory details are implicated in patterns of historical change that link local communities more and more to a wider capitalist economy and to the experience of modernity. While female modes of resistance cannot be seen as independent of power relations, she appropriately remarks that we should in general terms give the women involved 'credit for resisting in a variety of ways the power of those who control so much of their lives, without either misattributing to them forms of consciousness or politics that are not part of their experience – something like a feminist consciousness or feminist politics – or devaluing their practices as prepolitical, primitive, or even misguided' (1990: 42 and 47; see also Lazreg, 1988 and 1994b).

This is not only a more stimulating application of Foucault than Scott's (see, for example, Scott, 1986), but is also welcome for the note of respect it strikes for historical experience in its social and cultural specificity and in its self-articulated terms. Abu-Lughod's caveat is directed to alien interpretations, and in her full-length ethnography she calls for a 'tactical humanism' to give a moral dimension to diagnostics of power (Abu-Lughod, 1992: 28–9; cf. Stanley and Wise, 1993: 205–6). Although this point is not fully developed, it is nevertheless a telling one. Abu-Lughod does not present us, as in Foucault, with 'intentionality without a subject, a strategy without a strategist' (Dreyfus and Rabinow, 1982: 187; cf. Anderson, 1983: 54; Taylor, 1985: 152–84: and Habermas, 1987: 238–93). Foucault's genealogy made for 'a form of history which can account for the constitution of knowledges . . . without having to make reference to a subject' (Foucault, 1980: 117). As Milner puts it, poststructuralism in this way 'brings into play all the indeterminacy of phenomenological culturalisms, but without any corresponding sense of the practical creative efficacy of the human subject' (1991: 76). What is challenging about Foucault's work is its unconventionality, its challenges to the conventions and presuppositions of Annaliste and Marxist historical analysis, and its attempt to extend the boundaries of history as a discipline. Yet for him questions of experience and agency were irrelevant (O'Brien, 1989: 46; and see Weightman, 1989).[4] The medical anthropologist Byron Good supports this evaluation in noting that Foucault's work 'excludes the centrality of experience and in large measure the dialogical qualities of discourse. For the anthropologist, this inattention to the lived experience of the subject is ultimately untenable' (Good, 1994: 69). The same can arguably be said of the historian who seeks to go beyond accounts of 'the conversation of the people who counted' (Young, 1978: 18) into an exploration of the rhythms and textures of the everyday lives of ordinary people in different places and periods of the past.

Keeping Faith with History's Many Others

Starting from experience is simply to utilise a resource. As someone who continuously makes uneasy and troubled passes between history and sociology, I find it a challenging unit of analysis. It is challenging because it raises some of the most abiding problems in social and cultural analysis, those

of typicality and generalisability being only the most obvious. Its value even at a more straightforwardly empirical level
of analysis is that it provides a distinctive mode of access
into cultural theories and the construction of historical accounts. Its necessary engagement with the local and particular can lead to the questioning and modification of such
theories and accounts, as for instance in the way women's
experience has destabilised social class as a 'master' category
of analysis, or the way in which working-class and black ethnic
experience has subverted feminist accounts of the family,
'modelled as they have been on the middle-class white
family' (Wolff, 1995: 29). Janet Wolff's view is that
poststructuralism has too quickly aligned the concept of
'experience' with 'a suspect essentialism which posits the
self and its experiences as an already constituted and centred entity'. She goes on to say that we do not need to
succumb to essentialism or 'to pre-theoretical humanism in
order to start from (or include) experience in cultural
analysis':

> Indeed, it should be possible to demonstrate the constituted
> nature of experience in the process of its exploration. I would
> stress, then, that the model I am discussing, which moves from
> the abstractions of cultural theory to the experiential, is *not*
> one which substitutes the autobiographical narrative for theory.
> It is the *meeting point* of theory, social history and the particu-
> lar (the 'micrological').

This is very much in line with the general approach I have
been outlining thus far. Poststructuralism and postmodernism
have been critical of conceptions of experience (too often
lumped together, holus-bolus, under the cardinally sinful
label of humanism) on the grounds that these presuppose
linear and unitary connections between experience and
knowledge, assume progressive and cumulative increments
in knowledge on the basis of expansions in experience or
accredited experience, and enact a closure around experience as lived by human subjects because of its taken-for-
granted authoritative status. I have tried to show that these
claims, among others, are unfounded. Their shadow claims
derive from linguistic determinism, endorsing the assumption that, for instance, subjectivities are *produced by* particu-

lar discursive practices. As Christine Stansell observes, this is 'simply the flip side of crude materialism': 'Language is still separated from the social, but the causality is reversed: Now language determines the form of social relations rather than vice versa' (1987: 27).[5] Against this position, I have argued for an approach to ideology and discourse which is compatible with the ways that people, in the hurly-burly of their everyday social interactions, actively use language, and so both actively reproduce ideological meanings and values and come to argue against them, in thinking through contradictions or inconsistencies, or in trying out alternative ways of defining certain situations, categories or relations. Language use is in this view not only culturally varied but also capable of being varied because people habitually converse, exchange and contrast experiences, differ in opinion and point of view, dig into and under received sense, and engage in what Billig calls the 'open-palmed playfulness of witcraft' (1987: 100). This being so, we need not reduce experience and the subject to an effect of the play of words and language alone, for as Giddens puts it: 'meaning is not constructed by the play of signifiers, but by the intersection of the production of signifiers with objects and events in the world, focused and organised via the acting individual' (1987: 91). Language, as Cameron reminds us, is not the first cause (1985: 169).

Reconstructions of time's traces, whether in social history, historical sociology, cinematic narrative, or autobiography, obviously make certain claims or operate with certain presuppositions about referentiality, about objects and events in the world. This is not necessarily the same as mistaking such constructions for the past itself, or for 'reality' itself, and not necessarily the same as assuming that any such construction provides direct, unmediated access to the past or to 'reality'. The conflation of narrative constructions and such mistakes, the assumption that such assumptions have been made as the epistemological initial premise of the process of accounting for the past or constructing stories of past events and experience, often in fact stems from the theoretical critique itself, rather than the historical practice. The analysis of popular experience and popular culture solely in terms of the structures of their available discourses stands in grave danger of becoming intellectual-ist, of subjecting them to 'fundamentally academic ways of thinking' (Savage and Miles, 1994: 18). It is also to assume that referentiality presuppositions or claims may never de-rive from awareness of the artifice of historical re-membering and re-making what is past, from knowing not only that time's traces are fragmented and coherent only as segments or se-quences, but also always questioningly or questionably con-nected to our contemporary political context. If this is never the case, then anyone concerned to make sense and mean-ing out of time's traces must be said not to possess such awareness in some form or other, not to think reflexively at all about their practice of reconstruction but be caught, transfixed like rabbits, in the headlights of their empirical objects of remembering and remaking. This would be an arrogant conjecture. Referentiality is a rhetorical tool of the narrative imagination, but imaginative re-constructions of past times, past cultures, past concatenations of events and cir-cumstances, require their referential claims to the extent that it is those lives, those cultures and those events and circumstances in their historical specificities which the re-constructions are rooted in, *and not some others or any others.* Neither social history, nor historical film, nor autobiogra-phy, could be constructed on a totally non-referential basis.

Historical practice is then, finally, about keeping faith with those ordinary men and women who, in their own times, have among other things struggled to form 'a picture of the organisation of society, out of their own experience and with the help of their hard-won and erratic education' (Thompson, 1968b: 782). It is their historical experience which we strive to reconstruct, however complex, fragmented and contradictory that experience may have been, and un-less we wish to jettison any sense that is *their* experience which is primarily in the frame, then we have to work with some epistemological claim to referentiality. It is on these grounds that history needs to be rescued from the enor-mous condescension of poststructuralism.

Notes

1 The reverse emphasis is characteristic of poststructuralism, which presumes this naive conception among its adversaries in contrast to its own burnished theoretical credentials. Among historians, Patrick Joyce's take is representative: 'The seemingly simple recognition that the category of "experience" (out of which historians such as E. P. Thompson argue comes class consciousness) is in fact not prior to and constitutive of language but is actively constituted by language, has increasingly been recognised as having far-reaching implications' (1991: 9).

2 In what follows, I concentrate on Scott because, among historians of an emphatic poststructuralist leaning, her critique of the category of experience has been the most challenging. In this, I am taking her critique as a test-case of the poststructuralist take on the category, and it is that take in general terms which I am finally concerned with, rather than her own particular articulation of it.

3 Cf. Anna Davin's recollection that at Warwick, Thompson stood out 'among teachers and historians as being continually aware that women too were part of history' (cited in Palmer, 1994: 114). One happy example of this is Thompson's self-deprecatory reference to Mabel Ashby's lifelong rejection of women's subordination, or 'in her own memorable phrase', her refusal on the part of women 'to accept their own lessness' (Thompson, 1974: ix). Sheila Rowbottom, Barbara Taylor, Sally Alexander and Judith Walkowitz have also acknowledged their debt to Thompson's work and its impact on feminist history and theory (see Trimberger, 1984: 238, 241 n86). Trimberger adds: 'Thompson's emphasis on the centrality of experience and the model of his interpretive theoretical approach are indeed especially applicable to the study of women' (ibid: 238). With respect to questions of class formation and identity, Scott's sub-Nietzschean hermeneutics of drastic suspicion have of course to be understood in the wider context of contemporary scepticism towards social class. It is undeniable that definite benefits have followed from this scepticism, one of the most important being the emergence of a much stronger concern with gender in historical and cultural studies, but questions of gender are not an exclusive poststructuralist preserve, and part of what I'm arguing against in this chapter is the subsumption of both experience and consciousness by texts and languages, or the idea that all the world's a page (and its analogue). For Thompson's initial response to Scott's critique, see Palmer, 1994: 185. See also ibid: 90, 94–5; and Palmer, 1990, chapters 2 and 5.

History, Experience and Cultural Studies

4 It should perhaps be noted that at times Foucault described his historical work as 'histories of experience'. This description can be applied, for instance, to his distinctions between Renaissance, Classical and modern experiences of madness, or to his conception of the historical character of the experience of sexuality. But there are, as Gutting has pointed out, variations in the sense of his use of the concept, so that in *The History of Madness* it evokes 'the notion of an anonymous subject of an age's thought and perception', whereas subsequent references are read in terms of 'nonsubjective linguistic structures' or discursive formations. In his later work on sexuality, 'experience' is once again 'located in individual persons, who are themselves, however, situated in the fields of knowledge and the systems of normativity that are the respective objects of archaeology and genealogy' (Gutting, 1994: 13). Despite these variations, neither experience grounded in actual historical lives nor experience as a component of social and cultural praxis were of much interest to him.

5 It is worth noting that despite this kind of comment, Stansell is herself at times prone to collapsing social experience into the effects of discourse, as for instance in her study of sex and class in antebellum New York, where she writes of factory girls created by 'a discourse, a representation of experience refracted through political concerns' (Stansell, 1986: 127, cited in Palmer, 1990: 162). This is directly parallel to Scott's critique of Linda Gordon's history of family violence in Boston from the 1880s to the 1960s where she describes agency as 'a discursive effect, in this case the effect of social workers' constructions of families, gender and family violence' (Scott, 1990: 851). This is not to deny either the force or consequences of these institutional representations, but rather to object to 'experience' and 'agency' being reduced to their 'effects'. As Gordon notes in her response to Scott, 'construing agency as "effect" drains that notion of any meaning'. Agency is instead better conceived as 'arising from conflict among the "constructions" of various parties, the subordinate no less than the superordinate' (Gordon, 1990: 853).

Bibliography

Abrahams, R. D. (1986) 'Ordinary and Extraordinary Experience', in Turner, V. and Bruner, E. (eds).

Abu-Lughod, L. (1990) 'The Romance of Resistance: Tracing Transformations of Power through Bedouin Women', *American Anthropologist*, 17.

Abu-Lughod, L. (1992) *Writing Women's Worlds*, London and Berkeley: University of California Press.

Agger, B. (1992) *Cultural Studies as Critical Theory*, London and Washington: The Falmer Press.

Alexander, S. (1994) *Becoming a Woman: and Other Essays in Nineteenth and Twentieth Century Feminist History*, London: Virago.

Alexander, S. and Davin, A. (1976) 'Feminist History', *History Workshop*, 1 (Spring).

Althusser, L. (1977) *Lenin and Philosophy and Other Essays*, London: New Left Books (orig. pub. 1971).

Anderson, P. (1980) *Arguments within English Marxism*, London: Verso.

Anderson, P. (1983) *In the Tracks of Historical Materialism*, London: Verso.

Angus, I. (1994) 'Inscription and Horizon: A Postmodern Civilising Effect?', in Simons and Billig (eds).

Aronowitz, S. and Giroux, H.A. (1991) *Postmodern Education*, Minneapolis: University of Minnesota Press.

Ashmore, M. (1989) *The Reflexive Thesis: Wrighting Sociology of Scientific Knowledge*, Chicago: University of Chicago Press.

Bailey, P. (1978) *Leisure and Class in Victorian England: Rational Recreation and the Contest for Control, 1830–1885*, London: Routledge.

Bailey, P. (ed.) (1986) *Music Hall: The Business of Pleasure*, Milton

Keynes and Philadelphia: Open University Press.

Bakhtin, M. M. (1981) *The Dialogic Imagination*, Austin: University of Texas Press.

Baldick, C. (1983) *The Social Mission of English Criticism*, Oxford: Clarendon Press.

Bamford, S. (1893) *Passages in the Life of a Radical*, 2 vols, London: Fisher Unwin.

Barnes, J. A. (1994) *A Pack of Lies: Towards a Sociology of Lying*, Cambridge: Cambridge University Press.

Barnett, A. (1976) 'Raymond Williams and Marxism: A Rejoinder to Terry Eagleton', *New Left Review*, 99 (September–October).

Baudelaire, C. (1972) *Selected Writings on Art and Artists*, Harmondsworth: Penguin.

Bauman, Z. (1978) *Hermeneutics and Social Science*, London: Hutchinson.

Becker, H. (1967) 'Whose Side Are We On?', *Social Problems*, 14 (Winter).

Becker, H. (1974) 'Reply to Riley's "Partisanship and Objectivity"' in Riley, G. (ed).

Bennett, T. *et al.* (eds) (1981) *Culture, Ideology and Social Process*, London: Batsford.

Bennett, T. *et al.* (eds) (1986) *Popular Culture and Social Relations*, Milton Keynes: Open University Press.

Benton, T. (1984) *The Rise and Fall of Structural Marxism: Althusser and His Influence*, London and Basingstoke: Macmillan.

Bhaskar, R. (1975) *A Realist Theory of Science*, Leeds: Leeds Books.

Bhaskar, R. (1989) *Reclaiming Reality*, London: Verso.

Billig, M. (1987) *Arguing and Thinking*, Cambridge and New York: Cambridge University Press.

Billig, M. (1991) *Ideology and Opinions*, London, Newbury Park, New Delhi: Sage.

Bland, L. (1995) *Banishing the Beast: English Feminism and Sexual Morality, 1885–1914*, London and New York: Penguin.

Bloom, A. (1987) *The Closing of the American Mind*, New York: Simon & Schuster.

Bocock, R. (1993) *Consumption*, London and New York: Routledge.

Bourdieu, P. (1977) *Outline of a Theory of Practice*, Cambridge, London and New York: Cambridge University Press.

Bourdieu, P. (1986) *Distinction: A Social Critique of the Judgement of Taste*, London and New York: Routledge & Kegan Paul.

Bourdieu, P. (1990) *The Logic of Practice*, Cambridge: Polity Press.

Bourdieu P. and Passeron, J. C. (1977) *Reproduction in Education, Society and Culture*, London and Beverly Hills: Sage.

Brantlinger, P. (1990) *Crusoe's Footprints*, New York and London: Routledge.

Brecht, B. (1964) *Brecht on Theatre: The Development of an Aesthetic*, London: Methuen.

Bruner, E. (1986) 'Experience and its Expressions', in Turner, V. and Bruner, E. (eds).

Buck-Morss, S. (1983) 'Benjamin's *Passagen-Werk*', *New German Critique*, 29.

Buckingham, D. (1990) 'English and Media Studies: Making the Difference', *The English Magazine*, Summer.

Buckle, H. T. (1904) *The History of Civilization*, London: Routledge.

Calder, A. and Sheridan, D. (eds) (1984) *Speak for Yourself*, London: Cape.

Cameron, D. (1985) *Feminism and Linguistic Theory*, New York: St Martins Press.

Chaney, D. (1994) *The Cultural Turn*, London and New York: Routledge.

Chaney, D. and Pickering, M. (1986) 'Authorship in Documentary: Sociology as an Art Form in Mass Observation', in Corner, J. (ed.).

Chartier, R. (1982) 'Intellectual History or Sociocultural History? The French Trajectories', in Dominick LaCapra and Steven L. Kaplan, *Modern European History: Reappraisal and New Perspectives*, Ithaca, New York: Cornell University Press.

Chun, L. (1994) *The British New Left*, Edinburgh: Edinburgh University Press.

Clark, A. (1995) *The Struggle for the Breeches: Gender and the Making of the British Working Class*, London: Rivers Oram Press.

Clarke, J. *et al.* (eds) (1979) *Working-Class Culture*, London: Hutchinson.

Collingwood, R. G. (1973) *The Idea of History*, London, Oxford and New York: Oxford University Press.

Connell, I. (1978) 'Monopoly Capitalism and the Media' in Hibben, S. (ed.), *Politics, Ideology and the State*, London: Lawrence & Wishart.

Connell, I. (1983) 'Commercial Broadcasting and the British Left', *Screen*, 24:6.

Connell, I. and Curti, L. (1986) 'Popular Broadcasting in Italy and Britain: Some Issues and Problems', in Drummond, P. and Paterson, R. (eds), *Television in Transition*, London: BFI.

Corner, J. (ed.) (1986) *Documentary and the Mass Media*, London: Edward Arnold.

Corner, J. (1991) 'Meaning, Genre and Context: The Problematics of Public Knowledge', in Curran, J. and Gurevitch, M. (eds),

Mass Media and Society, London: Edward Arnold.

Corrigan, P. and Sayer, D. (1978) 'Hindess and Hirst: A Critical Review', *The Socialist Register*.

Coward, R. (1990) 'Literature, Television and Cultural Values', *The Yearbook of English Studies*, 20.

Cunningham, H. (1980) *Leisure and the Industrial Revolution*, London: Croom Helm.

Dant, T. (1991) *Knowledge, Ideology and Discourse: A Sociological Perspective*, London: Routledge.

Davidoff, L. and Hall, C. (1987) *Family Fortunes: Men and Women of the English Middle Class, 1780–1950*, London: Hutchinson.

de Lauretis, T. (1984) *Alice Doesn't: Feminism, Semiotics, Cinema*, Bloomington: Indiana University Press.

Derrida, J. (1976) *Of Grammatology*, London: Johns Hopkins University Press.

Derrida, J. (1981) *Positions*, Chicago: Chicago University Press.

Dilthey, W. (1976) *Selected Writings*, Cambridge, London and New York: Cambridge University Press.

Disraeli, B. (1926) *Vivian Grey*, London: Peter Davies.

Dostal, R. (1990) 'Philosophical Discourse and the Ethics of Hermeneutics', in Wright, K. (ed.).

Downs, L. L. (1993a) 'If "Woman" is Just an Empty Category, Then Why Am I Afraid to Walk Alone at Night? Identity Politics Meets the Postmodern Subject', *Comparative Studies in Society and History*, 35:2.

Downs, L. L. (1993b) 'Reply to Joan Scott', *Comparative Studies in Society and History*, 35:2.

Dray, W. (1966) *Laws and Explanations in History*, Oxford: Clarendon Press.

Dreyfus, H. L. and Rabinow, P. (1982) *Michel Foucault: Beyond Structuralism and Hermeneutics*, Chicago: University of Chicago.

Eagleton, T. (1976) *Criticism and Ideology*, London: Verso.

Eagleton, T. (1982) 'The End of Criticism', *English in Education*, 16:2 (Summer).

Eagleton, T. (1983) *Literary Theory*, Oxford: Basil Blackwell.

Eagleton, T. (1989) *Raymond Williams: Critical Perspectives*, Cambridge, Polity.

Eagleton, T. (1990) *Ideology of the Aesthetic*, Oxford: Basil Blackwell.

Eagleton, T. (1991) *Ideology*, London and New York: Verso.

Easthope, A. (1991) *Literary into Cultural Studies*, London and New York: Routledge.

Easton, S. *et al.* (1988) *Disorder and Discipline: Popular Culture from 1550 to the Present*, Aldershot: Temple Smith.

Eco, U. (1976) *A Theory of Semiotics*, Bloomington: Indiana University Press.

Education Group (1981) *Unpopular Education*, London: Hutchinson.

Education Group (1990) *Education Ltd*, London: Routledge.

Eisenstein, M. and Jardine, A. (1980) *The Future of Difference*, Boston: G. K. Hall & Co.

Eldridge, J. and Eldridge, L. (1994) *Raymond Williams: Making Connections*, London and New York: Routledge.

Elias, N. (1987) *Involvement and Detachment*, Oxford: Blackwell.

Elias, N. (1994) *Reflections on a Life*, Cambridge: Polity.

Elton, G. R. (1991) *Return to Essentials*, Cambridge and New York: Cambridge University Press.

Engels, F. (1969) *The Condition of the Working Class in England*, London: Panther.

Fairclough, N. (1989) *Language and Power*, London and New York: Longman.

Featherstone, M. (1991) *Consumer Culture and Postmodernism*, London, Newbury Park and New Delhi: Sage.

Fiske, J. (1989a) *Understanding Popular Culture*, Boston, London, Sydney, Washington: Unwin Hyman.

Fiske, J. (1989b) *Reading the Popular*, Boston, London, Sydney, Washington: Unwin Hyman.

Foot, P. (1980) *Red Shelley*, London: Sidgwick & Jackson.

Foucault, M. (1980) *Power/Knowledge: Selected Interviews and Other Writings, 1972–1977*, Brighton: Harvester Press.

Foucault, M. (1986) 'Nietzsche, Genealogy, History', in Rabinow, (ed.).

Foucault, M. (1990) *The History of Sexuality*, Volume 1, London: Penguin.

Frisby, D. (1984) *Georg Simmel*, London and New York: Tavistock.

Frisby, D. (1988) *Fragments of Modernity*, Cambridge: Polity.

Gadamer, H-G. (1975) *Truth and Method*, London: Sheed & Ward.

Gadamer, H-G. (1979) 'The Problem of Historical Consciousness', in Rabinow and Sullivan (eds).

Gallagher, C. (1980) 'The New Materialism in Marxist Aesthetics', *Theory and Society*, 9:4 (July).

Garnham, N. (1983) 'Towards a Theory of Cultural Materialism', *Journal of Communication*, 33:3.

Geertz, C. (1986) 'Making Experience, Authoring Selves', in Turner, V. and Bruner, E. (eds).

Geertz, C. (1993) *Local Knowledge*, New York: Basic Books (orig. pub. 1983).

Geist, H. (1983) *Arcades: The History of a Building Type*, Boston: MIT Press.

Giddens, A. (1977a) *Studies in Social and Political Theory*, London: Hutchinson.

Giddens, A. (1977b) *New Rules in Sociological Method*, London: Hutchinson.

Giddens, A. (1979) *Central Problems in Social Theory*, London and Basingstoke: Macmillan.

Giddens, A. (1983) *A Contemporary Critique of Historical Materialism*, London and Basingstoke: Macmillan.

Giddens, A. (1986) *The Constitution of Society*, Cambridge: Polity.

Giddens, A. (1987) *Social Theory and Modern Sociology*, Cambridge: Polity.

Giddens, A. (1991) *Modernity and Self-Identity*, Cambridge: Polity.

Gilroy, P. (1987) *There Ain't No Black in the Union Jack*, London, Melbourne, Sydney, Auckland, Johannesburg: Hutchinson.

Giroux, H. A. (1992) *Border Crossings*, New York: Routledge.

Giroux, H. A. and McLaren, P. (eds) (1994) *Between Borders: Pedagogy and the Politics of Cultural Studies*, New York and London: Routledge.

Gitlin, T. (1989) 'Postmodernism: Roots and Politics', in Angus, I. and Jhally, S., *Cultural Politics in Contemporary America*, New York and London: Routledge.

Good, B. (1994) *Medicine, Rationality, and Experience*, Cambridge: Cambridge University Press.

Goode, J. (1990) 'E. P. Thompson and "the Significance of Literature"', in Kaye and McClelland (eds).

Gordon, L. (1983) 'Interview', MARHO, *Visions of History*, Manchester: Manchester University Press.

Gordon, L. (1988) *Heroes of Their Own Lives: The Politics and History of Family Violence*, New York: Viking.

Gordon, L. (1990) 'Response to Scott', *Signs*, 15.

Gouldner, A. W. (1975) *For Sociology*, Harmondsworth: Penguin.

Graff, G. (1987) *Professing Literature: An Institutional History*, Chicago: University of Chicago Press.

Gramsci, A. (1978) *Selections from Prison Notebooks*, London: Lawrence & Wishart.

Green, M. (1982) 'The Centre for Contemporary Cultural Studies', in Widdowson, M. (ed), *Re-reading English*, London and New York: Methuen.

Greenblatt, S. (1990) 'Resonance and Wonder', in Collier, P. and Geyer-Ryan, H. (eds), *Literary Theory Today*, Cambridge: Polity.

Grondin, J. (1990) 'Hermeneutics and Relativism', in Wright, K. (ed.).

Grossberg, L. (1992) 'Is There a Fan in the House? The Affective

Sensibility of Fandom', in Lewis, L. A. (ed), *The Adoring Audience*, London and New York: Routledge.

Grossberg, L. (1993) 'The Formations of Cultural Studies' in Blundell, V. *et al.* (eds), *Relocating Cultural Studies*, London and New York: Routledge.

Gutting, G. (ed.) (1994) *The Cambridge Companion to Foucault*, Cambridge and New York: Cambridge University Press.

Habermas, J. (1972) *Knowledge and Human Interests*, London: Heinemann.

Habermas, J. (1977) 'A Review of Gadamer's *Truth and Method*', in Dallayr, F. and McCarthy, T. (eds), *Understanding and Social Inquiry*, Notre Dame, Ind.: University of Notre Dame Press.

Habermas, J. (1987) *The Philosophical Discourse on Modernity*, Cambridge, MA: MIT Press.

Habermas, J. (1990) *On the Logic of the Social Sciences*, Cambridge: Polity.

Hall, C. (1991) 'Politics, Post-Structuralism and Feminist History', *Gender and History*, 3:2 (Summer).

Hall, C. (1992) *White, Male and Middle Class: Explorations in Feminism and History*, Cambridge: Polity.

Hall, S. (1980a) 'Cultural Studies: Two Paradigms', *Media, Culture and Society*, 2:1 (January).

Hall, S. (1980b) 'The Williams Interviews', *Screen Education*, 34 (Spring).

Hall, S. (1981a) 'Notes on Deconstructing "the Popular"' in Samuel, R. (ed.)

Hall, S. (1981b) 'In Defence of Theory', in Samuel, R. (ed).

Hall, S. (1983) 'The Problem of Ideology: Marxism without Guarantees', in Mathews, B. (ed.), *Marx: A Hundred Years On,* London: Lawrence & Wishart.

Hall, S. (1989) 'Politics and Letters' in Eagleton, T. (ed.).

Hall, S. (1990) 'The Emergence of Cultural Studies and the Crisis of the Humanities', *October*, 53.

Hall, S. and Jefferson, T. (eds) (1977) *Resistance through Rituals*, London: Hutchinson (first pub. 1975).

Hall, S. and Whannell, P. (1964) *The Popular Arts*, London: Hutchinson.

Hall, S., Critcher, C., Jefferson, T., Clarke, J. and Roberts, B. (1978) *Policing the Crisis: Mugging, the State, and Law and Order*, London: Macmillan.

Hampton, C. (1990) *The Ideology of the Text*, Milton Keynes and Philadelphia: Open University Press.

Harding, S. and Hintikka, M.B. (1983) *Discovering Reality: Feminist*

Perspectives on Epistemology, Metaphysics, Methodology, and Philosophy of Science, Dordrecht: Reidel.

Harrison, J. F. C. (1963) *Learning and Living, 1790–1960*, London: Routledge & Kegan Paul.

Harrison, J. F. C. (1995) *Scholarship Boy*, London: Rivers Oram Press.

Harrisson, T. (1961) *Britain Revisited*, London: Gollancz.

Harvey, D. (1991) *The Condition of Postmodernity*, Cambridge MA and Oxford UK: Blackwell.

Hebdige, D. (1989) 'After the Masses', *Marxism Today*, January.

Hempel, C. G. (1942) 'The Function of General Laws in History', reprinted in Gardiner, P. (ed.) (1959) *Theories of History*, New York: Free Press.

Hempel, C. G. (1963) 'Reasons and Covering Laws in Historical Explanation', reprinted in Gardiner, P. (ed.) (1974) *Philosophy of History*, Oxford: Oxford University Press.

Hewison, R. (1995) *Culture and Consensus: England, Art and Politics since 1940*, London: Methuen.

Hindess, B. and Hirst, P. (1975) *Pre-Capitalist Modes of Production*, London: Routledge.

Hirsch, E. D. (1976) *Validity in Interpretation*, New Haven, Conn.: Yale University Press.

Hirsch, E.D. (1987) *Cultural Literacy*, Boston: Houghton Mifflin.

Hodges, H.A. (1952) *The Philosophy of Wilhelm Dilthey*, London: Routledge & Kegan Paul.

Hodges, H. A. (1969) *Wilhelm Dilthey*, London: Routledge & Kegan Paul.

Hoggart, R. (1957) *The Uses of Literacy*, London: Chatto & Windus.

Hoggart, R. (1973) *Speaking to Each Other* (2 vols), Harmondsworth: Penguin.

Hohendahl, P. U. (1983) 'Post-Revolutionary Literary History: The Case of Wilhelm Dilthey', in Schulze, L. and Wetzels, W., *Literature and History*, Lanham, New York and London: University Press of America.

Holborn, H. (1950) 'Wilhelm Dilthey and the Critique of Historical Reason', *Journal of the History of Ideas*, 11 (January).

Holborn, H. (1972) *History and the Humanities*, New York: Doubleday.

Honneth, A. (1986) 'The Fragmented World of Symbolic Forms: Reflections on Pierre Bourdieu's Sociology of Culture', *Theory, Culture and Society*, 3:3.

Hopper, S. (1995) 'Reflexivity in Academic Culture', in Adam, B. and Allan, S. (eds), *Theorising Culture, An Interdisciplinary Critique After Postmodernism*, London: UCL Press.

Horkheimer, M. (1939) 'The Relation between Psychology and

Sociology in the Work of Wilhem Dilthey', *Studies in Philosophy and Sociology*, 8:3.

Howkins, A. and Dyck, I. (1987) '"The Time's Alteration": Popular Ballads, Rural Radicalism and William Cobbett', *History Workshop*, 23 (Spring).

Hoy D. C. (1980) 'Hermeneutics', *Social Research*, 47 (Winter).

Hughes, H. S. (1967) *Consciousness and Society*, London: MacGibbon & Kee.

Hughes, J. (1990) *The Philosophy of Social Research*, London: Longman.

Hunt, L. (ed.) (1989) *The New Cultural History*, Berkeley, L.A. and London: University of California Press.

Iggers, G. G. (1968) *The German Conception of History*, Middletown, Conn.: Wesleyan University Press.

Inglis, F. (1982) *Radical Earnestness*, Oxford: Martin Robertson.

Inglis, F. (1993) *Cultural Studies*, Oxford, UK and Cambridge, USA: Blackwell.

Inglis, F. (1995) *Raymond Williams*, London and New York: Routledge.

Inglis, F. (1996) 'The Figures of Dissent', *New Left Review*, 215 (January/February).

Jackson, B. (1968) *Working Class Childhood*, London: Routledge & Kegan Paul.

Jackson, B. and Marsden, D. (1962) *Education and the Working Class*, London: Routledge & Kegan Paul.

Jameson, F. (1981) *The Political Unconscious*, Ithaca, New York: Cornell University Press.

Jameson, F. (1985) 'Class and Allegory in Contemporary Mass Culture: *Dog Day Afternoon* as a Political Film', in Nicholls, B. (ed.), *Movies and Methods*, II, Berkeley, L.A. and London: University of California Press.

Jefferies, R. (1883) *The Story of My Heart*, London: Longman, Green & Co.

Jeffrey, T. (1978) *Mass Observation: A Short History*, Birmingham: CCCS Occasional Paper, no. 55.

Jenkins, K. (1991) *Rethinking History*, London and New York: Routledge.

Jenkins, R. (1992) *Pierre Bourdieu*, London and New York: Routledge.

Johnson, L. (1979) *The Cultural Critics*, London, Boston and Henley: Routledge & Kegan Paul.

Johnson, R. (1978) 'Thompson, Genovese, and Socialist-Humanist History', *History Workshop*, 6 (Autumn).

Johnson, R. (1979a) 'Histories of Culture/Theories of Ideology: Notes on an Impasse', in Barrett, M. (ed.), *Ideology and Cultural Production*, London: Croom Helm.

Johnson, R. (1979b) 'Culture and the Historians', in Clarke, J. *et al.* (eds), *Working Class Culture*, London: Hutchinson.

Johnson, R. (1986/7) 'What is Cultural Studies Anyway?', *Social Text*, 16 (Winter), pp. 38–80.

Johnson, R. (1994) 'Cultural Studies: Tradition or Process?', *Curriculum Studies*, 2:3.

Johnson, R. *et al.* (eds) (1982) *Making Histories*, London: Hutchinson.

Joyce, P. (1991) *Visions of the People*, Cambridge and New York: Cambridge University Press.

Kaern, M. *et al.* (eds) (1990) *Georg Simmel and Contempory Sociology*, Dordrecht, Boston, London: Kluwer Academic Publishers.

Kaplan, C. (1986) *Sea Changes: Culture and Feminism*, London: Verso.

Kaye, H. and McClelland, K. (eds) (1990) *E. P. Thompson, Critical Perspectives*, Cambridge: Polity.

Kenny, M. (1995) *The First New Left: British Intellectuals After Stalin*, London: Lawrence & Wishart.

Kernan, A. (1990) *The Death of Literature*, New Haven: Yale University Press.

Koonz, C. (1989) 'Post Scripts', *Women's Review of Books*, 6:4 (January).

La Rochefoucauld (1931) *Maxims*, London: Haworth Press.

LaCapra, D. (1985) *History and Criticism*, Ithaca and London: Cornell University Press.

Langer, S. (1953) *Feeling and Form*, New York: Scribner.

Lazreg, M. (1988) 'Feminism and Difference: The Perils of Writing as a Woman on Women in Algeria', *Feminist Studies*, 14:1.

Lazreg, M. (1994a) 'Women's Experience and Feminist Epistemology', in Lennon and Whitford, pp. 45–62.

Lazreg, M. (1994b) *The Eloquence of Silence*, New York and London: Routledge.

Leavis, F. R. (1930) *Mass Civilisation and Minority Culture*, Cambridge: Gordon Fraser.

Leavis, F. R. (1976) *The Common Pursuit*, Harmondsworth: Penguin.

Lennon, K. and Whitford, M. (eds) (1994) *Knowing the Difference: Feminist Perspectives in Epistemology*, London and New York: .

Lévi-Strauss, C. (1969) *The Raw and the Cooked*, London: Cape.

Lévi-Strauss, C. (1972) *The Savage Mind*, London: Weidenfeld & Nicolson.

Lewis, J. (1985) 'The Debate on Sex and Class', *New Left Review*, 149 (January/February).

Lloyd, C. (1986) *Explanation in Social History*, Oxford: Blackwell.

Lodge, D. (1989) *Nice Work*, London: Penguin.

Lovell, T. (1989) 'Knowable Pasts, Imaginable Futures', *History Workshop*, 27 (Spring).

Lovell, T. (ed.) (1990) *British Feminist Thought: A Reader*, Oxford: Blackwell.

Lowenthal, D. (1976) 'Heroes and History: A Commentary', in Moore, G. T. and Golledge, R. G. (eds), *Environmental Learning*, Stroudsberg, PA: Dowden, Hutchinson & Ross.

MacCabe, C. (ed.) (1988) *Futures for English*, Manchester: Manchester University Press.

MacIntyre, A. (1976) 'Contexts of Interpretation', *Boston University Journal*, 27:1.

MacIntyre, A. (1985) *After Virtue*, London: Duckworth.

MacKenzie, J. M. (1995) *Orientalism: History, Theory and the Arts*, Manchester and New York: Manchester University Press.

Makkreel, R.A. (1975) *Dilthey, Philosopher of the Human Studies*, Princeton, N.J.: Princeton University Press.

Mangena, O. (1994) 'Against Fragmentation', in Lennon and Whitford (eds).

Marcus, G. E. and Fischer, M. J. (1986) *Anthropology as Cultural Critique*, Chicago and London: University of Chicago Press.

Marlow, J. (1970) *The Peterloo Massacre*, London: Rapp & Whiting.

Martin-Barbero, J. (1988) 'Communication from Culture', *Media, Culture and Society*, 10:4.

Marx, K. (1977) *Grundrisse*, Harmondsworth: Penguin.

Mason, T. (1995) *Nazism, Fascism and the Working Class*, Cambridge: Cambridge University Press.

Mass Observation (1939) *Britain*, Harmondsworth: Penguin.

Masterman, L. (1980) *Teaching about Television*, London and Basingstoke: Macmillan.

Masterman, L. (1986) *Teaching the Media*, London: Comedia.

Masur, G. (1952) 'Wilhelm Dilthey and the History of Ideas', *Journal of the History of Ideas*, 13:1 (January).

Masur, G. (1963) *Prophets of Yesterday, Studies in European Culture 1890–1914*, Weidenfeld & Nicolson, London.

Maynard, M. (1994) 'Methods, Practice and Epistemology: The Debate About Feminism and Research', in Maynard, M. and Purvis, J. (eds), *Researching Women's Lives from a Feminist Perspective*, London: Taylor & Francis.

McClintock, A. (1995) *Imperial Leather: Race, Gender and Sexuality in the Colonial Contest*, New York and London: Routledge.

McDermott, J. (ed.) (1967) *The Writings of William James*, New York: Random House.

McDermott, J. (ed.) (1981) *The Philosophy of John Dewey*, New York: Putnam's.

McGuigan, J. (1992) *Cultural Populism*, London and New York: Routledge.

McGuigan, J. (1993) 'Reaching for Control: Raymond Williams on Mass Communication and Popular Culture' in Morgan, W. J. and Preston, P. (eds).

McIlroy, J. and Westwood, S. (eds) (1993) *Border Country: Raymond Williams in Adult Education*, Leicester: National Institute of Continuing Adult Education.

McLennan, G. (1981) *Marxism and the Methodologies of History*, London: Verso.

McRobbie, A. (1980) 'Settling Accounts with Subcultures', *Screen Education*, 34.

McRobbie, A. and Garber, J. (1976) 'Girls and Subcultures', in Hall and Jefferson (eds).

Meiskins Wood, E. (1982) 'The Politics of Theory and the Concept of Class: E. P. Thompson and his Critics', *Studies in Political Economy*, 9 (Fall).

Mennell, S. (1992) *Norbert Elias: An Introduction*, Oxford UK and Cambridge USA: Blackwell.

Merrill, M. (1976) 'Interview with E.P. Thompson', *Radical History Review*, 3:4.

Middleton, P. (1989) 'Why Structure Feeling?', *News From Nowhere*, 6.

Mill, J.S. (1910) *Utilitarianism, Liberty, Representative Government*, London: Dent.

Milner, A. (1991) *Contemporary Cultural Theory*, Sydney: Allen & Unwin.

Milner, A. (1993) *Cultural Materialism*, Carlton, Victoria: Melbourne University.

Mitchell, J. (1984) *Women: The Longest Revolution*, London: Virago.

Moretti, F. (1983) *Signs Taken for Wonders*, London: Verso.

Morgan, W. J. and Preston, P. (eds) (1993) *Raymond Williams: Politics, Education, Letters*, Houndmills and London: Macmillan/St Martin's Press.

Morris, W. (1979) *Political Writings of William Morris*, London: Lawrence & Wishart.

Mulkay, M. (1985) *The Word and the World, Explorations in the Form of Sociological Analysis*, London: Allen & Unwin.

Murdock, G. (1989) 'Cultural Studies at the Crossroads', *Australian Journal of Communication*, 16.

Murdock, G. (1993) 'Communications and the Constitution of Modernity', *Media, Culture and Society*, 15:4 (October).

Myerhoff, B. and Ruby, J. (1982) 'Introduction' to Ruby (ed.), *A Crack in the Mirror*, Philadelphia: University of Philadelphia Press.

Nash, D. and Wintrob, R. (1972) 'The Emergence of Self-Consciousness in Ethnography', *Current Anthropology*, 13:5.

Nathanson, M. (1974) 'Solipsism and Sociality', *New Literary History*, 5:2.

Nava, M. (1987) 'Consumerism and its Contradictions', *Cultural Studies*, 1:2 (May).

Nedelmann, B. (1990) 'On the Concept of "Erlaben" in Georg Simmel's Sociology', in Kaern, M. *et al.*

Needham, R. (1972) *Belief, Language, and Experience*, Oxford: Basil Blackwell.

Newton, J., Ryan, M. P. and Walkowitz, J. R. (1983) *Sex and Class in Women's History*, London: Routledge & Kegan Paul.

O'Brien, P. (1978) 'Crime and Punishment as a Historical Problem', *Journal of Social History*, 11.

O'Brien, P. (1989) 'Michel Foucault's History of Culture', in Hunt (ed.).

O'Connor, A. (1989) *Raymond Williams: Writing, Culture, Politics*, Oxford and New York: Basil Blackwell.

Ohmann, R. (1976) *English in America: A Radical View from the Profession*, New York: Oxford University Press.

Ortega y Gasset (1963) *Concord and Liberty*, New York: W.W. Norton.

Outhwaite, W. (1975) *Understanding Social Life*, London: Allen & Unwin.

Outhwaite, W. (1994) *Habermas*, Cambridge: Polity.

Palmer, B. (1981) *The Making of E. P. Thompson: Marxism, Humanism and History*, Toronto: New Hogtown Press.

Palmer. B. (1990) *Descent into Discourse*, Philadelphia: Temple University Press.

Palmer, B. (1994) *E. P. Thompson: Objections and Oppositions*, London: Verso.

Philp, M. (1990) 'Michel Foucault', in Skinner, Q. (ed.), *The Return of Grand Theory in the Human Sciences*, Cambridge: Cambridge University Press.

Pickering, M. (1987) 'The Past as a Source of Aspiration: Popular Song and Social Change', in Pickering and Green (eds).

Pickering, M. (1990) 'Mass Communications and the Quest for Cultural Identity', *Sites, A Journal for South Pacific Cultural Studies*, 21 (Spring).

Pickering, M. (1991) 'Social Power and Symbolic Sites', *Sites, A Journal for South Pacific Cultural Studies*, Spring.

Pickering, M. and Chaney, D. (1986) 'Democracy and Communication: Mass Observation 1937–1943', *Journal of Communication*, 36:1.

Pickering, M. and Green, T. (1987a) 'Studying the Everyday Arts', in Pickering and Green (eds).

Pickering, M. and Green, T. (1987b) 'Towards a Cartography of the Vernacular Milieu', in Pickering and Green (eds).

Pickering, M. and Green, T. (eds) (1987c) *Everyday Culture*, Milton Keynes and Philadelphia: Open University Press.

Pollner, M, (1987) *Mundane Reason*, Cambridge: Cambridge University Press.

Poovey, M. (1990) 'Cultural Criticism: Past and Present', *College English*, 52:6 (October).

Prawer, S. S. (1978) *Karl Marx and World Literature*, Oxford, New York, Melbourne: Oxford University Press.

Pusey, M. (1987) *Jürgen Habermas*, Chichester, London and New York: Ellis Harwood/Tavistock.

Rabinow, P. (ed.) (1986) 'Introduction' to *The Foucault Reader*, Harmondsworth: Peregrine.

Rabinow, P. and Sullivan, W. M. (eds) (1979) *Interpretive Social Science*, Berkeley, Los Angeles, London: University of California Press.

Radhakrishnan, R. (1993) 'Cultural Theory and the Politics of Location', in Dworkin, D. L. and Roman, L. G. (eds), *Views Beyond the Border Country*, New York and London: Routledge.

Rée, J. (1984) *Proletarian Philosophers*, Oxford: Clarendon Press.

Reinharz, S. (1983) 'Experiential Analysis: A Contribution to Feminist Research', in Bowles, G. and Duelli Klein, R. (eds), *Theories of Women's Studies*, London: Routledge & Kegan Paul.

Rickman, H.P. (1960) 'The Reaction against Positivism and Dilthey's Concept of Understanding', *British Journal of Sociology*, 11.

Rickman, H. P. (1961) *Meaning in History: W. Dilthey's Thoughts on History and Society*, London: George Allen & Unwin.

Rickman, H. P. (ed.) (1976) *Wilhelm Dilthey: Selected Writings*, Cambridge, London and New York: Cambridge University Press.

Rickman, H. P. (1979) *Wilhelm Dilthey: Pioneer of the Human Studies*, London: Paul Elek.

Riley, D. (1987) 'Does a Sex Have a History? "Women" and Feminism', *New Formations*, 1.

Riley, D. (1988) *Am I That Name? Feminism and the Category of 'Women' in History*, Houndmills: Macmillan.

Riley, G. (1974a) 'Partisanship and Objectivity in the Social Sciences', in Riley. G. (ed.).

Riley, G. (ed.) (1974b) *Values, Objectivity and the Social Sciences*, London: Addison-Wesley.

Roberts, H. (ed.) (1992) *Doing Feminist Research*, London: Routledge.

Robins, K. and Webster, F. (1987) 'The Communications Revolution: New Media, Old Problems', *Communication*, 10.

Rorty, A. O. (ed.) (1980) *Explaining Emotions*, Berkeley, CA: University of California Press.

Rosaldo, M. Z. (1980) *Knowledge and Passion: Ilongot Notions of Self and Social Life*, Cambridge, London and New York: Cambridge University Press.

Rosaldo, M. Z. (1984) 'Towards an Anthropology of Self and Feeling', in Shweder, R. A. and Levine, R. A. (eds), *Culture Theory: Essays on Minds, Self, and Emotion*, London and New York: Cambridge University Press.

Rowbottom, S. (1977) *Hidden from History*, London: Pluto (orig. pub. 1973).

Rowbottom, S. (1979) 'The Women's Movement and Organising for Socialism', in Rowbottom *et al.*, *Beyond the Fragments*, London: Merlin Press.

Ryan, A. (ed.) (1973) *The Philosophy of Social Explanation*, London: Oxford University Press.

Said, E. (1978) *Orientalism*, London: Routledge & Kegan Paul.

Said, E. (1982) 'Opponents, Audiences, Constituencies, and Community', *Critical Inquiry*, 9:1 (September).

Said, E. (1983) *The World, the Text and the Critic*, Cambridge, MA: Harvard University Press.

Said, E. (1985) *Beginnings, Intention and Method*, New York: Columbia University Press.

Said, E. (1989) 'Representing the Colonised: Anthropology's Interlocutors', *Critical Inquiry*, 15:2.

Said, E. (1994) *Culture and Imperialism*, London: Vintage.

Samuel, R. (1981a) 'People's History', in Samuel, R. (ed.).

Samuel, R. (ed.) (1981b) *People's History and Socialist Theory*, London and Boston: Routledge & Kegan Paul.

Samuel, R. (1989) '"Philosophy Teaching by Example": Past and Present in Raymond Williams', *History Workshop*, 27 (Spring).

Samuel, R. and Stedman Jones, G (1976) 'Sociology and History', *History Workshop*, 1 (Spring).

Sartre, J.-P. (1963) *The Problem of Method*, London: Methuen.

Sarup. M. (1993) *An Introductory Guide to Post-Structuralism and Post-Modernism*, New York, London: Harvester/Wheatsheaf.

Saunders, N.J. (1995) 'Minds Ancient and Modern', *The Times Higher*, 13 October.

Savage, M. and Miles, A. (1994) *The Remaking of the British Working Class, 1840–1940*, London and New York: Routledge.

Scannell, P. (1986) '"The Stuff of Radio": Developments in Radio

Features and Documentaries Before the War', in Corner, J. (ed.).

Scannell, P. and Cardiff, D. (1991) *A Social History of British Broadcasting, Volume One: Serving the Nation*, Oxford, UK and Cambridge, Mass.: Oxford University Press.

Scott, J. (1986) 'Gender: A Useful Category of Historical Analysis', *American Historical Review*, 91 (October).

Scott, J. (1988) *Gender and the Politics of History*, New York: Columbia University Press.

Scott, J. (1990) Review of Linda Gordon's *Heroes*, *Signs*, 15.

Scott, J. (1991) 'The Evidence of Experience', *Critical Inquiry*, 17 (Summer).

Scott, J.W. (1993) 'The Tip of the Iceberg', *Comparative Studies in Society and History*, 35:2.

Sheridan, A. (1980) *Michel Foucault: The Will to Truth*, London and New York: Tavistock.

Shields, C. (1994) *The Stone Diaries*, London: Fourth Estate.

Shotter, J. (1992) 'Bakhtin and Billig: Monological versus Dialogical Practices', *American Behavioural Scientist*, 36:1.

Shurmer-Smith, P. and Hannam, K. (1994) *Worlds of Desire, Realms of Power*, London and New York: Edward Arnold.

Simons, H. W. and Billig, M. (eds) (1994) *After Postmodernism*, London, Thousand Oaks, New Delhi: Sage.

Skeggs, B. (1992) 'Paul Willis, *Learning to Labour*', in Barker, M. and Beezer, A. (eds), *Readings into Cultural Studies*, London and New York: Routledge.

Smith, A. C. H., Blackwell, T. and Immirzi, E. (1975) *Paper Voices*, London: Chatto & Windus.

Smith, D. (1979) 'A Sociology for Women', in Sherman, J. A. and Beck, E. T. (eds), *The Prism of Sex*, Madison, WI: University of Wisconsin Press.

Smith, D. (1987) *The Everyday World as Problematic*, Boston: Northeastern University Press.

Smith, P. (1885) *Glossary of Terms and Phrases*, London: Kegan Paul, Trench & Co.

Soper, K. (1990) *Troubled Pleasures*, London: Verso.

Spivak, G. C. (1987) *In Other Worlds: Essays in Cultural Politics*, London and New York: Methuen.

Stallybrass, P. and White, A. (1986) *The Politics and Poetics of Transgression*, London: Methuen.

Stanford, M. (1994) *A Companion to the Study of History*, Oxford, UK and Cambridge USA: Blackwell.

Stanley, L. and Wise, S. (1993) *Breaking Out Again: Feminist Ontology and Epistemology*, London and New York: Routledge.

Stansell, C. (1986) *City of Women: Sex and Class in New York, 1789–1860*, New York: Knopf.

Stansell, C. (1987) 'A Response to Joan Scott', *International Labour and Working Class History*, 31 (Spring).

St Aubyn, G. (1958) *A Victorian Eminence, The Life and Works of Henry Thomas Buckle*, London: Barrie.

Stedman Jones, G. (1983) *Languages of Class*, Cambridge: Cambridge University Press.

Steedman, C. (1986) *Landscape for a Good Woman*, London: Virago.

Steedman, C. (1990) *Childhood, Culture and Class in Britain: Margaret McMillan 1860–1931*, London: Virago.

Steedman, C. (1992a) 'La Théorie Qui N'En Est Pas Une, Or, Why Clio Doesn't Care'. *History and Theory*, 31.

Steedman, C. (1992b) *Past Tenses: Essays on Writing, Autobiography and History*, London: Rivers Oram Press.

Steedman, C. (1994) 'The Price of Experience: Women and the Making of the English Working Class', *Radical History Review*, 59.

Stein, L. (1924) 'Historical Optimism: Wilhelm Dilthey', *Philosophical Review*, 33:4 (July).

Stent, G. (1975) 'Limits to the Scientific Understanding of Man', *Science*, 187.

Swingewood, A. (1977) *The Myth of Mass Culture*, London and Basingstoke: Macmillan.

Swingewood, A. (1984) *A Short History of Sociological Thought*, London and Basingstoke: Macmillan.

Tapper, B. (1925) 'Dilthey's Methodology of the *Geistwissenschaften*', *Philosophical Review*, 34.

Taylor, B. (1983) *Eve and the New Jerusalem, Socialism and Feminism in the Nineteenth Century*, London: Virago.

Taylor, C. (1985) *Philosophy and the Human Sciences: Philosophical Papers 2*, Cambridge: Cambridge University Press.

Thompson, E. P. (1957) 'Socialist Humanism', *New Reasoner*, 1 (Summer).

Thompson, E. P. (1968a) *Education and Experience*, Leeds: Leeds University Press.

Thompson, E. P. (1968b) *The Making of the English Working Class*, Harmondsworth: Penguin.

Thompson, E. P. (1974) 'Introduction' to Ashby, M.K., *Joseph Ashby of Tysoe, 1859–1919*, London: Macmillan Press.

Thompson, E. P. (1976a) 'Interview', *Radical History Review*, 3:4.

Thompson, E. P. (1976b) 'Romanticism, Utopianism and Moralism: The Case of William Morris', *New Left Review*, 99 (September–October).

Thompson, E. P. (1977a) *William Morris: Romantic to Revolution-ary*, London: Merlin Press (orig. pub. 1955).

Thompson, E. P. (1977b) *Whigs and Hunters*, Harmondsworth: Penguin.

Thompson, E. P. (1978) *The Poverty of Theory*, London: Merlin Press.

Thompson, E. P. (1982) *Beyond the Cold War*, London: Merlin Press.

Thompson, E. P. (1994) *Persons and Polemics*, London: Merlin Press.

Tosh, J. (1984) *The Pursuit of History*, London and New York: Longman.

Tredell, N. (1990) *Uncancelled Challenge: The Work of Raymond Williams*, Nottingham: Paupers Press.

Trimberger, E. K. (1984) 'E. P. Thompson: Understanding the Process of History', in Skocpol, T. (ed.), *Vision and Method in Historical Sociology*, Cambridge, London and New York: Cambridge University Press.

Truzzi, M. (1974) *Verstehen*, Reading, Mass., London: Addison-Wesley.

Turner, G. (1990) *British Cultural Studies*, Boston, London, Sydney, Wellington: Unwin Hyman.

Turner, V. (1982) *From Ritual to Theatre: The Human Seriousness of Play*, New York: Performing Arts Journal Publications.

Turner, V. (1986) 'Dewey, Dilthey, and Drama: An Essay in the Anthropology of Experience', in Turner, V. and Bruner, E. (eds).

Turner, V. and Bruner, E. (eds) (1986) *The Anthropology of Experience*, Urbana and Chicago: University of Illinois Press.

Tweedie, J. (1980) 'What Every Fragment Knows', *The Guardian*, 29 January.

Urry, J. (1990) *The Tourist Gaze: Leisure and Travel in Contemporary Societies*, London: Sage.

Volosinov, V. N. (1986) *Marxism and the Philosophy of Language*, Cambridge, Mass: Harvard University Press.

Wallis, M. (1993) 'Present Consciousness of a *Practical* Kind: Structure of Feeling and Higher Education Drama', in Morgan, W. J. and Preston, P. (eds), *Raymond Williams: Politics, Education, Letters*, Houndmills: Macmillan.

Warnke, G. (1987) *Gadamer: Hermeneutics, Tradition and Reason*, Cambridge: Polity.

Weightman, J. (1989) 'On Not Understanding Michel Foucault', *American Scholar*, Summer.

Westcott, M. (1979) 'Feminist Criticism of the Social Sciences', *Harvard Educational Review*, 49:4 (November).

White, P. (1985) *On Living in an Old Country*, London: Verso.

Whitehead, A. N. (1928) *Symbolism*, Cambridge: Cambridge University Press.

Whitelegg, E. *et al.* (eds) (1984) *The Changing Experience of Women*, Oxford: Martin Robertson.

Wiehl, R. (1990) 'Schleiermacher's Hermeneutics', in Wright, K. (ed.).

Wilkinson, S. (1988) 'The Role of Reflexivity in Feminist Psychology', *Women's Studies International Forum*, 11:5.

Williams, R. (1958) *Culture and Society, 1780–1950*, London: Chatto & Windus (also various Penguin editions).

Williams, R. (1961) *The Long Revolution*, London: Chatto & Windus (also various Penguin editions).

Williams, R. (1968) *Drama from Ibsen to Brecht*, London: Chatto & Windus.

Williams, R. (1970) 'Recent English Drama', in Ford, B. (ed.), *The Pelican Guide to English Literature*, 7, *The Modern Age*, Harmondsworth: Pelican.

Williams, R. (1973) *The Country and the City*, London: Chatto & Windus.

Williams, R. (1976) *Keywords*, Glasgow: Fontana.

Williams, R. (1977) *Marxism and Literature*, Oxford: Oxford University Press.

Williams, R. (1978) *Orwell*, Glasgow: Fontana/Collins.

Williams, R. (1979) *Politics and Letters*, London: New Left Books.

Williams, R. (1980) *Problems in Materialism and Culture*, London: Verso.

Williams, R. (1981) *Culture*, Glasgow: Fontana.

Williams, R. (1983a) *Towards 2000*, London: Chatto & Windus.

Williams, R. (1983b) *Cobbett*, Oxford and New York: Oxford University Press.

Williams, R. (1987) *Keywords*, London : Fontana (revised edition).

Williams, R. (1989a) *Resources of Hope*, London and New York: Verso.

Williams, R. (1989b) *The Politics of Modernism*, London and New York: Verso.

Williams, R. and Orrom, M. (1954) *Preface to Film*, London: Film Drama.

Williams, R. H. (1982) *Dream Worlds: Mass Consumption in Late Nineteenth Century France*, Berkeley: California University Press.

Willis, P. (1978) *Profane Culture*, London, Henley and Boston: Routledge & Kegan Paul.

Willis, P. (1979) *Learning to Labour*, Farnborough: Saxon House.

Willis, P. (1980) 'Notes on Method', in Hall, S. *et al.* (eds), *Culture, Media, Language*, London: Hutchinson.

Wolff, J. (1981) *The Social Production of Art*, London and Basingstoke: Macmillan.

Wolff, J. (1983) *Aesthetics and the Sociology of Art*, London, Boston and Sydney: George Allen & Unwin.

Wolff, J. (1995) *Resident Alien: Feminist Cultural Criticism*, Cambridge: Polity.

Wolff, K. (ed.) (1964) *The Sociology of Georg Simmel*, London: Collier-Macmillan.

Wollheim, R. (1980) 'On Persons and Their Lives', in Rorty, A. O. (ed.), *Explaining Emotions*, Berkeley, CA: University of California Press.

Women's Study Group, Centre for Contemporary Cultural Studies (1978) *Women Take Issue*, London: Hutchinson.

Woolgar, S. (1989) 'The Ideology of Representation and the Role of the Agent', in Lawson, H. and Appignanesi, L. (eds), *Dismantling Truth: Reality in the Postmodern World*, London: Weidenfeld & Nicholson.

Wright, K. (ed.) (1990) *Festivals of Interpretation, Essays on Hans-Georg Gadamer's Work*, Albany: State University of New York Press.

Wright, P. (1985) *On Living in an Old Country*, London: Verso.

Yeo, E. J. (1996) *The Contest for Social Sciences: Relations and Representations of Gender and Class*, London: Rivers Oram Press.

Young, G. M. (1978) *Victorian England*, Oxford: Oxford University Press.

Name Index

Abrahams, Roger 102
Abu-Lughod, Lila 240–1
Adorno, Theodor W. 82, 186,
    191, 222
Agger, Ben 177
Alexander, Sally 245n3
Althusser, Louis 17, 19, 43, 62,
    163, 165, 182, 186–7, 189,
    197, 204
Anderson, Perry 195–6
Aristotle 51
Arnold, Mathew 58, 67
Ashby, Mabel 245n3
Ashmore, Malcolm 149

Bakhtin, Mikhail 199
Bailey, Peter 5
Bamford, Jemima and
    Samuel 224
Barnett, Anthony 164, 189
Barthes, Roland 165
Baudrillard, Jean 64
Baumann, Zygmunt 127, 135
Becker, Howard 159n7
Bennett, Tony 165
Berger, John 98
Bergson, Henri 127
Bhaskar, Roy 178, 229
Billig, Michael 47, 83, 243
Blackstone, Sir William 195–6
Blake, William 16
Bourdieu, Pierre 121–2n1
Brecht, Bertolt 140
Buckingham, David 78
Buckle, Henry Thomas 116

Burke, Edmund 16, 154

Caesar 134
Cameron, Deborah 243
Cardiff, David 212
Carlyle, Thomas 28
Chaney, David 177, 199
Chartier, Roger 230
Cobbett, William 25, 27
Collingwood, R. G. 159n5
Connell, Ian 81
Comte, Auguste 109, 113, 115,
    159n4
Coward, Ros 79

Dant, Tim 233
Davidoff, Leonore 19, 22
Davin, Anna 245n1
Derrida, Jacques 20, 168, 240
Dewey, John 94–5
Dilthey, Wilhelm 15–16, 95–101,
    104–21, 125–42, 144, 147,
    151–4, 161, 167, 172, 180,
    182, 194, 197, 201, 207n4,
    236
Disraeli, Benjamin 93
Dostal, Robert 155
Douglas, Mary 71
Downs, Laura Lee 174, 211,
    227–8, 237
Durkheim, Emile 115

Eagleton, Terry 57, 61, 154,
    158n1, 164, 179, 181–8,
    207n5, 239

Easthope, Anthony 72–5, 198
Elias, Norbert 132–3, 147
Eliot, T. S. 38
Elton, Geoffrey 166
Engels, Frederick 213–4
Evans, Malcolm 71

Fairclough, Norman 148
Ferdinand, Franz
    Archduke 119–20, 196
Feuerbach, Ludwig 84
Fischer, Michael 203
Fish, Stanley 73
Fiske, John 81–2, 191
Freud, Sigmund 158n3
Foucault, Michel 5, 20, 165,
    199, 221–3, 225, 138–9, 145,
    152–8, 158n8, 207n4, 219

Gadamer, Hans-Georg 16, 126,
    128–9, 138–9, 145, 152–8,
    158n3, 159n8, 207n4, 219
Garfinkel, Harold 109
Geertz, Clifford 71, 104, 207n3
Giddens, Anthony 1, 150, 186,
    196–8, 200, 207n6, 7 and 8,
    243
Giroux, Henry A. 90n9
Goethe, Johann Wolfgang
    von 96, 127
Good, Byron 241
Gordon, George 86
Gordon, Linda 19, 246n5
Graff, Gerald 87
Gramsci, Antonio 4, 47, 63, 66,
    165
Green, T. H. 98
Greenblatt, Stephen 70
Grossberg, Lawrence 55, 62, 235
Gutting, Gary 246n4

Habermas, Jürgen 126, 128,
    137–8, 145, 154–6, 158n3
Hall, Catherine 19–22, 221
Hall, Stuart 2, 4–5, 17, 63,
    80, 162, 164–5, 171,
    200–201
Hegel, Georg Wilhelm
    Friedrich 113, 129

Heidegger, Martin 152
Hempel, Carl 128
Hirsch, E. D. 152
Hobsbawm, Eric 4
Hodges, H. A. 101, 117
Hoggart, Richard 56–7, 75–8, 85
Holborn, Hajo 116, 159n5
Hönigswald, Richard 133
Horkheimer, Max 158n3, 191,
    222
Humboldt, Wilhelm 133
Hume, David 108
Husserl, Edmund 137, 152

Iggers, Georg 159n5
Inglis, Fred 43, 189

Jackson, Brian 85
James, William 107
Jameson, Frederic 4, 61
Jefferies, Richard 97
Jenkins, Keith 166
Johnson, Richard 5, 12, 16,
    71–2, 145, 147, 164, 166,
    200–201
Jones, Gareth Stedman 166
Joyce, Patrick 166, 245n1

Kant, Immanuel 99–100, 132–3,
    152
Kaplan, Cora 21
Kuhn, Thomas 238

Lacan, Jacques 68, 165
Langer, Suzanne 235
Lauretis, Teresa de 225–6
Lazreg, Marnia 177–8
Leavis, F. R. 38–9, 56–8, 76, 83,
    87, 137, 182, 190
Lévi-Strauss, Claude 163, 165,
    168, 233, 238
Littlewood, Joan 213
Lodge, David 69
Lovell, Terry 25, 29

MacCabe, Colin 70
MacIntyre, Alisdair 123n4, 131,
    154
Madge, Charles 126

Makkreel, Rudolf 137
Mangena, Oshadi 175–6
Mao Tsetung 83
Marcus, George 203
Marcuse, Herbert 222
Marx, Karl 3, 78, 80, 113,
  169–71
Mason, Tim 212
Masterman, Len 78
Masur, Gerhard 114, 159n4
  and 5
Mattelart, Armand 191
McClintock, Anne 22
McGuigan, Jim 46, 51, 80, 142
McLean, Tony 90n7
Middleton, Peter 50–1
Mill, John Stuart 93, 108, 115n4
Milner, Andrew 16, 241
Mitchell, Juliet 17–18
Moretti, Franco 70
Morris, William 27–28, 62, 98
Mulkay, Michael 149
Murdock, Graham 79

Nava, Mica 82
Needham, Rodney 92
Nietzsche, Friedrich 108, 223,
  239

O'Connor, Alan 45
Ohmann, Richard 74
Ortega y Gasset 158n1
Outhwaite, William 138–9

Pareto, Vilfredo 128
Parsons, Talcott 188–9
Plato 51, 134

Rabinow, Paul 137
Ranke, Leopold von 109, 117,
  129
Reinharz, Shulamit 176
Richards, I. A. 58, 87
Rickert, Heinrich 132
Rickman, H. P. 114, 134
Riley, Denise 20
Riley, G. 159n7
Rorty, Richard 73
Rousseau, Jean-Jacques 96

Rowbottom, Sheila 17, 245n3
Rudé, George 4
Ruskin, John 28
Ryan, Alan 141
Ryle, Gilbert 123n4

Sahlins, Marshall 71
Said, Edward 20, 59, 179
St. Simon, Henri 113
Samuel, Raphael 25, 28, 144
Sapir, Edward 109
Sartre, Jean-Paul 118, 126
Saunders, Nicholas J. 160n9
Saussure, Ferdinand de 167, 170
Scannell, Paddy 212–16
Schiller, Herbert 191
Schleirmacher, Friedrich 99–100,
  110, 133, 144, 158n3
Scott, Joan 19–20, 166, 211–12,
  220–1, 223–8, 230–1, 240,
  245n1, 3 and 5
Shakespeare, William 71, 78
Shapley, Olive 212–16, 219
Shelley, Percy Bysshe 78
Shields, Carol 106
Simmel, Georg 113, 134
Simons, Herbert 83
Smith, Dorothy 205
Southcott, Joanna 172
Spivak, Gayatri Chakravorty 211
Stallybrass, Peter 70
Stanford, Michael 120
Stanley, Liz 179–80
Stansell, Christine 2, 243,
  246n5
Steedman, Carolyn 8, 21, 179,
  216
Sullivan, William 137
Swingewood, Alan 158n3

Taylor, Barbara 245n3
Thompson, Edward Palmer 4–5,
  15, 27, 43, 45, 78, 85, 98,
  110, 172, 180–97, 207n4, 219,
  221, 245n1 and 3
Tredell, Nicholas 39, 41
Trimberger, Ellen Kay 245n3
Turner, Graeme 11, 161
Turner, Victor 71, 95, 105, 117

Vico, Giambattista 121
Volosinov, V. N. 51, 170–71

Walkowitz, Judith 245n3
Warnke, Georgia 106, 129, 184
Weber, Max 137, 139, 222
White, Allon 70
White, Patrick 3
Whitehead, Alfred North 55, 100
Wiehl, Reiner 158n1
Wilkinson, Sue 149
Williams, Raymond 9, 14–16, 18,
    21, 23–56, 60, 63, 67, 75, 78,

80, 84–5, 94, 98, 100–101,
    105, 112, 145, 161, 164,
    180–95, 207n5, 235
Willis, Paul 81, 200–205, 207n8
Windelband, Wilhelm 132
Wise, Sue 179–80
Wittgenstein, Ludwig 131, 139
Wolff, Janet 155, 176, 179–80,
    242
Woolgar, Steve 149
Wordsworth, William 123n4

Yeo, Eileen Janes 88

Subject Index

agency 5, 44, 50, 67, 114, 119, 145, 162–5, 168–9, 171, 186, 192, 196–8, 202–3, 207n6, 220, 229, 241, 246n5
anthropology 13, 16, 22, 71, 84, 98, 185, 207n3
apriorism 98, 122n2, 132–3
authenticity 13, 80–2, 103, 153, 171, 174
autobiography 101–2, 107, 214–19, 243–4

base–superstructure model 38, 46, 62, 79–80, 186

capitalism 15, 22, 26–7, 60, 69, 191, 201, 240
Centre for Contemporary Cultural Studies 3, 76, 164–5
Chartism 86
Christian Socialism 86
common sense 47, 204
communication 43, 67–9, 71, 103–4, 112, 117, 132, 138, 152, 154, 165, 167, 169
Coronation Street 214
culture
  as art 16, 29, 38–41, 54, 60–2, 78, 97, 185, 194
  as ordinary 40, 47, 54–89, 102, 144, 181, 198, 206
  as way of life 16, 54, 181, 184–5, 200
  consumer 82, 191

emergence and 14, 23–4, 29, 33–4, 38, 41, 48–51, 55, 94, 104–5, 188, 190, 210
  popular 3–5, 14, 40, 45, 49, 66, 69, 74, 76, 79, 81, 84, 87, 144, 146–7, 165, 181, 191, 193, 202, 243
  populism and 15, 42, 78, 81–2, 84, 173, 181, 184, 212
  working-class 57, 76, 81, 84–5, 193, 200–1, 234
  see also ideology
cultural analysis 8, 10–14, 32–3, 41, 49–50, 58–9, 61, 63, 65, 67, 84–5, 91, 104, 125, 141, 150, 152–3, 171, 180, 184–5, 190, 197–8, 200, 206, 224, 230–1, 233–4, 241–2
cultural change 14, 23–4, 29, 34, 41–2, 45, 49–50, 93, 161, 181, 187, 190, 210
  see also structure of feeling
cultural criticism 3, 16, 187, 219
cultural theory 15, 18, 29, 242
cultural reproduction 186, 188, 200–2, 204, 229, 243
culturalism 11–17, 21–2, 162–6, 171, 192, 195, 200–201, 210

deconstruction 20, 72, 221, 224, 237–8
difference 21, 58–9, 67, 82, 99, 120, 137, 140, 151, 157, 168–9, 170, 175, 178, 183,

271

difference – *continued*
185, 191, 193, 209, 220,
223–4, 230, 238
domination 48, 66, 141, 143,
155, 168, 191, 194, 211, 222,
235
dual focus in cultural
studies 64–7, 146
duality of structure 195–206

education 14–15, 18, 40, 43, 51,
68, 83–9, 143, 181, 200–2,
244
empathy 16, 19, 21, 25, 52n1,
97, 110, 112, 127, 135–7, 141,
148, 151–2
empiricism 18, 43, 59, 68, 97–8,
108, 111, 116, 128, 148, 151,
166, 179, 187, 192, 224–5
English 14–15, 40, 56–89
epistemology 2–3, 44, 98, 146,
148, 178, 184, 209–10, 225,
229, 232, 243–4
Erlebnis 95, 100–1, 105–6, 110,
116, 137–8, 141, 197–8, 210
essentialism 19–20, 59, 63, 69,
73, 81–2, 150, 174, 176, 210,
224, 227–8, 242
ethnicity 20–2, 41, 66, 175, 238,
242
ethnography 21, 57, 67, 81,
200–4, 206, 208, 230
experience
lived 15, 24, 31–2, 34–5, 42–5,
54, 61, 93–4, 99, 105–6, 132,
135–6, 139, 144, 147, 164,
171, 173, 176, 179–80, 182,
187–8, 190, 192, 200, 208,
241
commodification of 14, 79–83
concept of 12–16, 92–121,
125–58, 161–7, 175–81, 206,
208–9, 220–1, 225–6
gender and 19, 174–7, 180
historical 2, 19, 54, 126, 205
temporal structure of 107,
117–18
transcendent 56–9, 67, 70,
73–4, 99, 132–3, 151, 176

experiential sentimentalism
102–4, 134, 154, 157, 189
expression and expressive
form 10, 50, 54, 59, 104–7,
112, 117–19, 123n4, 130,
132, 135, 140–1, 145–6, 150,
161–2, 167, 169, 171, 177,
186, 200, 210, 228, 235–6

First World War 119
feeling 16, 20–21, 26, 37, 50–51,
57, 78, 94, 98, 108, 110–11,
117–18, 139, 151, 176–7, 194,
235
see also structure of feeling
feminism 12, 17–22, 40, 60, 64,
67, 69, 71–2, 147–9, 162, 165,
173–5, 176–7, 179–80, 211,
226–8, 240, 242, 245n3
see also history
formalism 10, 24, 43, 72, 75, 89,
129, 187

Geisteswissenschaften 115–16, 128,
130, 151
generation 31–2, 34, 41–2, 120,
133, 159n4, 188, 199, 216
gender 20–2, 41, 60, 66, 74,
174–5, 178, 204, 221, 223–4,
234, 240, 245n3

habitus 96, 121–2n1, 154, 160n10
hegemony 46–8, 63, 66–7, 185,
187, 190, 194
hermeneutics 12, 16, 85, 97,
111–12, 131, 134, 138–9,
144–6, 150–58, 167, 169–70,
172, 176–7, 182, 188, 199,
230–1, 233–4
historiography 3, 8, 11, 15,
17–18, 21, 31, 75, 166, 170,
173, 197, 205, 210–11, 241
history
feminist 12, 17–22, 143–4,
154, 172, 176
'history from below' 4, 57,
143, 191
labour 19
oral 9, 143, 234

social   1, 4–5, 9, 11–12, 16, 18,
    21, 29, 33, 119, 131, 142–5,
    154, 162, 166, 172–3, 190,
    205, 210–11, 219–20, 224,
    231, 234, 242–4
History Workshop   4–5, 18, 143

identity politics   63–4, 66, 68,
    174–5, 178, 238–9
ideology   5, 35–6, 43, 47, 60,
    62–3, 65–7, 71–2, 74, 76, 84,
    136, 150, 154, 161, 163,
    165–6, 184, 186–7, 189–90,
    194, 202, 204, 211, 224–7
imperialism   22
industrialism   15, 22, 29
inequality   20, 48, 60, 66, 84,
    149, 154, 171, 202, 204
interpretation   16, 19, 42, 65,
    73, 85, 95, 97, 99, 110, 114,
    116–7, 120, 122n2, 131,
    134–5, 137–9, 141–2, 145,
    148, 150–3, 155, 168–9, 173,
    179–80, 182, 186, 193, 231–4,
    237, 241
    see also hermeneutics

language   30, 43, 58, 71, 76, 92,
    108, 131, 136, 139, 141, 152,
    157, 166–71, 179, 186, 201,
    208–11, 224–5, 228–30, 239,
    243
linguistics   19, 30, 44, 69–70, 99,
    167–8, 170, 203n3, 229, 233,
    242
literary studies   *see* English

Marxism   3–4, 12, 43, 46, 59,
    61–2, 64, 67, 71, 75, 180,
    189, 192, 194–5, 223, 241
mass media   26, 28–9, 42, 59, 61,
    64–7, 69, 76, 81, 84, 87, 137,
    157, 181, 191, 199, 212–19,
    243–4
Mass Observation   87, 90n5, 214
media studies   9, 29, 64, 69, 78,
    81, 89
mediation   131, 138, 141, 157,
    186, 190, 192, 219–20

memory   106, 108
    collective   41, 65, 119
    historical forgetting   74
    popular   3
    see also nostalgia
methodology   7–8, 24, 50, 57,
    60–1, 63, 71, 77, 97, 99,
    111–12, 127–8, 130, 134,
    148, 167, 176, 192, 200,
    231–2
modernity   16, 22, 27, 82–4,
    150–1, 154, 222, 240

Nacherleben   137–8
    see also empathy
New Criticism   59
New Historicism   71
New Left   87–8
Newbolt Report   86
nostalgia   26–8, 57, 70, 156

objectivity   18, 31, 98–9, 116,
    128–9, 134, 148, 154–5,
    174–7, 199, 232, 237, 239
Open University   5, 165
ordinariness   14–15, 39–40,
    54–89, 102, 143–4, 193, 198
    see also culture
Otherness   21, 78, 81, 178, 209,
    211, 238

Peterloo (1819)   224
pluralism   61, 177
popular leisure   4–5, 86
positivism   97, 111, 116, 128,
    139, 145–6, 151, 155, 176,
    189
postmodernism   25, 64, 75, 79,
    82–4, 228, 238, 242
poststructuralism   19–20, 75, 108,
    165, 167, 170, 178, 208–9,
    232–4, 236–42, 244
poverty   213–19
power   52, 56, 66–7, 76, 84, 128,
    141–2, 147, 163–4, 171, 176,
    179, 181, 191, 204, 209,
    222–3, 228, 230, 238, 239–40
prejudice   153–5, 201
presentism   19–20, 22, 227

race   22, 60, 175
   see also ethnicity
racism   22, 82, 174, 184, 201, 204
realism   16, 82
referentiality   168, 170, 232,
      243–4
reflexivity   16, 106–7, 111, 141,
      149–50, 151, 155, 188–9, 198,
      230–33
relativism   113–15, 127, 170,
      176–7, 183, 191, 193, 227,
      237
residual   28–9, 188–9, 235
Romanticism   15, 28, 94, 96–9,
      127–8, 153, 170–1, 195

semiotics   43–4, 63, 68, 70, 75,
      168, 170–1, 191, 198, 226,
      229–30
sexuality   20–2, 66, 82, 222, 238,
      246n4
social change   25–7, 28–30, 45,
      50, 96, 126, 170, 182–3, 199,
      210, 223, 226
social class   18–20, 22, 26–7, 41,
      46, 62–3, 66, 85–6, 172, 175,
      185, 193–6, 201, 204–5, 216,
      221, 223–4, 242, 245n3
social sciences   1–2, 10, 18, 24–5,
      70, 74–5, 77, 97, 108, 112,
      115, 122–3n3, 128, 132, 145,
      150, 155, 197, 241, 243
social theory   3, 155, 161, 183,
      192, 206
socialist-humanism   17, 62, 67,
      194, 197
sociology   *see* social sciences
structure of feeling   14, 21,
      31–52, 54–5, 94, 104–5, 126,
      136, 151, 159n4, 161, 171,
      185, 171, 185, 190, 193, 201
structuralism   11, 17, 21–2, 43–4,
      63, 68, 89, 108, 110, 162–71,
      182, 189, 192, 197, 200–1,
      229, 232–4, 238
subjectivity   19–22, 51, 59, 63–5,
      71–2, 74, 98, 113, 116, 118,
      143–5, 174, 176–8, 202, 211,
      220, 223–6, 233, 238, 242

tradition   26–8, 49, 52n2, 56, 74,
      129, 138–9, 153–6, 158, 173,
      219
tragedy of finitude   96, 129, 180,
      201

Verstehen   16, 116, 124n6, 137,
      151–2, 159n6, 217
voluntarism   42, 131–2, 188–91,
      199, 210, 229

youth   2, 65, 81, 199–205, 234